Table of Contents:

How I Learned About the Tones   2

How to Find the Tones in the Bible   13

The Degree Circle and Compass   35

The Binaural Beats   50

The Cube   68

Torsion Physics and the Merkaba   79

Binary Code and Trinary Code   86

The Net   94

Science of the Song of Degrees   119

Number Patterns and Geometry   138

The 360 Day Calendar   164

Music Clues   172

The Science of Sound   192

Afterword   201

Dedicated to God, the Holy Spirit, Jesus Christ, the Angels and the 144,000.

How I Learned About the Tones

In December of 2004, I made a decision that changed the entire course of my life. My eyes were opened to a new way of seeing, and my heart was open to a new way of feeling. I've always walked with God, but now I walk with him with a sense of purpose in this madness that we call life.

In 2004, I was in a small car accident with my son. It really wasn't like an accident at all! The whole experience seemed to be more like a dream than reality. It was late at night, and I was trying to get us home quickly. We had an exercise machine in the back seat of the car. My mom thought that we should tie it down, but somehow I thought it would be okay to just put it back there without strapping it down. It turned out that she was right. We were traveling along a country back road that was a short cut back to our house. Suddenly, I saw a deer along the side of the road, and I decided to brake fearing that the deer was going to leap out in front of us. The funny thing about the whole event is that the deer stayed along the side of the road and apparently had no intentions of crossing out in front of us. My braking was for no apparent reason other than the fear that he would. When I hit the brake, the exercise machine got dislodged from its position and came hurling forward into the back of my head and my son's head. I was immediately thrust into the steering wheel with such a strong force, and then my head bounced backwards. My first thought was that someone is trying to knock some sense into me, and I even chuckled inside my mind at that thought. It amused me! I was still in a daze as I looked over to see the deer watching our current predicament. He was strangely calm as he watched us intently from the side of the road. I gained my composure and asked my son if he was okay. He said that he was, but I knew that he had been hit in the back of his head too, and I was worried about him. I suddenly started to feel a liquid running down my face, and I realized that it was blood washing over me. I asked Brian to look at me to see if I was bleeding, and he told me that there was a gash just above my eye. I asked him for a tissue or napkin, so that I could place it on the wound to stop the bleeding, and he handed me something. We were only a few miles from home, so I started to drive home. We passed some foxes that were traveling along the side of the road. It was interesting to me that there was so much wildlife out on this road. I wasn't feeling good at all! There was a few times that I got woozy on the drive back home, but each time I would talk myself into being strong and to just keep driving the few miles left for home. I knew that I needed to get my son home safely, so I drove extremely slowly. I was afraid that I could pass out at any moment. We got home, and I checked my son's blood sugar before he went to bed. I was so tired that I decided after I cleaned and bandaged my wound that I would just go straight to bed. I knew the smart thing would have been to go to the emergency room, but I didn't want to do that because I was just so sleepy. I thought, "Well, if it is time for me to go, than I will move on while I sleep." I woke up the next morning, and I was fine. It was interesting to me that the whole experience seemed more like a dream. During the entire experience, it almost felt like I was in the hazy twilight period of just waking up from sleep. It felt like that groggy period in the morning when you don't know if you are awake or still asleep, and so you lay there in bed trying to figure out if you are still dreaming, or if you have just woken up. Even now as I think back, I still wonder if it was a dream and had it not been for the very real gash on my forehead just above my eye, I may have dismissed the whole thing as a hallucination in the darkness of night.

I wasn't prepared for the lingering effects that the accident was going to have on me. I started getting daily headaches that were annoying me, so I made the decision to go to a doctor to get some help. My doctor ordered a CT scan and an MRI to make sure that there was no damage done to my neck or brain from the accident. Both tests came out fine, and there was no significant damage that they could find. My doctor also noticed that I had a lot of anxiety and depression, so she placed me on two different medications to help me out with those problems. The medications were useless to me because I had terrible side effects with them both, and they didn't solve my headache problem at all.

I had read about a mysterious substance that was called white powder gold years ago, and somehow in my research to find an alternative medicine to help me, I was led to more information about this substance. I had never wanted to take this stuff before, but suddenly I was attracted to the idea of trying this ancient medicine to try to cure the headache problem. I just intuitively thought that it might help me with these awful headaches. At the time, I had no idea about what I was about to get myself into, and how this one decision was going to change the rest of my life.

This white powder gold was used by the ancient high priest and was rediscovered by a man named David Hudson. The only verse that tells about how the showbread is made was mysteriously told about in a story in the book of Exodus, which tells about how the Israelites were worshipping a golden calf when Moses came down from the mountain to bring them the tablet with the commandments of God. He saw them worshipping the golden calf and broke the tablets upon throwing them down in anger, and then he took the golden calf and burned it in the fire, ground it into a powder, threw it in the water and then made the Israelite people drink the powder in the water. This helped the Israelite people to turn back to God and to quit worshipping the false idol.

Exodus 32:20

[20] *And he took the calf which they had made, and burnt it in the fire, and ground it to powder, and strawed it upon the water, and made the children of Israel drink of it.*

When I first started taking the powder, I noticed that my head felt like it had a hat or rubber band around it, and I could feel this constriction for about a month until it finally went away. At the time, I didn't really know why the powder made my brain feel this way, but later on I went to the website about *Etherium Gold* and read an article about their research, which showed that this powder was making both hemispheres of the brain work together in a perfect balance. In other words, this powder was affecting the way my brain functions and making me think more whole brained rather than with a left or right dominance of the hemispheres of my brain.

I started to feel tingling sensations around certain parts of my body, and I thought that it was quite odd since I had never had this experience before. Slowly over time I started to realize that this was happening around the chakra points of the body, which I had read about on the internet, but I had never felt them before. The chakras are a Hindu and Buddhist belief, and they are not taught to Christians, so many people in the western world are not familiar with these concepts of there being energy zones within the body. I looked up graphics to see where these specific locations of the body were, and to my surprise it was exactly the places that I was experiencing these ongoing tingling sensations. This experience certainly made me a big believer in the chakras, because for the first time I was feeling these energy zones within my body. Prior to this experience I had read about the chakras, but I never really believed that they actually existed. I thought that it was some kind of religious belief or mystical stories that had no actual basis in reality. It is interesting that a Christian prophet and psychic named Edgar Cayce believed that these energy zones are related to 7 special endocrine glands within the body. Over time, I realized that the 7 Menorah lamps in the Tabernacle and the Temples were a blueprint for the human body. Jesus had followed that blueprint within his own body, and he became a living Temple that served God. In order for a high priest to set up his temple body, it is a requirement to awaken these 7 energy zones within the body. The showbread or white powder gold is used to light the 7 Menorah lamps of the 7 chakra zones.

I could literally feel energy or electricity pulsing through my body on a regular basis during this experience, and I felt like it was literally awakening my body to some very shocking conclusions (pun intended). Somehow this substance was increasing the energy within my body and almost like it was charging my body much in the same way that we recharge our batteries, computers and cell phones today in our modern age.

I started to become almost obsessed with reading about the near death experience, and I read several books about actual experiences of people, and one book from a doctor researching about his patients that had died and came back to life. I read them through the two and a half months that I took the powder, and I became really fascinated by this phenomenon. What I learned from these books is that after some people die, their souls leave their body and actually travel through a tunnel to another place that is filled with light. It was an eye opening experience for me, considering that my parents were both raised as Jehovah's Witness, and they were taught that this would not happen until a future time when the resurrection of dead Christian's bodies from the graves will occur. My mom had told me about what she was taught in the JW's, but also that she questioned those beliefs after my grandfather's death. Her dad had died in 1970, and she was astonished to discover that she still felt his presence very strongly after he died, which went against everything that her church had taught her. At some point later, my mom and I were reading Matthew 27 and realized that the actual resurrection occurred when Jesus died over 2,000 years ago and still occurs today.

Matthew 27

[52] *And the graves were opened; and many bodies of the saints which slept arose,*

[53] *And came out of the graves after his resurrection, and went into the holy city, and appeared unto many.*

At some point during my experience, I began to recognize that I was having thoughts that were not my own. This did not scare me in the least bit, because I recognized that these thoughts were positive, instructive and uplifting. I began to call these pearls of wisdom that were being given to me….."the Holy Spirit instruction". It seemed more and more as if I was being led towards certain books and information for a specific reason. I was now starting to feel like I was being guided and led like a shepherd leads a lamb, and I wrote this down in the diary that I was keeping of my white powder gold experiences.

About a month after taking this mysterious powder, I started to hear an interesting background sound that I had never heard before. I had remembered from my research that somebody had also heard a sound after they started taking the white powder gold. I went back to a website to reread that information. I started to ponder on what the meaning of this sound could possibly be, and at some point I found a verse that described this sound perfectly. Jesus had said to the Apostles that to be born again is like hearing the wind blow and not being able to tell where the sound is coming from and where it is going. This one verse explained the sound better than I ever could. It can sound like white noise, the wind, bees buzzing and sometimes like crickets chirping, but you can never really tell where the sound originates. For me, this wind sound kept howling consistently day and night, and it was the most relaxing and calming to listen to this sound especially at nighttime or early morning when no other sounds filled the air around me. In the Hindu and Buddhist religions it is called the nada sound that someone hears when they meditate for awhile.

John 3:8

[8] The wind bloweth where it listeth, and thou hearest the sound thereof, but canst not tell whence it cometh, and whither it goeth: so is every one that is born of the Spirit.

I started to compare this sound to be like the sound that is heard when we used to hook up to the internet over the phone lines. In the past before high speed internet, we always knew that we were hooked up to the net when we heard those peculiar tones and beeping sounds. The powder I was taking seemed to be hooking me up to a spiritual internet system that linked up with the Holy Spirit. I also began to believe that this stuff had opened up a mini-wormhole to the other side, and it turned out that years later I was able to prove this theory to be correct. I read the book *Lost Secrets of the Sacred Ark* by Laurence Gardner, and he told about experiments that were done with the white powder gold. The conclusions of these experiments found this substance to actually be exotic matter that was capable of bending space-time and existing in two different dimensions at one time. This means that this powder was opening wormholes to a higher dimension beyond our own. For the first time, I realized that the information that was coming through to me in my thoughts were in fact true. I came to the realization that the Holy of Holies in the Tabernacle and the Temples was symbolic of the wormhole. Holy is a homophone for holey. The tunnel that the near death experience people go through is in fact the Holy or holey of Holies, and the sound that I was hearing was coming from this Holy of Holies too. I had somehow found a way to hook up my temple body to God's net, which is very different from our internet system. This took surfing the net to a whole new level!

Matthew 13:47
Again, the kingdom of heaven is like unto a net, that was cast into the sea, and gathered of every kind:

One day I was thinking about how crazy everything is on the earth right now and about all of the suffering that my son and I had gone through together. I decided that I was going to pray to God and to talk to Jesus about what I was feeling. I told Jesus that I wanted to do whatever I could to help with these last day events, and that I would help him with the harvest or whatever he needed me to do. I just sincerely wanted to do something to help out with the process, because I had become so disillusioned with the ways of this world and the suffering that I was seeing all around me.

During the total experience, I was not only being taught concepts that I had never heard of before, but I was also being told some things that I would be doing with my life in the future. Again, these ideas came to me from within my thoughts, as I have never heard any booming voice talking to me from a burning bush or from Heaven above. This all came to me like a radio signal being sent out to a receiver, only God and His team were the transmitters, and I was the receiver.

I was told specifically about three things that were going to happen to me. I was told that I was going to assist the 144,000, that I was going to go back to Zion National Park, and that I was going to be a teacher. These were the very thoughts that came to me at some point during my experience with the gold powder. I didn't believe any of them. The funniest one to me was that I was going to become a teacher. I hate public speaking and would always shake anytime I had to give a speech in front of the classroom in school, so I really found this amusing. I also didn't want to go back to college to get a teaching degree, so I was just so sure that these thoughts were coming to me from my overactive imagination instead of the Holy Spirit. I also kept getting this persistent thought to research more about Zion National Park, and I was told in my thoughts that I would be going back there to sing. I had no idea what this meant, and I kept telling myself that I would never have enough money to travel out west again and that I was lucky enough to go to Zion National Park the first time that I went there. I did not believe that I would ever have another opportunity to go back there again, so I did not believe that this was going to happen either. The thing about assisting the 144,000 really threw me for a loop, and I just thought this was the craziest thing ever. I had never really thought much about the 144,000, so this idea seemed like it was really out of the reach for me. My mom has always thought that my grandfather could be one of the 144,000, and he was an exceptional man when he lived on the earth. I am just an ordinary person that has been pushed into extraordinary circumstances for most of my adult life, and that has made it impossible for me to live a normal life. I am probably more known for the odd problems that I have had in my life than for my spiritual nature. I have never belonged to a religion or church, nor had I ever preached. Why would God want for me to assist the 144,000? That was pretty much my take on these prophetic thoughts at the time. Not that I didn't have faith in God at that time, but I just didn't believe that these thoughts came from God.

I was able to eventually achieve all of the three goals that were told to me in that period of time from December 2004 to February 2005, so eventually I did begin to realize that these three prophecies for me were given to me by the Holy Spirit. It took years for all of these things to come to pass even though all of these things were told to me in just the two and a half months that I took the powder.

During my white powder gold experience, I started researching sound therapy and found out about six tones that were encoded in the book of numbers in the Bible. I can remember on one of these websites I was able to listen to the six tones, and I remember that I liked them. It wasn't until a year or two later that I started to work with the math of the tones. This book will cover all of the discoveries that I have made with the encoded information in the Bible and the encoded information that I found hidden within the math of the tones.

I never became a teacher in the sense of a traditional job of teaching within schools, but what did happen to me was even more remarkable. I started to work with the math of the tones, and I began to find some very interesting patterns within the tones which led me to add three more tones. I brought the tones up to 9 with just recognizing the pattern, and later on I saw on the internet where others had done that too. I made a website to display my Solfeggio tones research and noticed that I was getting a lot of hits on that page. In a sense, I was teaching others about these tones. I also started to write online research books that I was putting on the internet for other people to read, and eventually that led to doing a You Tube channel and publishing books on Createspace, Amazon and Kindle Books. I had become a teacher of a different kind!

There was an interesting event that occurred with my Solfeggio tones research page. At one point, my son was being bullied on the internet. This guy was going into my son's website, my websites and my parent's websites. We all started to take our websites down, and the only website that I was unable to take off the internet was the Solfeggio tones website. For some unknown reason it remained on the internet despite the fact that I went into my account and had taken it down with all of the others. It became obvious to me that God and Jesus wanted for it to stay on the net, so I never contacted the website owners about the problem, and I left that one website on the net.

I had studied sound therapy and the science of cymatics extensively over the years, and I had learned enough to know that our bodies can be tuned up much like we tune up musical instruments. I came to the conclusion that the atonement (a-tone-ment) mentioned in the Bible was prophetic of using these tones to tune up our bodies into higher frequencies. I read a book called *Mary Magdalene: The Illuminator* by William Henry. In this book, he explained that Mary's last name Magdalene could have shown that she came from the fishing town called Magdala. In the Jewish Talmud this name is spelled differently, and it means the "Fish Tower". Mr. Henry goes on to explain about the mysterious story in John 9:1-7 where Jesus heals a blind man by putting clay and saliva on his eyes, and then he asked him to go wash in the pool of Siloam. He mentions another verse in Luke 13:4 that talks about a tower falling in Siloam. His theory was that this tower emitted a healing frequency or frequencies. I got the idea from reading his book and from my research of the Solfeggio tones that we could tune our body into a "Fish Tower" like Mary Magdalene. Mary Magdalene's name had implied that she was a tower for the fish, and Jesus said that he would teach the apostles to be fishers of men. Could Magdalene have tuned herself into higher frequencies and transformed her temple body into a tower that transmitted these healing tones? I realized through all of my research that the tones make up the fishing net of John 21, so it seemed as if all of my research was leading me to realize one thing. You can sing a song to catch the fish or play the tones to lift them into God's net. It almost was like the old myth of mermaids singing to catch the fish. I could tune my body up by listening to the tones, and then my body temple would then become a tower for the fish. Through a scientific process called resonance, anyone near me would hopefully start resonating with the tones or sounds that I was emitting. I will explain the science in much more depth later on in this book.

Jesus Christ is the Light, but Mary Magdalene is the Sound. Jesus was the fisherman, and Mary was the tower for the fish. In terms of yin and yang or masculine and feminine, the sound or tones represents the feminine side of God, and the light or EM scale represents the masculine side of God.

In 2010, I went on a trip back out west again, and as we were planning the route, I realized that we were going to go right past the area that Zion National Park was located in Utah, so I added it to our itinerary. It's interesting to note that many of the names of places in Zion National Park were given to us by the Mormons, and therefore, a lot of the names reflect stories and places in the Bible. There are names like the Court of the Patriarchs, which represents Abraham, Isaac and Jacob and other places are named the Great White Throne, Angel's Landing, North and South Guardian Angels, Tabernacle Dome, the East and West Temples, the Altar of Sacrifice, The Pulpit and Cathedral Mountain. Rev. Frederick Vining named many of the places in Zion National Park, such as Angels Landing and the Great White Throne. He believed that Angels would never land on the nearby Great White Throne, which was a seat for perhaps Jesus, but that they would instead" reverently pause at the foot to pay their obeisance from Angels Landing". It's interesting that the Mormons felt the need to link this area with Zion in Jerusalem.

I had learned that the Temple of Sinawava was a natural amphitheater at the end of the canyon, and it was named after the Coyote god of the Paiute Indians that occupied the canyon prior to the Mormon settlers. The name alone reminded me of sine waves, as if it was some kind of clue. All sound is in the form of sine waves which looks like waves on a graph. I instinctively knew that if I had to sing or emit the tones in the park that the Temple of Sinawava seemed to be the place to get that done. On that trip, I listened to the Solfeggio tones the night before going to Zion, which tuned my body temple into those higher frequencies. My body was tuned up, and I was singing! We went to the Great Salt Lake that morning, and I waded in the salty waters of this mighty inland sea that was similar to the Dead Sea in Israel, and later that day I was walking around in the Temple of Sinawava emitting the tones from my perfectly tuned body like a musical instrument from God. The Virgin River flows into the Zion Narrows at the end of the canyon in the Temple of Sinawava, so it seemed like this was a good place to emit these tones from my temple body or "Fish Tower". The symbolism alone in the names of the places seemed to imply that the 144,000 virgins would also one day use these tones when singing the new song. Although I still to this day do not know why it was important for me to go there to do this job, however, when God tells you that you are going to do something……you will do it with no questions asked. I had done exactly what the Holy Spirit had told me that I would do, and I was astounded and pleased to do this for Him. Perhaps this was merely a symbolic gesture or test to show how these tones will one day be used by the 144,000 to sing the new song at Mount Sion.

Matthew 7:14

Because strait is the gate, and narrow is the way, which leadeth unto life, and few there be that find it.

Later on, I realized that Zion National Park was located in a special place in Utah. I had found that there was a star map and timeline encoded within the Tabernacle pattern that God gave to the Israelites. The Incense Altar and the Bronze Altar represented the star constellations of Taurus and Aries. I had made contact with the author Gary A. David of the book *The Orion*

Zone. He had found a star map on the ground in Arizona that was made by the Hopi Indians by following a star in the sky. It turned out that this star map contained the very same constellations that were in the Tabernacle star map. Zion National Park seems to be sitting just above the Incense Altar or Taurus and Aries in the star map, which is the same as the Bronze Altar in this star map on the ground. Perhaps Zion National Park was positioned on a leyline or has some other unknown purpose for God.

Of course, at some point it became clear to me that working with these tones and decoding the math and science involved with them was helping me to accomplish my third goal to assist the 144,000 with their work. It has become obvious to me that this great work that I have undertaken with decoding the math and science within these tones is accomplishing the goal or prophecy that I was given in 2005 when I was told that I would be assisting the 144,000. All of the research in this book was guided and taught to me by the Holy Spirit and by all of God's team. When I was in school, I hated math, and most of the time I made just average grades; however, since I was set forth on this spiritual path, I have discovered complex mathematical patterns hidden within the structure of these tones. I have been pleasantly surprised by the change that has occurred within me, and now I truly love math for the first time in my life.

I understand that my experiences with the Holy Spirit and taking the ancient showbread that the high priest took will make some people skeptical. I too am a skeptic by nature and question many things that I hear and read every day. I believe that this is the healthy thing to do. No one should believe every story they hear or read, and I know that I don't. At this point, I ask the reader to continue to read the book and the information that is contained therein, and then you can decide for yourself whether I was guided by the Holy Spirit or not within my endeavors. Believe me, when I say that there were many times that even I questioned whether this was all real or not, and I am the one that has lived through this experience. I never questioned the many mystical and magical stories in the Bible of Angels appearing to people, or of God talking to certain people in the Bible, nor have I ever questioned the future stories told by the prophets. If we believe that all of those experiences took place in the ancient biblical times, then why would we think that in our modern times that none of that can happen now? I do believe that God, the Holy Spirit, Jesus Christ and the Angels are real, and I do believe in mystical and spiritual experiences. Sadly to say, there are many Christians that believe in the Bible's stories, but that do not believe that those same spiritual experiences can happen to us today. God is forever, and He walks with us forever, and I believe that He still communicates with us today. All I can say to my readers is to read my research about the tones encoded within the book of Numbers and the Song of Degrees, and if this does not seem good to you or does not prove to you that I was led by the Holy Spirit, then walk away from it.

1 Thessalonians 5:21 (KJV)

Prove all things; hold fast that which is good.

God placed math and science within the Bible because they do not lie. In math, one plus one will always be two, and in scientific laws, if we drop an apple from our hand it will always fall down to the earth due to the pull of gravity. Math and science hold the truth within their special languages, and so this is the most direct way that God can show proof that He is the Creator of the universe. No matter how many times the Bible has been edited, verses deleted and books taken out of the Bible; the science and math encoded in the stories of the Bible will still reveal core information that was not recognized by those that sought to erase these truths. This is why this information was written in the form of stories because simple stories would not be thought of as containing significant knowledge to the mysteries of the universe. God reveals precious information to the masses in such a way that it is only revealed to those that have a higher understanding. Those that have sought to manipulate God's word in such a way to control the masses for their own secret agendas have never understood that the Bible was written in such a way that it reveals truths even if it is chopped apart and edited or translated to other languages. If you divide a hologram, you will still have the whole picture in half of the hologram, and likewise, if you cut out certain books or stories of the Bible, you will still have the whole picture of information in the parts that remain. Every story of the Bible is filled with encoded science or math, and therefore, you can not erase all of this information that shows humankind the truth.

John 8:32

And ye shall know the truth, and the truth shall make you free.

Most people don't see that there is math and science in the Bible, because most people are reading it as a book of morals and spirituality. The Bible is written in such a way that we can learn from it at a literal perspective and from a symbolic perspective. As a child we all read the Bible from the simplified literal interpretations, and we all learned many moral and ethical lessons, but as we got older many people start to realize that there is a whole new level to the Bible in the form of symbolism and allegory. Once you begin to realize that the Bible was written in such a way that it conveys many different perspectives or levels of information within one story, you can start to become acquainted with a whole new book.

The key to learning from the Bible is that we can literally view it as more of an encyclopedia, then as just one book; although the information is compacted all together in a multi-layer conglomerate of information. It literally is like your cable or satellite TV or even the internet if you know how to work with this information. When we watch TV, we look on our TV guides to see what is on, and then we decide what we want to watch. We have many different varieties of genres to choose from, and so we have to decide what we are in the mood to watch. Do we want to watch comedy, drama, reality, documentaries, sci-fi or something else? Do we want to watch a movie or a show? Only we can decide what we want to watch and which channel we will change on our remote control. While there is only one TV, there can be as many as a hundred or more channels to watch. Well, the Bible is the same way. One day I might need to learn from a story from a literal perspective, because it can answer a question I have for my individual life, but another day I might need to read that same story from a symbolic level. From a symbolic perspective, the Bible can actually be interpreted from many different subject levels ranging from spirituality and morality to the more advanced mathematical and scientific levels. The key to unlocking the different levels is that you have to have some kind of knowledge in the field of study that you are trying to unlock. In other words, you can't find information in astronomy, unless you already have some knowledge in that area. For instance, I can't unlock the significance of verses about Orion and the Pleiades without knowing some information in astronomy about the constellations or Precession of the Equinoxes. This means that I already need to understand some of the subject matter being presented to me, so that I will know what to look for in my research. Also I have to be willing to research the scientific information that is being presented to me.

For example: in Job 38:31, we are asked *"Canst thou bind the sweet influences of Pleiades, or loose the bands of Orion?"* How can I answer that question if I have no knowledge of those star constellations and their positions in the sky? It would be helpful to already know that Orion is a star constellation or that the Pleiades is a star group in the Taurus Constellation, but there are many people that would not know what these names are about. The biggest key to decoding the science and math in the Bible is to research the subject matter that is being presented to us in the verses or the stories. If you do not research those clues, then you will not find those treasures that are hidden just below the layer of the text. In order to find these buried treasures of knowledge, you have to be able to dig into the information in much the same way that a rock hound sifts through layers of dirt to find a precious gemstone. You need to know what you are looking for in your research and why. Another useful tool in researching a certain verse or story is to look for other similar verses or stories with the same subject matter. In other words, you can look up the word Orion in a Bible concordance or online at certain websites such as Bible Gateway that allow you to look up how many verses contain the word Orion. This will give you many more clues to look for in your research in an attempt to answer the question that is posed to us in Job 38:31. Once you start to research these star constellations, then you are suddenly getting an astronomy lesson from the Bible, and you will begin to understand the underlying science that is embedded into the words of the Bible.

You have to understand that the Bible isn't just a book to read, it is a workbook filled with plenty of homework assignments for anyone to do. Once you come to that conclusion, then you are ready to unlock the many hidden doors that lead to secret rooms filled with volumes of information that you never even knew was in the Bible. It can be so exciting to take that journey of a massive treasure hunt within the Bible's magical pages and to collect those many treasures that can be neither lost nor stolen.

It is a shame that most churches do not even teach the scientific and mathematical perspective of the Bible, and what most people need to realize is that the Bible was written from a multi-layer view of information. Each story is a parable similar to the stories that Jesus taught, and it is up to each individual as to how many layers they are able to uncover. In Luke 8:10, we are told that the mysteries of the kingdom of God are in the parables, but only if people see them and hear them in a special way. It is up to the astute student to decipher all of the deeper meanings that are embedded just below the surface of each story and to discover the very mysteries of the universe.

Luke 8:10

And he said, Unto you it is given to know the mysteries of the kingdom of God: but to others in parables; that seeing they might not see, and hearing they might not understand.

In my journey to discover the true meaning of these tones or numbers that are encoded in Numbers 7 of the Bible, I have been astonished at the things that I have learned. When I first started this journey about 10 years ago, I had no idea what I would find and how complex the information was going to get, but nevertheless, I have continued to do my research and to see where this information encoded in the Bible was going to lead. This is a journey not taken by most Christians, Jews or Muslims, and so it has been mostly a solitary journey in this work, although along the way I have been inspired by a few authors that have written about their research of these tones and by some websites and forums that talk about these tones. The Holy Spirit guided me along the way to discover more and more about these tones, and I have joyfully followed that guidance and inspiration.

I eventually bought and read the book *Healing Codes for the Biological Apocalypse* by Dr. Leonard G. Horowitz and Dr. Joseph S. Puleo. I learned that these tones were given specifically to Dr. Puleo by Jesus Christ and the Angels. It is an astonishing story, and so I encourage anyone interested in this topic to read this book. This book only told about the 6 tones and how to find them, but it did not go beyond the basic lesson so as to start the reader on his own discovery to find more tones.

If you choose to use this level of the Bible as a workbook and do all of the homework assignments that are given to the reader in chapter 7 of the book of Numbers and in other books, then you will discover a whole new world of learning that goes far beyond anything that you were taught in the schools of this physical life. I discovered through years of listening to these 9 main tones that the key to understanding the tones themselves can be understood through just listening to them. Listening to the tones is like unlocking the mystery to the tones themselves, and it almost seems to me like the tones are actually capable of explaining themselves to the listener. I know this might sound quite astonishing, but I believe this to be true. I have found that there is a parallel between the tones and the white powder gold, and that parallel is that when we use these tools within our lives, these tools end up helping us build a spiritual plateau in our lives that goes well beyond the physical use of the tools. This is quite a paradox to our physical life in that if we use a hammer to build a house, we will never have the hammer start to build the house for us. However, when I started listening to the tones, it almost seemed like I was then able to explain them. In other words, listening to the tones themselves is the key to understanding how to find more tones and what we need to do with them. Therefore, I would encourage the reader to not only read this book, but to experience the tones as well. If you have not already listened to the tones, then please start listening to the tones on a daily basis to help you along your journey.

This book will describe how to find the tones encoded in the Bible, the degree math associated with the tones, the encoded numbers of the skip rates, torsion physics encoded in the tones, binaural beats hidden within the tones, the net symbolism of John 21 and the binary code encoded in the skip rates of the tones, as well as the scientific principles behind the tones. Some of the information in this book may seem complex at first, but please first read over all of the information included, and eventually you will start to see the many connections and how this all relates.

How to Find the Tones in the Bible

I will attempt to lay out the methods for finding the tones encoded in the Bible as simply as I can. Please take your time with this information and work out these methods for yourself. The fun is in decoding this information in a step by step process. As I have explained before, I am not a mathematical genius by any means, so if I can decode this information, then so can you. The math used to find the tones is actually very simple math, so there is nothing to stress over.

There are two methods to find these tones that are encoded within the Bible. Each method shows a pattern, which can be easily deciphered by reading the clues carefully. When I first started to research these tones, which are now termed the Solfeggio tones, I learned from a website how to find the six tones encoded in the seventh chapter of the book of Numbers. This method was quite easy to figure out, and after having read chapter seven of Numbers, it began to appear more obvious to me that the story was designed to be repetitive for the reason of hiding the tones. The whole chapter mostly consists of describing a period of twelve days where the princes offer their offering for the dedicating of the altar. The offerings are always the same for each day, and the only difference is the name of the prince for each day is different. If you read Numbers 7, you will see that the repetitive story for each day is somewhat mundane, and it makes you wonder why did the writer go through the same detail for every single day. It becomes very obvious that the repetitive story is meant to get our attention to focus us on the encoded message that is layered just beneath the literal translation of the story.

I had read on the website that I had found back then that we are suppose to look at the verse number and add the numbers together until we have reduced it to a single digit. This method is called the Pythagorean mathematical skein. After each number is reduced to a single digit, the numbers consists of 1,2,3,4,5,6,7,8 and 9, which are really the only true numbers, as all other numbers are multiples of those 9 numbers. I was instructed on the website to start at the first day on verse 12 and to start numbering them by reducing them to a single digit. The website explained that the tones are spaced apart by six lines, and this was due to God creating the heavens and the earth in six days, as He rested on the seventh day. For someone like me that is really good at recognizing patterns, it seems obvious that each similar verse is put together to create the number of the tone. In other words, the verses that talk about the first day, second day, third day etc. all go together to create one of the repeating tones.

Example:

Verse 12: 1+2=3

Verse 18: 1 + 8=9

Verse 24: 2+4=6

The first tone is 396 Hz!

Numbers 7: 12, 18 & 24

¹² And he that offered his offering the first day was Nahshon the son of Amminadab, of the tribe of Judah: (1+2=3)

¹⁸ On the second day Nethaneel the son of Zuar, prince of Issachar, did offer: (1 + 8=9)

²⁴ On the third day Eliab the son of Helon, prince of the children of Zebulun, did offer: (2+4=6)

You can number verses 12 through 83 and construct the tone numbers by going down every 6th verse or by connecting the repetitive verses together to find the tones. Once you do the math from verse 12 through 83, you will find 6 repeating tones. Remember to reduce the numbers to a single digit.

Numbers 7:12-83 (KJV)

¹² And he that offered his offering the **first day** was Nahshon the son of Amminadab, of the tribe of Judah: **(1+2= _)**

¹³ And his offering was one silver charger, the weight thereof was an hundred and thirty shekels, one silver bowl of seventy shekels, after the shekel of the sanctuary; both of them were full of fine flour mingled with oil for a meat offering: **(1+3= _)**

¹⁴ One spoon of ten shekels of gold, full of incense: **(1+4= _)**

¹⁵ One young bullock, one ram, one lamb of the first year, for a burnt offering: **(1+5= _)**

¹⁶ One kid of the goats for a sin offering: **(1+6= _)**

¹⁷ And for a sacrifice of peace offerings, two oxen, five rams, five he goats, five lambs of the first year: this was the offering of Nahshon the son of Amminadab. **(1+7= _)**

¹⁸ On the **second day** Nethaneel the son of Zuar, prince of Issachar, did offer: **(1+8= _)**

¹⁹ He offered for his offering one silver charger, the weight whereof was an hundred and thirty shekels, one silver bowl of seventy shekels, after the shekel of the sanctuary; both of them full of fine flour mingled with oil for a meat offering: **(1+9= __ reduce to a single digit 1+0 = _)**

²⁰ One spoon of gold of ten shekels, full of incense: **(2+0= _)**

²¹ One young bullock, one ram, one lamb of the first year, for a burnt offering: **(2+1= _)**

²² One kid of the goats for a sin offering: **(2+2= _)**

²³ And for a sacrifice of peace offerings, two oxen, five rams, five he goats, five lambs of the first year: this was the offering of Nethaneel the son of Zuar. **(2+3= _)**

²⁴ On the **third day** Eliab the son of Helon, prince of the children of Zebulun, did offer: **(2+4=**

_ First Tone Example: First Day 3, Second Day 9 & Third Day 6 First Tone ___)

²⁵ His offering was one silver charger, the weight whereof was an hundred and thirty shekels, one silver bowl of seventy shekels, after the shekel of the sanctuary; both of them full of fine flour mingled with oil for a meat offering: **(2+5= _)**

²⁶ One golden spoon of ten shekels, full of incense: **(2+6= _)**

²⁷ One young bullock, one ram, one lamb of the first year, for a burnt offering: **(2+7= _)**

²⁸ One kid of the goats for a sin offering: **(2+8= __)**

²⁹ And for a sacrifice of peace offerings, two oxen, five rams, five he goats, five lambs of the first year: this was the offering of Eliab the son of Helon. **(2+9= __)**

³⁰ On the fourth day Elizur the son of Shedeur, prince of the children of Reuben, did offer: **(3+0= _)**

³¹ His offering was one silver charger of the weight of an hundred and thirty shekels, one silver bowl of seventy shekels, after the shekel of the sanctuary; both of them full of fine flour mingled with oil for a meat offering: **(3+1= _)**

³² One golden spoon of ten shekels, full of incense: **(3+2= _)**

³³ One young bullock, one ram, one lamb of the first year, for a burnt offering: **(3+3= _)**

³⁴ One kid of the goats for a sin offering**: (3+4= _)**

³⁵ And for a sacrifice of peace offerings, two oxen, five rams, five he goats, five lambs of the first year: this was the offering of Elizur the son of Shedeur. **(3+5= _)**

³⁶ On the fifth day Shelumiel the son of Zurishaddai, prince of the children of Simeon, did offer: **(3+6= _)**

³⁷ His offering was one silver charger, the weight whereof was an hundred and thirty shekels, one silver bowl of seventy shekels, after the shekel of the sanctuary; both of them full of fine flour mingled with oil for a meat offering: **(3+7= __)**

³⁸ One golden spoon of ten shekels, full of incense: **(3+8 = __)**

³⁹ One young bullock, one ram, one lamb of the first year, for a burnt offering: **(3+9= __)**

⁴⁰ One kid of the goats for a sin offering: **(4+0= _)**

⁴¹ And for a sacrifice of peace offerings, two oxen, five rams, five he goats, five lambs of the first year: this was the offering of Shelumiel the son of Zurishaddai. **(4+1= _)**

⁴² On the sixth day Eliasaph the son of Deuel, prince of the children of Gad, offered: (4+2= _)

⁴³ His offering was one silver charger of the weight of an hundred and thirty shekels, a silver bowl of seventy shekels, after the shekel of the sanctuary; both of them full of fine flour mingled with oil for a meat offering: (4+3= _)

⁴⁴ One golden spoon of ten shekels, full of incense: (4+4= _)

⁴⁵ One young bullock, one ram, one lamb of the first year, for a burnt offering: (4+5= _)

⁴⁶ One kid of the goats for a sin offering: (4+6= __)

⁴⁷ And for a sacrifice of peace offerings, two oxen, five rams, five he goats, five lambs of the first year: this was the offering of Eliasaph the son of Deuel. (4+7= __)

⁴⁸ On the seventh day Elishama the son of Ammihud, prince of the children of Ephraim, offered: (4+8= __)

⁴⁹ His offering was one silver charger, the weight whereof was an hundred and thirty shekels, one silver bowl of seventy shekels, after the shekel of the sanctuary; both of them full of fine flour mingled with oil for a meat offering: (4+9= __)

⁵⁰ One golden spoon of ten shekels, full of incense: (5+0= _)

⁵¹ One young bullock, one ram, one lamb of the first year, for a burnt offering: (5+1= _)

⁵² One kid of the goats for a sin offering: (5+2= _)

⁵³ And for a sacrifice of peace offerings, two oxen, five rams, five he goats, five lambs of the first year: this was the offering of Elishama the son of Ammihud. (5+3= _)

⁵⁴ On the eighth day offered Gamaliel the son of Pedahzur, prince of the children of Manasseh: (5+4= _)

⁵⁵ His offering was one silver charger of the weight of an hundred and thirty shekels, one silver bowl of seventy shekels, after the shekel of the sanctuary; both of them full of fine flour mingled with oil for a meat offering: (5+5= __)

⁵⁶ One golden spoon of ten shekels, full of incense: (5+6= __)

⁵⁷ One young bullock, one ram, one lamb of the first year, for a burnt offering: (5+7= __)

⁵⁸ One kid of the goats for a sin offering: (5+8= __)

⁵⁹ And for a sacrifice of peace offerings, two oxen, five rams, five he goats, five lambs of the first year: this was the offering of Gamaliel the son of Pedahzur. (5+9= __)

⁶⁰ On the ninth day Abidan the son of Gideoni, prince of the children of Benjamin, offered: **(6+0= _)**

⁶¹ His offering was one silver charger, the weight whereof was an hundred and thirty shekels, one silver bowl of seventy shekels, after the shekel of the sanctuary; both of them full of fine flour mingled with oil for a meat offering: **(6+1= _)**

⁶² One golden spoon of ten shekels, full of incense: **(6+2= _)**

⁶³ One young bullock, one ram, one lamb of the first year, for a burnt offering: **(6+3= _)**

⁶⁴ One kid of the goats for a sin offering: **(6+4= __)**

⁶⁵ And for a sacrifice of peace offerings, two oxen, five rams, five he goats, five lambs of the first year: this was the offering of Abidan the son of Gideoni. **(6+5= __)**

⁶⁶ On the tenth day Ahiezer the son of Ammishaddai, prince of the children of Dan, offered: **(6+6= __)**

⁶⁷ His offering was one silver charger, the weight whereof was an hundred and thirty shekels, one silver bowl of seventy shekels, after the shekel of the sanctuary; both of them full of fine flour mingled with oil for a meat offering: **(6+7= __)**

⁶⁸ One golden spoon of ten shekels, full of incense: **(6+8= __)**

⁶⁹ One young bullock, one ram, one lamb of the first year, for a burnt offering: **(6+9= __)**

⁷⁰ One kid of the goats for a sin offering: **(7+0= _)**

⁷¹ And for a sacrifice of peace offerings, two oxen, five rams, five he goats, five lambs of the first year: this was the offering of Ahiezer the son of Ammishaddai. **(7+1= _)**

⁷² On the eleventh day Pagiel the son of Ocran, prince of the children of Asher, offered: **(7+2= _)**

⁷³ His offering was one silver charger, the weight whereof was an hundred and thirty shekels, one silver bowl of seventy shekels, after the shekel of the sanctuary; both of them full of fine flour mingled with oil for a meat offering: **(7+3= __)**

⁷⁴ One golden spoon of ten shekels, full of incense: **(7+4= __)**

⁷⁵ One young bullock, one ram, one lamb of the first year, for a burnt offering: **(7+5= __)**

⁷⁶ One kid of the goats for a sin offering: **(7+6= __)**

⁷⁷ And for a sacrifice of peace offerings, two oxen, five rams, five he goats, five lambs of the first

year: this was the offering of Pagiel the son of Ocran. (7+7= __)

⁷⁸ On the twelfth day Ahira the son of Enan, prince of the children of Naphtali, offered: (7+8= __)

⁷⁹ His offering was one silver charger, the weight whereof was an hundred and thirty shekels, one silver bowl of seventy shekels, after the shekel of the sanctuary; both of them full of fine flour mingled with oil for a meat offering: (7+9= __)

⁸⁰ One golden spoon of ten shekels, full of incense: (8+0= _)

⁸¹ One young bullock, one ram, one lamb of the first year, for a burnt offering: (8+1= _)

⁸² One kid of the goats for a sin offering: (8+2= __)

⁸³ And for a sacrifice of peace offerings, two oxen, five rams, five he goats, five lambs of the first year: this was the offering of Ahira the son of Enan. (8+3= __)

You should have found these six repeating tones below.

1. 396 Hz
2. 417 Hz
3. 528 Hz
4. 639 Hz
5. 741 Hz
6. 852 Hz

Now when you focus on those 6 tones, a pattern should emerge. I noticed a pattern that I now call the wraparound effect. If you look at 396 Hz and 639 Hz, then you can see that the last number in 396 gets moved to the front of the number in 639. Now continue that pattern with all the numbers, and you will end up with 9 main Solfeggio tones which are listed below. Fill in the blanks below:

396, 639, ___

417, 741, ___

528, 852, ___

It appears this is a simple math lesson in pattern recognition. It becomes apparent that the purpose of this story is to convey this mathematical pattern, so the reader can find the numbers or tones that are encoded. We have just stumbled onto a mathematical lesson that is encoded in the book of Numbers, so the title of this book should alert us that we are studying the subject of number patterns in the universe. The next step is to put the numbers in order from the lowest tone to the highest tone, which was one of the first things I did with the 9 tones. This lesson will go beyond the nine numbers that we have here, but for now we will stick with these nine tones, until I can explain all of the mathematical patterns that are encoded within the divine nine.

The Nine Solfeggio Tones

1. 174 Hz
2. 285 Hz
3. 396 Hz
4. 417 Hz
5. 528 Hz
6. 639 Hz
7. 741 Hz
8. 852 Hz
9. 963 Hz

The wraparound method will be used throughout the mathematical patterns found within the first 18 Solfeggio tones. In the Greek letters Alpha is the first letter, and Omega is the last letter in that alphabet. In this pattern the last number becomes the first number in the next tone; therefore, we use the Alpha or first number and the Omega or last number for each tone to find the next one. Jesus Christ refers to himself as being the Alpha and the Omega, and his tones also have the Alpha and the Omega patterns wrapping around to create the tones. Figure 1 shows the wraparound pattern with the 9 main Solfeggio tones. Just study this pattern, and you will understand how easy it is to recognize it after you start to look for this pattern within the tones. This pattern will continue not only throughout these first tones, but also in the skip rates, which I will explain later.

THE WRAPAROUND PATTERN OF THE SOLFEGGIO TONES

Revelation 22:13
I am Alpha and Omega, the beginning and the end, the first and the last.

9 TONE SCALE

1. 174 2. 285 3. 396

4. 417 5. 528 6. 639 The last number in the first row becomes the first number in the second row.

7. 741 8. 852 9. 963 The last number in the second row becomes the first number in the third row.

Figure 1

When I first found this pattern, I was so astonished at how easy it was to recognize this specific pattern that was hidden within the first 6 tones. The first 6 tones were not put there in Numbers 7 to give you all that you need to know, but instead they beckon you to look deeper within the pattern to pull out more tones. It becomes obvious that God has given us a mathematical lesson to discover, but only if we are capable of looking beyond the parable to find the mysteries of the kingdom of God, as Jesus told the Apostles. The verses of the Bible at one time were not numbered, but here we can see in this lesson that there is a reason why man decided to number each verse in the Bible. Later on in this chapter, I will explain that these tones are also encoded in another area of the Bible, so this is just one place and one method for unlocking these powerful tones.

I will lead you carefully through every stage that I was led through by the Holy Spirit, and by all the work and research that I did on my own. The Holy Spirit didn't just give me fish, but it taught me how to fish on my own. This book will lead you through the steps, but you also need to work out the math on your own if you are to get a better understanding. This is a workbook!

First, let me say one thing before I move onto the next lesson in the math of these tones. The writers of the book *Healing Codes of the Biological Apocalypse* made it clear in their book that they believed that these tones would be used by the 144,000. It is apparent from my studying of the Bible that the 144,000 have to learn the new song. It is not going to be zapped into their brain automatically upon the sealing of these people, but it is to be learned. In this book, it is my intention to teach the readers the information that needs to be learned to help them with the new song. It will not only help you to learn, but it should propel you to go beyond what is merely given here and to work out the lessons for yourself. The best way to learn is not merely through reading alone, but it is to do the work yourself, so that you can better assimilate the information. As you continue to work with these tones, you will eventually be able to recognize the numbers anytime you see them in the clocks or elsewhere. You will eventually be able to memorize the main tones, and this is what needs to happen. In Revelation 14:3 it says that no man could learn the song, but the 144,000. This verse implies that it is a song that is learned, which means it will take some time and effort to receive this song.

Revelation 14:3 *And they sung as it were a new song before the throne, and before the four beasts, and the elders: and no man could learn that song but the hundred and forty and four thousand, which were redeemed from the earth.*

The next step that I took was simply to follow a thought that I had, which was to see what the spacing is in between the tones. I do not know if this idea was my own, or that the Holy Spirit led me to this conclusion, but I can say that there was something very significant to find in between the tones. I simply began by subtracting the higher number tone from the lower number tone in order from the highest to the lowest, and what I found was simply amazing. There was another pattern underlying beneath the simple layer of the tones. Do the simple subtraction problems below to find another pattern within the tones.

Finding the Skip Rates

285-174= ___

396-285= ___

417-396= ___

528-417= ___

$$639-528=\_\_\_$$

$$741-639=\_\_\_$$

$$852-741=\_\_\_$$

$$963-852=\_\_\_$$

After I worked on the subtraction of the tones, I discovered a really interesting pattern. It was that pattern that eventually helped me to understand that there were more tones. Also there was another pattern that I also realized was beckoning me to add more tones to the 9 main tones. Together with both clues I was able to go beyond the 9 main tones. I will discuss the process first, so that you the reader will understand each step and each level of realization based on diverse perspectives. There are two different ways to come up with the next 9 tones, and there are other clues that lead to even more tones. I will cover every way and clue that I have discovered, so that you will understand all of the clues involved. This may seem to get quite complex, however; it is all based on either pattern recognition or simple mathematical problems using subtraction.

If you did your math correctly, then you will come up with the same pattern below. I call it the skip rates of the tones, but basically this is the pattern between the tones. For example, the number 111 is added to 174 to make the next tone of 285, so this shows another pattern within the tones.

Pythagorean Math		Skip Rates
1) 1+7+4 = 12 = 1+2 = **3**	174
		---------------------------------------+111
2) 2+8+5 = 15 = 1+5 = **6**	285
		---------------------------------------+111
3) 3+9+6 = 18 = 1+8 = **9**	396
		---------------------------------------+21
4) 4+1+7 = 12 = 1+2 = **3**	417
		---------------------------------------+111
5) 5+2+8 = 15 = 1+5 = **6**	528
		---------------------------------------+111
6) 6+3+9 = 18 = 1+8 = **9**	639
		---------------------------------------+102
7) 7+4+1 = 12 = 1+2 = **3**	741
		---------------------------------------+111
8) 8+5+2 = 15 = 1+5 = **6**	852
		---------------------------------------+111
9) 9+6+3 = 18 = 1+8 = **9**	963

Figure 2

In figure 2, you can see the pattern hidden within the 9 tones. When I looked at this pattern the 102 and 21 stood out as being different, so I wanted to subtract them to see what number would come up. This was the next mathematical problem that seemed to beckon me to continue my work on the math within the tones.

$$102-21=\underline{}$$

The numbers 21 and 102 also shows another pattern, which I will discuss after the next math problems that I found. I began to see that there was another pattern within the 9 tones, and that had to do with another pattern recognition exercise. I realized that I could group the 9 patterns into 3 groups that I began to call the triplet numbers.

Group the triplet numbers together by recognizing the numbers that are the same.

Finding the Triplet Numbers

1. 174 Hz _____ _____
2. 285 Hz _____ _____
3. 396 Hz _____ _____
4. 417 Hz
5. 528 Hz
6. 639 Hz
7. 741 Hz
8. 852 Hz
9. 963 Hz

Eventually I realized that I needed to see what the skip rates were with the triplet numbers, so I subtracted the smaller numbers from the bigger ones and found another pattern. This pattern was also the key to adding more tones, and it also verified that I was on the right track in following the patterns that I was seeing.

These patterns within the skip rates of the 9 tones and within the triplet numbers offer another lesson in pattern recognition. It seemed as if the spacing of the number patterns were as important as the tones themselves, and so later on I will explain more about the scientific importance of the math within these numbers. I couldn't help but wonder why it was so important to encode these numbers or tones within the book of Numbers, when it was related to the new song of the 144,000. However, what I began to realize over the years is that these numbers are really even more than just these tones, so it seemed within these mathematical patterns there is information being conveyed that went beyond music and more into the realm of codes within the matrix of the universe or creation itself. The encoded math within the tones were there to represent the underlying fabric of perhaps space-time, as the fabric of our universe consists of specific repeating numbers in various multiples that are also conveyed within the tones. Physicists tell us that the universe is made up of vibrations or sound in theories like string theory, which I will cover in another chapter.

The next mathematical assignment within the tones after you have worked out the triplet numbers is to subtract the lowest from the highest to find their skip rates.

Subtraction of the Triplet Numbers

741- 417= ___

417-174= ___

852-528= ___

528-285= ___

963-639= ___

639-396= ___

After you do these subtraction problems, you will start to see another pattern that requires pattern recognition again, and you can use the wraparound method to decode the last number in the series. Now we can begin to see that two different patterns have emerged within the tones with the 21 and 102, and with the 243 and the 324. All that is needed is to subtract the skip rates of the triplet numbers to find the same number as the skip rate of the numbers 21 and 102.

324- 243= ___

Now, as you can see this skip rate number matches the skip rate number with the numbers of 21 and 102, which are found in the skip rates of the tones. This is not a coincidence. Later on I will show you how it all ties into the mathematical patterns within the tones. All of these number patterns in the skip rates are significant to the encoded information. The skip rates are the key to continuing the tones pattern.

The pattern recognition tests and the wraparound patterns are simple to recognize and to work with in the tone math. At every step in the process, you will find it to be rather simple and straightforward. This is far from the complex mathematics of Algebra or Geometry, so it is just a matter of taking these simple steps at every point within the process. I hated math when I was at school, but I found this math to be rather simple and with a great purpose. I can remember back when I was in school, and we always had to do a lot of problems for math class. I would always get so bored with doing the math problems because there was no goal to achieve. The math was hardly ever applied to real life, and even the word problems didn't impress me. If math was taught with a purpose for our life, then it would have been more fun to me, but it was always just about doing a page full of math problems to solve. I have found that working with the math within the tones has made me feel more like I was on a treasure quest to find more information encoded within the tones. It has been exciting and intriguing to follow the clues to see where they will lead next. The goal was to find more tones, but also in the process I started to find information that was so pertinent to the structure of the universe. I will cover that information in another chapter.

Okay, once you do those math exercises you should have all of the skip rates that are in the graphic below. You should start to notice another pattern emerging with the skip rate numbers.

Pythagorean Math	Skip Rates		Triplet Skip Rates	
1) 1+7+4 = 12 = 1+2 = **3**	174		174	
	--------+111			
2) 2+8+5 = 15 = 1+5 = **6**	285		285	
	--------+111	**>243**		
3) 3+9+6 = 18 = 1+8 = **9**	396		396	
	--------+21		**>243**	
4) 4+1+7 = 12 = 1+2 = **3**	417		417	
	--------+111		**>243**	
5) 5+2+8 = 15 = 1+5 = **6**	528		528	324
	--------+111	**>324**		-243
6) 6+3+9 = 18 = 1+8 = **9**	639		639	**81**
	--------+102	**>324**		
7) 7+4+1 = 12 = 1+2 = **3**	741		741	
	--------+111		**>324**	
8) 8+5+2 = 15 = 1+5 = **6**	852		852	
	--------+111			
9) 9+6+3 = 18 = 1+8 = **9**	963		963	
		102		
		-21		
		81		

Figure 3

I started to see a pattern with the skip rate numbers as well. The next lesson in pattern recognition was to continue the skip rate patterns on to the next number in the sequence. Down below you can finish the pattern yourself to see what you will find.

21, 102, ___

243, 324, ___

Once again, we find that the wraparound pattern is needed, but in the case of the number 21 revolving to 102, we can clearly see that a 0 is added as a place holder. Otherwise, if the 0 had not been added, then we would have revolved to 12, rather than to 102. Remember in this wraparound pattern of the first 9 tones, we always take the last number and wrap it around to the first number in the next skip rate. It's a simple pattern to recognize, and once you learn the wraparound method, you will easily recognize it when it comes along again.

The Numbers 210 & 432

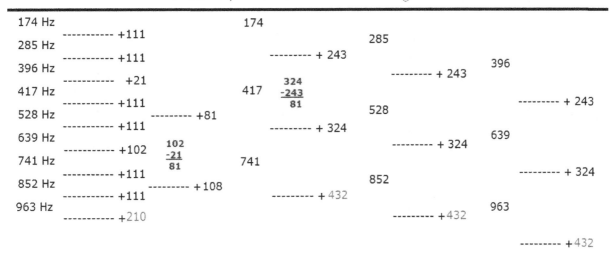

Figure 4

Now, we can clearly see that the next key is to add 210 to 963 to come up with the next tone in the series. This new tone should add the new skip rate number of 432, which completes the skip rate pattern of the triplet numbers. As we can see the wraparound patterns for the skip rate numbers are both solved, and they do not go beyond these patterns, as 210 becomes 21 and 432 becomes 243. These cycle back to the first number in the skip rate patterns to form a loop.

The next step is to add the number 210 to the last tone of 963, and then to continue the pattern of adding 111 twice to the next 2 tones.

$$963 + 210 = \underline{\qquad}$$

$$\underline{\qquad} + 111 = \underline{\qquad}$$

$$\underline{\qquad} + 111 = \underline{\qquad}$$

I found out later that the 210 skip rate is also encoded in chapter 7 of the book of Numbers, so if someone didn't pick up on the pattern recognition tests, then they may be able to decode the verses and find the clue to add 210 to the last tone.

Numbers 7

*[13] And his offering was one silver charger, the weight thereof was an **hundred and thirty shekels**, one silver bowl of **seventy shekels**, after the shekel of the sanctuary; both of them were full of fine flour mingled with oil for a meat offering:*

*[14] One spoon of **ten shekels** of gold, full of incense:*

The first hint of the 210 skip rate is given in verse 13 and 14. We are supposed to add the shekels together to help us to find the next tone in the series.

130 shekels + 70 shekels + 10 shekels= ___

There is another test for pattern recognition that emerges within the skip rate numbers of 21, 102 and 210. We have to complete the pattern by subtracting 102 from 210 to find the next number after 81. This also completes the skip rates for those numbers and clearly shows the wraparound effect again with the zero being held as a place marker in the second number.

102 – 21= ___   324-243= ___

210 - 102= ___   432-324= ___

The First Twelve Tones

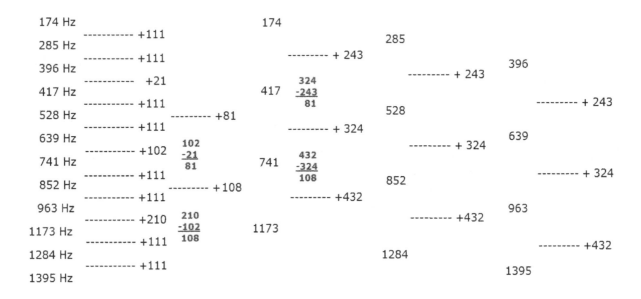

Figure 5

This completes the pattern for the skip rates of the Solfeggio tones; however, we are not done with the Solfeggio tones yet. As it turns out, we only have one side for the tones, and we need to begin to work on the other side.

You may have already noticed that there is a pattern with the triplet numbers that is not yet complete. The triplet numbers for the first 9 tones are only half of the different combinations, that you can get using those exact numbers altogether. In other words, there are 9 more numbers that complete the pattern of the triplet numbers, and you have to figure out the combinations that haven't been used yet with those specific numbers. This is another pattern recognition test for those who have eyes to see that there is more to that pattern. The next set of problems will test your pattern recognition skills again. Find all of the combinations of these numbers.

1. 174 Hz ___
2. 285 Hz ___
3. 396 Hz ___
4. 417 Hz ___
5. 528 Hz ___
6. 639 Hz ___
7. 741 Hz ___
8. 852 Hz ___
9. 963 Hz ___

After you have the next 9 tones in the right column, then you need to go through the same process as we did for the first 9 tones. You need to add the number 210 to the last tone in the right column and then add 111 twice to the next 2 tones. This will bring you up to 24 tones. I will go over the significance of this number in another chapter.

THE WRAPAROUND PATTERN OF THE SOLFEGGIO TONES

Revelation 22:13
I am Alpha and Omega, the beginning and the end, the first and the last.

9 TONE SCALE

1. 174 2. 285 3. 396
   ↙   ↙   ↙
4. 417 5. 528 6. 639 The last number in the first row becomes the first number in the second row.
   ↙   ↙   ↙
7. 741 8. 852 9. 963 The last number in the second row becomes the first number in the third row.

81 & 108 SKIP RATE

81
↙
108 The zero is used as a placeholder when moving into the triple digits. The last number in the first row becomes the first number in the second row.

21, 102 & 210 SKIP RATE

21
↙
102 The zero is used as a placeholder when moving into the triple digits. The last number in the first
↙   row becomes the first number in the second row.
210 The last number in the second row becomes the first number in the third row.

243, 324 & 432 SKIP RATE

243
↙
324 The last number in the first row becomes the first number in the second row.
↙
432 The last number in the second row becomes the first number in the third row.

Figure 6

The 111 skip rate is also encoded in chapter 7 of the book of Numbers, so this is another clue. Verse 15 and its repetitive verses of the 12 days is a very clever clue that was encoded there to let us know that we are on the right track if we get the number 111 in the skip rate of the tones. Later on I will talk about the significance of the binary code connection in another chapter.

Numbers 7:15 (KJV)

[15] **One** young bullock, **one** ram, **one** lamb of the first year, for a burnt offering:

Now if you have all 24 tones, notice how the wraparound effect has changed in these tones. It is now a different pattern. The numbers 21 and 102 have changed places and the numbers 243 and 324 have changed places also. This is a clue to something I discovered later on.

THE OTHER 12 SOLFEGGIO TONES

```
147 Hz                              147
          ---------- +111                     258
258 Hz                                      --------- + 324
          ---------- +111                                        369
369 Hz                                                 --------- + 324
          ---------- +102
471 Hz                              471                                       --------- + 324
          ---------- +111 --------- +81
582 Hz                                      --------- + 243     582
          ---------- +111
693 Hz                                                 --------- + 243         693
          ---------- + 21
714 Hz                              714
          ---------- +111                    825                              --------- + 243
825 Hz                          --------- +189
          ---------- +111                  --------- +432
936 Hz                                                 --------- +432          936
          ---------- +210
1146 Hz                             1146
          ---------- +111                                                     --------- +432
1257 Hz                                     1257
          ---------- +111
1368 Hz                                                        1368
```

Figure 7

Later on, I realized that this information with the tones was also given in another book of the Bible. The key to picking up on this clue was to realize that the name of the song is a clue of how to find the notes or tones for the actual song itself. This clue can be found in the book of Psalms in chapters 120 through 134. These fifteen chapters make up the entire Song of Degrees, which in some chapters is also called the Song of Degrees of David. I realized at some point that this song is actually talking about the degrees of a circle. We actually get the degrees of a circle from the ancient Sumerians, which divided up the circle into 360 degrees or segments. Six of the tones can be found within the 360 degree circle. There is a certain technique that is needed to find them, and the biggest clue is hidden in the number of the chapters within the song. Since there are 15 chapters of the song, which is a big clue that we need to divide the degree circle into 15 degree intervals. I actually got this clue from studying the pattern for Ed Leedskalnin's magnetic flywheel at Coral Castle. He had divided up his magnetic flywheel into 15 degree intervals to place his 24 magnets around the wheel, and somehow he was able to generate electricity with his invention. I realized after reading the Song of Degrees that the 15 chapters was a clue to divide up the degree circle by degrees of 15 all around.

We have to use the Pythagorean mathematical skein once again after the circle is divided into 15 degree sections. Remember that you must add the digits to reduce it to a single digit number.

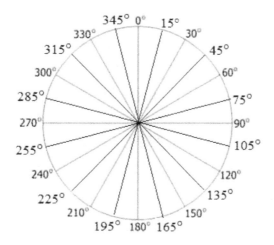

Figure 8

Pythagorean Mathematical Skein Pattern of the Song of Degrees

1+5=_

3+0=_

4+5=_

6+0=_

7+5=__

9+0=_

1+0+5=_

1+2+0=_

1+3+5=_

1+5+0=_

1+6+5=__

1+8+0=_

1+9+5=__

2+1+0=_

2+2+5=_

2+4+0=_

2+5+5=__

2+7+0=_

2+8+5=__

3+0+0=_

3+1+5=_

3+3+0=_

3+4+5=__

Remember to keep reducing the number by adding the digits until you have ended up with only a one digit number. If you have done your math work properly, then you will end up with a series of 3, 6 and 9 numbers going all around the degree circle.

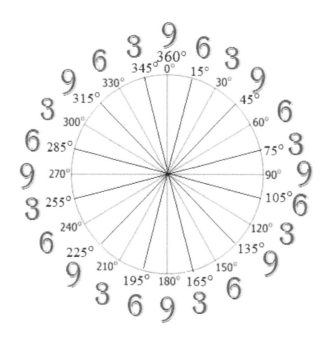

Figure 9

When I first came up with this pattern of numbers, I put them around the degree circle and recognized a 639 pattern that repeated around the circle starting from the 15 degree interval.

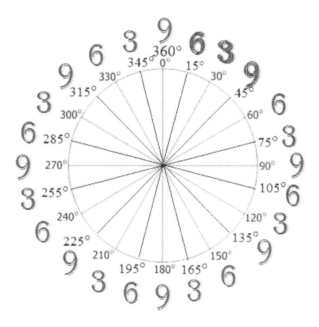

Figure 10

However, upon further inspection and focus on this degree circle, I realized that all of the 3, 6 & 9 combinations were revealed within the 15 degree interval circle. I just had to pick them out in such a way that left a gap between the 6 numbers. If you gaze on the degree circle above, you will start to pick them out too.

At some point during my project to decode the Solfeggio tones, I got picked to do some research on a geometry project called the *Seed Abba* by Debra Mahara Mahar. I showed her my graphics on the degree circle math I was researching, and she discovered something really interesting. If you count those 3, 6 & 9 numbers going around the 15 degree interval circle, you will get the number 144. This number is mentioned in Revelation 21:17 in the Bible and is also a Fibonacci number. I will get more into the symbolism of this verse in another chapter, however, for now it is relevant to mention that this number is the measure of the wall around New Jerusalem. This measurement is measured in cubits, which is a clue to the Holy of Holies cube, and later on I will show you how the cube fits into the Solfeggio tones patterns. There is a lot of sacred geometry within the tones, and that geometry is not limited by our three dimensional universe.

144 Degree Circle Math Code

6+3+9+6+3+9+6+3+9+6+3+9+6+3+9+6+3+9+6+3+9+6+3+9=___

Revelation 21:17 (KJV) *And he measured the wall thereof, an hundred and forty and four cubits, according to the measure of a man, that is, of the angel.*

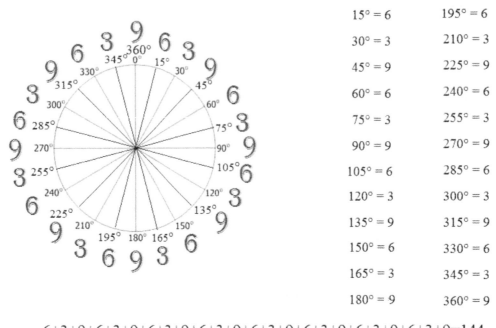

Add all of the 3, 6 & 9's to get the number 144.

15° = 6	195° = 6
30° = 3	210° = 3
45° = 9	225° = 9
60° = 6	240° = 6
75° = 3	255° = 3
90° = 9	270° = 9
105° = 6	285° = 6
120° = 3	300° = 3
135° = 9	315° = 9
150° = 6	330° = 6
165° = 3	345° = 3
180° = 9	360° = 9

6+3+9+6+3+9+6+3+9+6+3+9+6+3+9+6+3+9+6+3+9+6+3+9=144

Figure 11

The graphic below displays all the sequences of the 3, 6 & 9 numbers within the 15 degree interval circle. Notice that I have included the geometry of the Star of David within the degree circle.

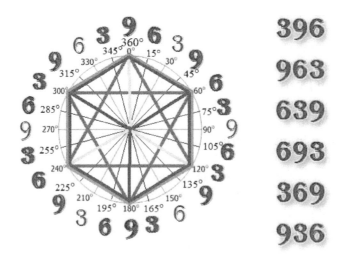

396
963
639
693
369
936

Figure 12

It's interesting that the Psalms clue in the Song of Degrees is also showing that the encoded information within the tones is based on a 3, 6 & 9 pattern when we use the Pythagorean mathematical skein of reducing the numbers to single digit integers. Therefore, the Song of Degrees is not only encoding six of the tones, but it is also encoding the underlying mathematical code of the 3, 6 & 9 pattern within the tones.

The 3, 6 & 9 Pattern in the Tones

1) 1+7+4 = 12 = 1+2 = **3**   1) 1+4+7=12= 1+2=**3**

2) 2+8+5 = 15 = 1+5 = **6**   2) 2+5+8=15=1+5=**6**

3) 3+9+6 = 18 = 1+8 = **9**   3) 3+6+9=18=1+8=**9**

4) 4+1+7 = 12 = 1+2 = **3**   4) 4+7+1=12=1+2=**3**

5) 5+2+8 = 15 = 1+5 = **6**   5) 5+8+2=15=1+5=**6**

6) 6+3+9 = 18 = 1+8 = **9**   6) 6+9+3=18=1+8=**9**

7) 7+4+1 = 12 = 1+2 = **3**   7) 7+1+4+12=1+2=**3**

8) 8+5+2 = 15 = 1+5 = **6**   8) 8+2+5=15+1+5=**6**

9) 9+6+3 = 18 = 1+8 = **9**   9) 9+3+6=18=1+8=**9**

Figure 13

"If you only knew the magnificence of the 3, 6 and 9, then you would have a key to the universe."

-Nikola Tesla

It was also interesting to me to learn that Nikola Tesla may have had knowledge in regards to the encoded information of the Song of Degrees in Psalms and the tones encoded in Numbers 7. After reading a quote that Tesla made about the magnificence of the 3, 6 and 9, I decided to look more into the life of Nikola Tesla. I was excited to find out that Tesla's father Milutin was an Orthodox priest, and so it would hardly seem surprising to wonder if perhaps Tesla may have decoded this very same information from the Bible. I'm sure he would have studied the Bible quite often when he was a child, and his work as an adult would seem to confirm that maybe he was able to successfully decode the tones for himself. Although this is purely conjecture on my part, I do believe that Tesla must have become aware of this encoded information either from Psalms 120-135 or from Numbers 7.

The Star of David within the degree circle is always drawn with placing two equilateral triangles perfectly within the circle, so that its vertices touch at 60°, 120°, 180°, 240°, 300° and 360°/0°. The vertices in the Star of David, and the hexagon points out each sequence of the 3, 6 & 9 tones, and the Star of David also does encode the Holy of Holies cube. Another interesting pattern that I found within this degree circle shows that each tone has three lines pointing towards the number. This could be an encoded reference to the trinity, but also I believe it has something to do with the Hebrew letter of Shin.

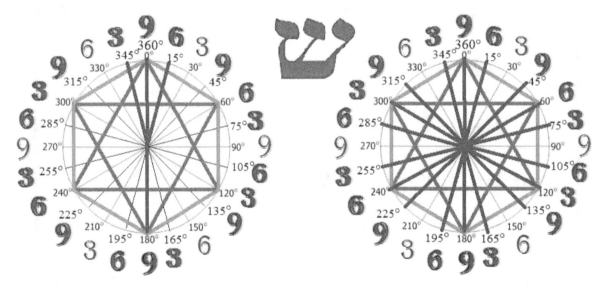

The Tridents of the Solfeggio Tones around the Degree Circle

Figure 14

The Song of Degrees helped me to realize that the degree circle is associated with the math of the tones of Numbers 7, and it also helped me to understand the underlying geometry that is associated with the tones, the Holy of Holies and New Jerusalem. I have come to understand that the degree circle math encodes a lot of additional information that is also associated with the mathematical numbers in our Solar System. In the next chapter I will go over more information about the degree circle as well as the compass. Through my research into the Jericho story in the Bible, I was able to realize more of the connections within the degree circle math.

The Degree Circle and Compass

I was reading the story about Jericho for some more clues because I realized that the story was about how the Israelites used sound to bring down the walls of Jericho. As I read the story again, I realized that there was another clue about the tones within this story. The clue was so subtle that it could be easily overlooked, if I did not know what I was looking for in this story, so if anyone was reading the story from a literal perspective and not looking for clues as to how the sounds brought down the walls, then they would miss this clue altogether.

Joshua 6:4 *And seven priests shall bear before the ark seven trumpets of rams' horns: and the seventh day ye shall compass the city seven times, and the priests shall blow with the trumpets.*

When I had read the story before, I was not aware of how the Solfeggio tones and the degree circle were related, nor was I aware of how the compass fits into the degree circle. This clue seemed to leap out to me as if it was beckoning me to explore this information further, and I did. It was amazing to me because it all seemed so easy to understand now. I realized that I had to explore what the numbers were if I rotated around the compass seven times just as the clue told me to do. When I looked at the numbers that resulted from the 7th rotation of the compass, I realized that when I went around the degree circle seven times, that it ended up with a very significant number that is encoded in Numbers 7. I had never understood why this number was encoded in Numbers 7 before, but now I completely understood the meaning of this clue that had perplexed me in the past. The clue in Joshua 6 and Numbers 7 was showing the reader that the numbers involved in these mysterious tones were associated with the degree circle and the compass. The rotations of the compass brought the numbers beyond the mere 360 degrees of a circle that the ancient Sumerians used and showed an underlying math that was the key to the creation of our universe. The longer and longer I delved into the mysteries of the degree circle math, the more I began to realize that our creation was based upon the rotation of circles, and that sacred geometry arose from them. My research was going around in circles (pun intended).

In this chapter I will explain step by step the twist and turns that I took to find all of the clues that were laid out before me. Each step shows another clue that we must take on our journey to find the purpose of these mysterious tones.

On my first step I wanted to understand what the numbers would add up to if I kept doubling the 360 degrees of a circle for each rotation, so I did the math to see what would happen. This is the next step for the reader as well. Below is the next mathematical exercise.

First Rotation: 360

Second Rotation: 360+360=___

Third Rotation: ___+360=___

Fourth Rotation: ___+360=___

Fifth Rotation: ___+360=___

Sixth Rotation: ___+360=___

Seventh Rotation: ___+360=___

In the verses below, the clue is encoded by adding the shekels together to get the sum for the seventh rotation of the compass. You can work out the math below in the next mathematical problem.

Numbers 7:85-86

[85] *Each charger of silver weighing an hundred and thirty shekels, each bowl seventy: all the silver vessels weighed* **two thousand and four hundred shekels**, *after the shekel of the sanctuary:*

[86] *The golden spoons were twelve, full of incense, weighing ten shekels apiece, after the shekel of the sanctuary: all the gold of the spoons was an* **hundred and twenty shekels**.

$$2400+120=\_\_\_\_$$

This clue to rotating the compass seven times in Numbers 7 is located right after the 6 encoded tones which ends at verse 83. I had remembered seeing a website that talked about how adding the shekels in these two verses gave the number 2,520 shekels, but the website never mentioned that this number has to do with the seventh rotation of the degree circle. When I worked out the math up to the seventh rotation, I recognized that number. I knew I had seen it before, so I looked it up and realized this was another encoded number in Numbers 7, but I never knew what it meant until now. I had finally understood the secret.

The story of Jericho was repeating the same clue as Numbers 7 but in a completely different way. Now I was sure more than ever that Numbers 7, Psalms 120-134 and Joshua 6 were all encoding these tones that are found within the degree circle with the rotation of the compass. Apparently, these tones were used to bring down the walls of Jericho, but it was more than just using the 24 tones that I had deciphered from the clues. I realized that the 24 tones only brought me up to the fourth rotation; so therefore, there must have been more tones. I needed to continue the pattern and go beyond the 24 tones to get to the seventh rotation. This was when I realized that there was another clue in verse 84 that suggested that I needed to add more tones. Looking at the pattern of the 24 tones is the key to working our way up to higher tones, and again this was another lesson in pattern recognition.

Numbers 7:84 This *was the dedication of the altar, in the day when it was anointed, by the princes of Israel:* **twelve** *chargers of silver,* **twelve** *silver bowls,* **twelve** *spoons of gold:*

$$12+12+12=\underline{}$$

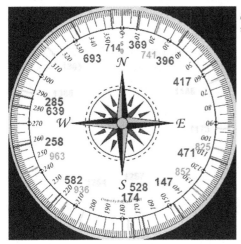

Go around the compass seven times.

First Rotation
0-360 degrees
Second Rotation
360-720 degrees
Third Rotation
720-1080 degrees
Fourth Rotation
1080-1440 degrees
Fifth Rotation
1440-1800 degrees
Sixth Rotation
1800-2160 degrees
Seventh Rotation
2160-2520 degrees

Joshua 6:4 *And seven priests shall bear before the ark seven trumpets of rams' horns: and the seventh day ye shall **compass the city seven times**, and the priests shall blow with the trumpets.*

Numbers 7

85 Each charger of silver weighing an hundred and thirty shekels, each bowl seventy: all the silver vessels weighed two thousand and four hundred shekels, after the shekel of the sanctuary:

86 The golden spoons were twelve, full of incense, weighing ten shekels apiece, after the shekel of the sanctuary: all the gold of the spoons was an hundred and twenty shekels.

2400 shekels + 120 shekels = 2520

Figure 15

As you can see from the graphic above, the 24 tones go up to the fourth rotation of the compass, so this is a clue that we need to finish the pattern within the 24 tones and bring the number of tones up to 36 as the clue in verse 84 is telling us to do.

The first thing to do when looking at the first 24 tones is to recognize that the last 3 tones in each column do not follow the pattern of the previous 9 tones; therefore, we need to group the first 9 tones together with the second 9 tones in the other column. This means that the last 3 tones in both columns are the first of a new series with their own pattern. The 18 triad numbers have the wraparound pattern, so now we have to figure out what the pattern of the next 18 tones is going to be by the 6 tones that we have so far.

The First Eighteen Tones

```
174                 147
      -------111         ------111
285                 258
      -------111         ------111
396                 369
      -------21          ------102
417                 471
      -------111         ------111
528                 582
      -------111         ------111
639                 693
      -------102         ------21
741                 714
      -------111         ------111
852                 825
      -------111         ------111
963                 936
      -------210         ------210
```

Figure 16

Now if we look at the pattern within the first 18 tones, we can see that we need to follow this same pattern within the next 18 tones to bring us up to the 36 tones pattern. In the left column we have a number pattern of 111,111, 21, 111, 111 102, 111, 111 and 210. In the right column we have a number pattern of 111, 111, 102, 111, 111, 21, 111, 111 and 210. Notice that the 21 and 102 numbers change positions from the left column to the right column. It seems obvious that we must keep this pattern with the second 18 tones, since the first 2 tones on the left and right side start out with a skip rate of 111 two times.

This exercise will reveal the next 12 tones, which brings the total up to 36 tones altogether.

Left Column	Right Column
1173 +111=1284	1146+111=1257
1284+111=1395	1257+111=1368
1395+21=____	1368+102=____
____+111=____	____+111=____
____+111=____	____+111=____
____+102=____	____+21=____
____+111=____	____+111=____
____+111=____	____+111=____
____	____

Once I had the 36 tones, I wanted to plot them on the degree circles and see where I ended up. This was no easy task, as I had to keep zooming into the graphic to count the tiny lines on the degree circle and highlight it with a color. After I completed plotting the tones on the rotations of the compass, I saw that there was nothing on the 7th degree circle. I was perplexed as to why the clue led me to believe that bringing the total up to 36 tones would end at the 7th degree circle with the total of 2,520 degrees. After a lot of brain storming, I realized that it possibly symbolized the creation of the heavens and the earth which God made in 6 days, as He rested on the 7th day. The Jericho story was showing that the symbolism of the story was not just about the Israelites conquering the city, but prophetic of God conquering Satan's fallen warped creation and freeing His people to return them back home. These tones have the power to destroy the wall that was placed between us and God as a result of the fall of mankind. These tones have the power to free us all, and that is why the 144,000 will sing the new song with these tones. Apparently, the 36 tones have the power to break down any walls or barriers, therefore, waking people up to our connection with God.

Here is a graphic of the second 18 tones. As you can see there is a new pattern to figure out, since these tones do not have the same wraparound pattern as the first 18 tones in the triad numbers. I call these the "one plus" numbers. Here is an example: (1173 is 1+173=174). Notice that this connects the second 18 tones with the first 18 tones.

The Second Eighteen Tones

```
1173            1146
   -------111      -----111
1284            1257
   -------111      -----111
1395            1368
   -------21       -----102
1416            1470
   -------111      -----111
1527            1581
   -------111      -----111
1638            1692
   -------102      -----21
1740            1713
   -------111      -----111
1851            1824
   -------111      -----111
1962            1935
   -------210      -----210
```

Figure 17

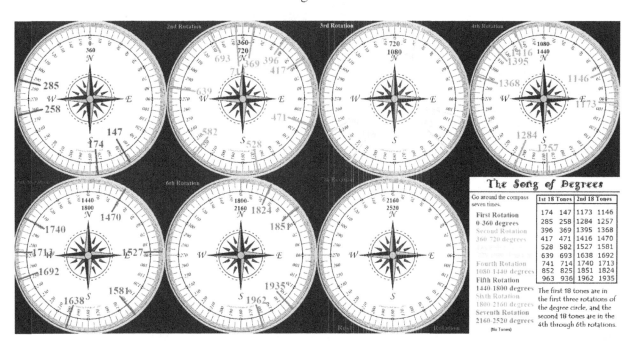

Figure 18

The degree circle is also associated with sacred geometry. It can help people to draw a perfect Star of David, which is another reason why the Song of Degrees is sometimes called the Song of Degrees of David. Now remember Jesus Christ was a descendant of King David, so it makes sense that the tones would be associated with the new song of the 144,000 followers of Christ.

In the next interactive exercise, you will draw a Star of David within the degree circle and compass. First, start at 120 degrees and draw a straight line to 240 degrees to the left, then draw a line to the 0 or 360 degrees at the top of the circle. The next step is to complete the triangle pointing up by connecting the 0 line to 120 degrees. Now you can start the triangle pointing down by starting at 60 degrees and connecting a line to 180 degrees, then connect a line from 180 degrees to 300 degrees and from the 300 degrees mark, you can connect the line back to 60 degrees to complete the triangle pointing down. You have just made a perfect Star of David!

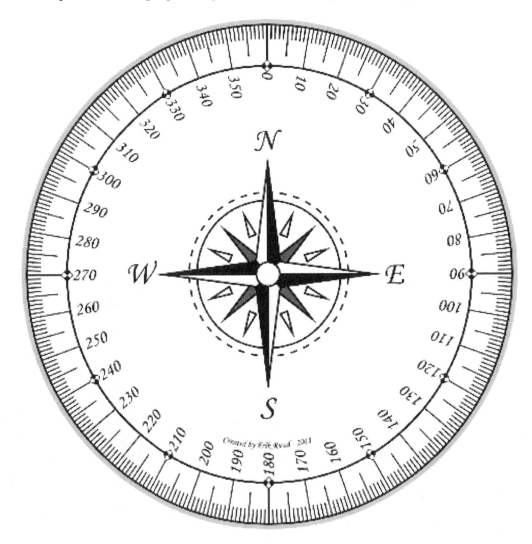

Now the next step is to find the Holy of Holies cube in the same degree circle above. It is easy! First, you will trace out a hexagon by starting at 0 degrees and connecting a line to 60 degrees, and then you can connect a line from 60 degrees to 120 degrees. The next line should start at 120 degrees and go to 180 degrees, then from 180 degrees draw a line to 240 degrees. The next line will start at 240 degrees and go to 300 degrees, and then you can trace out your final line from 300 degrees to 0 or 360 degrees to complete your hexagon. The next step is to connect a line from 0 degrees to the center of the degree circle which would be the center point of the compass drawing in the center. Draw a line from 60 degrees, 120 degrees, 180 degrees, 240 degrees and 300 degrees to the center. You have drawn the Holy of Holies cube.

Figure 19

Figure 20

You may be wondering why this is significant to the Song of Degrees, as I have stated before, sometimes the verses in Psalms 120-134 also call it the Song of Degrees of David, so therefore, this is a clue to draw the Star of David in the 15 degree interval circle with the 3, 6 and 9 tones. If you remember from the previous chapter, each vertex of the Star of David points out one of the six 3, 6 & 9 tones. This can only mean that the geometry that is being hinted at in the Song of Degrees is a clue to something else that we have to decipher.

As I began to see the connections between the geometry of the Star of David, the Holy of Holies cube and the Song of degrees, I suddenly realized one day that these tones are related to the city of New Jerusalem that is mentioned in Revelation 21 of the last book in the Bible. Both the Holy of Holies and New Jerusalem are in the shape of a cube, because the length, width and height are equal. In 1 Kings 6:20, we are told that the oracle or Holy of Holies is 20 cubits length by 20 cubits breadth by 20 cubits height. Notice that the ancient measurements of the cubit sounds like "cube it" and this is what we did to the Star of David in the degree circle. We turned it into a two dimensional cube. By comparison, Revelation 21:16 also states that the length, breadth and height of New Jerusalem is equal, therefore, this verse is implying that this future city is in the shape of a cube. It is kind of hard to actually visualize a city that is cube shaped, but it could be talking about the city being circular. We have seen that we can make a two dimensional cube inside of a circle.

1 Kings 6:20

*And the oracle in the forepart was **twenty cubits in length, and twenty cubits in breadth, and twenty cubits in the height** thereof: and he overlaid it with pure gold; and so covered the altar which was of cedar.*

Revelation 21:16 (KJV) *And the city lieth foursquare, and the length is as large as the breadth: and he measured the city with the reed, twelve thousand furlongs.* ***The length and the breadth and the height of it are equal.***

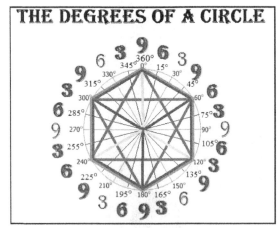

Revelation 21:17 *And he measured the wall thereof, an hundred and forty and four cubits, according to the measure of a man, that is, of the angel.* (angel/angle anagram)

Add all of the 3, 6 & 9's to get the number 144.

15° = 6	195° = 6
30° = 3	210° = 3
45° = 9	225° = 9
60° = 6	240° = 6
75° = 3	255° = 3
90° = 9	270° = 9
105° = 6	285° = 6
120° = 3	300° = 3
135° = 9	315° = 9
150° = 6	330° = 6
165° = 3	345° = 3
180° = 9	360° = 9

6+3+9+6+3+9+6+3+9+6+3+9+6+3+9+6+3+9+6+3+9+6+3+9=144

Figure 21

It was the hint of the 15 chapters in the Song of Degrees that put us on this path to find the encoded tones within the 15 degree interval of a circle. We added the 3's, 6's and 9's, which is the clue in finding the number 144 in the verse of Revelation 21:17, and we followed the clue to cube it. In another chapter, we will indeed cube the Solfeggio tones and discover what other clues we can find.

In Leonard Horowitz book *Walk on Water*, he explains about the discovery of the infinity pattern made by Marko Rodin. Actually, this discovery is not a new one, and I will show you where you can find a hint to this pattern in Numbers 7. In Numbers 7 there are 2 verses that seem to be presenting a numerical pattern for us to decipher in the number of the wagons and oxen. The clue is so subtle that most people would never be able to pick up on it as being a clue to the Solfeggio tones. Pay very close attention to the pattern that is being presented to us in our mathematical lessons in Numbers 7. You may recognize another pattern within the numbers.

Numbers 7:7-8 (KJV)

*⁷ **Two** wagons and **four** oxen he gave unto the sons of Gershon, according to their service:*

*⁸ And **four** wagons and **eight** oxen he gave unto the sons of Merari, according unto their service, under the hand of Ithamar the son of Aaron the priest.*

The clue is to continue the pattern that is being presented to us. As you can easily decipher in this pattern recognition test each digit doubles. Continue the pattern below in the next interactive exercise of the Bible.

2, 4, 8......

2, 4, 8, __, __, __, ___, ___, ___, ___

You may already recognize these numbers as being the same numbers that are associated with your computers and memory cards. In addition to these numbers being associated with the infinity pattern that Rodin rediscovered, the numbers are also called binary byte numbers. It's interesting that the Bible actually shows us the template for our modern day binary code. We will go over binary code in another chapter. For now though, I will mention that the 111 skip rate in the Solfeggio tones is also a binary number.

Here is another exercise to work on below. According to Rodin's discovery, if we apply the Pythagorean mathematical skein to these numbers, then a repeating pattern will emerge. Reduce the numbers below to a single digit. You can then use those single digit numbers to create the infinity pattern. Notice how the pattern continues to repeat as you fill in the blanks below.

2, 4, 8, 16 (1+6=_), 32 (3+2=_), 64 (6+4=__ 1+0=_), 128 (1+2+8=__ 1+1=_), 256 (2+5+6=__ 1+3=_), 512 (5+1+2=_), 1024 (1+0+2+4=_) ....

You should get six repeating numbers that will go on forever if you continue the pattern of doubling the numbers.

Here is the answer:

2, 4, 8, 16 (1+6=**7**), 32 (3+2=**5**), 64 (6+4=10 1+0=**1**), 128 (1+2+8=11 1+1=**2**), 256 (2+5+6=13 1+3=**4**), 512 (5+1+2=**8**), 1024 (1+0+2+4=**7**) ………..

1, 2, 4, 8, 7, 5………

There are pictures of Rodin's infinity pattern on the internet. He used a circle labeled with 9 numbers. Really, there are only 9 numbers in our numeral system, as every other number is a multiple of the 9 main numbers. I looked at this pattern and realized that I needed to put the 9 numbers on a degree circle, but first I needed to figure out how many times 9 goes into 360 degrees, so that I could figure out the degree interval of how to space them.

$$360/9=\_\_$$

Once I had that number I could space them apart on the degree circle to see if there were any more clues. I found a significant clue in the geometry of the Star of David.

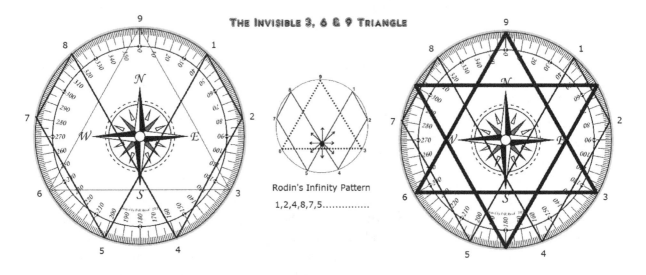

Figure 22

The infinity clue seems to be another template or exercise to get us to draw the Star of David within the degree circle. As you can see from the graphic above, I divided up the degree circle into 40 degree intervals, so that I would know where to put the 9 numbers around the degree circle. The first nine tones and the second nine tones of the Solfeggio scale are made up of all possible combinations of just the nine numbers in the 18 triad tones. There are graphics all over the internet showing the first 9 tones in a circle. It turns out that the infinity pattern which is presented in Numbers 7:7-8 is also a clue to putting the tones in the circle to make the Star of David pattern for the triad tones.

In the next exercise, you can draw the triangles and Star of David symbols within the degree circle. Remember to use a pencil in all of the exercises, so that you can erase any mistakes you make while you are learning these tones. Here are some hints that you need to know before you get started. It's easy to connect the triangles of the 1,4 &7 tones, 2,5 & 8 tones and the 3,6 & 9 tones, but it is a little harder to position the down triangle in the Star of David for each one. The line on all sides of the equilateral triangle is 120 degrees and the down pointing vertex is 180 degrees from the up pointing apex of the triangle pointing up. Make sure that your down triangle has those measurements, so that your Star of David will be perfectly aligned.

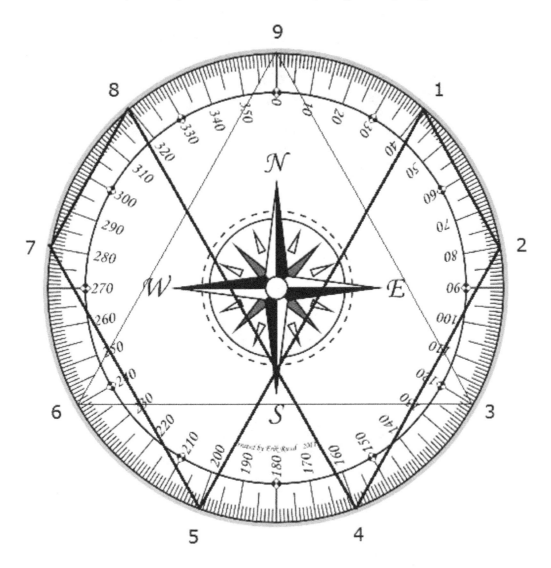

Once you have completed this exercise, you will have three Star of David symbols within the degree circle. You should then label each number with its 2 tones. For example: the number 1 should have all tones that start with the number 1, which would be 147 and 174. This will help you to get an idea of which triangle and Star of David goes with what tones. You can also use colored pencils to help to distinguish each triangle. Also, after you have completed the exercise, it would be wise to trace each tone around the triangles to get an idea of how you have to move around the degree circle to read them. Some of them are read clockwise, and some are read counterclockwise. Focus on this drawing to be able to understand the tones better, as this is God's way to help us to understand His creation and His tones with blueprints and pictures.

THREE TRIANGLES

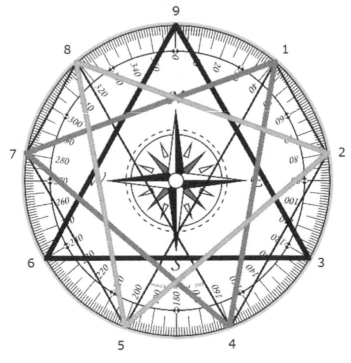

1,4 & 7 - 2,5 & 8 - **3,6 & 9**

THREE STAR OF DAVIDS

1,4 & 7 - 2,5 & 8 - **3,6 & 9**

Figure 23

After I worked on these drawings, I began to see that there is much more encoded within these graphics. This builds on another discovery that I had made previously. I will go into much more detail about the clockwise and counterclockwise patterns in another chapter. For now I will leave you with the graphic below.

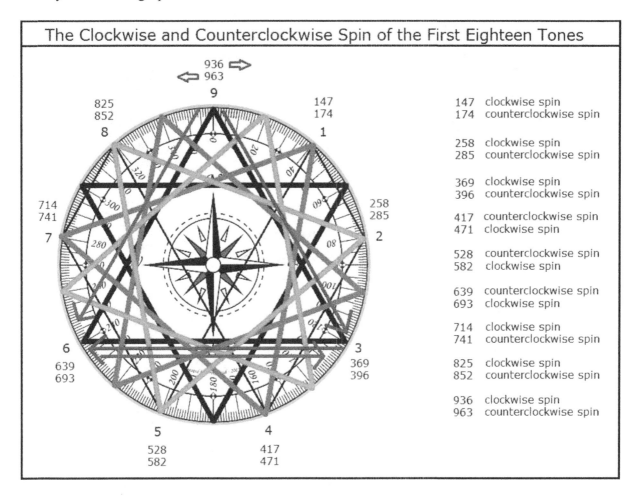

Figure 24

Another pattern that I have found from the infinity pattern was discovered after I wrote this chapter, and so I have had to add more information upon accidentally discovering that the degrees in this 40 degree interval circle also point out these numbers associated with all the triad tones. I decided to add all of the degrees that the 40 degree interval pointed out to make the triangles and Star of David within the 9 pointed circle. Once I added them all up, I realized that the 1, 4 &7 tones, 2, 5 & 8 tones and the 3, 6 & 9 are still clearly marked out at the triangles that are assigned to each triangle; however, they became reversed in the addition of the degrees. For example: the number 1 became 4, the number 4 became 7 and the number 7 became 1.

The next graphic shows how I used the Pythagorean mathematical skein to reduce the 9 numbers in the 40 degree interval circle for the infinity pattern. The numbers that I assigned as 1 through 9 around the circle changed when I reduced the degree numbers to 1 digit numbers, so this created another pattern that shows I was on the right track to divide the degree circle into 40 degree intervals. This pattern shows me that I was right to assign these triangles to the tones that we did, so therefore, this is a confirmation of this work.

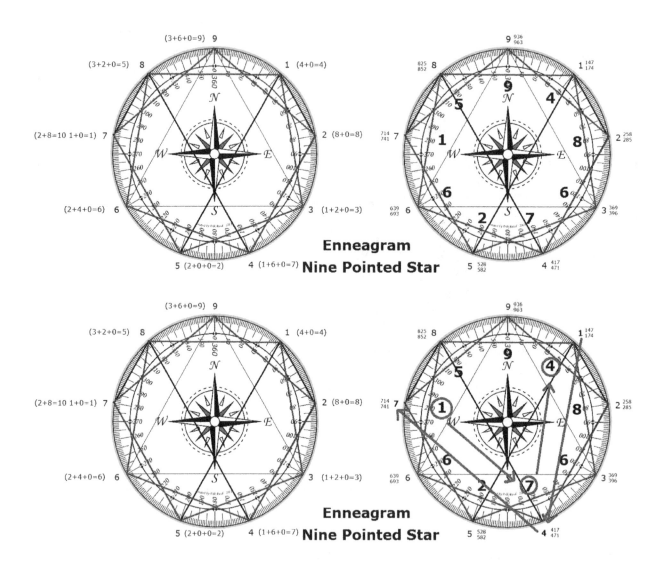

Figure 25

Another thing that I noticed after I reduced these 40 degree numbers to 1 digit is that we can trace out a 9 pointed star. If I had traced out the 1 through 9 patterns before, it would have traced out a 9 sided polygon called an enneagon. After I reassigned the numbers, I decided to see what they traced out, so I drew a line from the first number to the next consecutive number (1 to 2, 3 to 4….) until I got to the number 9 in the circle, and when I had finished I realized I had just drawn a 9 pointed star.

The 9 pointed star is called an enneagram, and I believe that this star represents the 9 segment columns that are found throughout the tones. The number 9 has been a big pattern with these tones, and it is geometrically associated with the enneagram. Just as the Star of David is associated with the triad tones as a six pointed star, the enneagram is associated with the 9 tones in each column within the tones. The 9 pointed star in the degree circle almost looks like a crown with 9 thorns. Is this an image of Jesus crown of thorns?

The Navajo have a prophecy that warns of the time of the end. One of the signs is that a nine pointed star will come from the east and unify all races and nations with love. One website also says that when the Pahana or Bahana returns again, who is the lost white brother of the Hopi, he will come from the father sun in the east, and a nine pointed star would be seen rising to herald his arrival. The Pahana or Elder Brother left for the east at the time that the Hopi entered the fourth world; however, the Hopi say that he will return again, and that he will destroy the wicked and usher in a new age of peace in the fifth world. Pahana sounds like Jesus Christ, and his name would be different due to the language of the Hopi people being different. If Jesus had indeed visited the Hopi people in the past, then this might confirm the book of Mormon that says that Jesus visited the people in the Americas after some of the Israelites had come over to colonize this part of the world.

In 1963, Grandfather David Monongye, which is the late spiritual elder of Hotevilla, Arizona, saw a nine pointed star rising in the sky. He realized that this must be the fulfillment of the star prophecy that the lost white brother Bahana will soon return. Notice that the year that he saw the nine pointed star was in 1**963**, and that the last three numbers is the 9th tone of 963.

Could the 9 tone design within the tones and the 9 pointed star within the 40 degree interval circle be a sign of the time of the end? Could the tones of this star unify all races with love?

There is a 9 candlestick Menorah that is used during Hanukkah, and I can't help but wonder if perhaps this is also a sign of the Divine nine within the tones. It was created to commemorate the victory of the Jewish Maccabees over the Greek and Syrians in 165 BC, when a miraculous burning of a one day supply of oil lasted for eight days. The ninth candlestick in the middle is called the "Shamash" and it is used to light the other 8 candlesticks. Could this 9 candlestick Menorah be symbolic and prophetic of the discovery of these mysterious tones in the end times?

As you can see the degree circle math is very important when learning about the tones, and within this simple system there is so much to discover. I believe the whole universe was designed with the math found within these tones and the Song of Degrees. I will be bringing out more information about the degree circle math in another chapter.

This concludes the chapter on the degree circle math, but in other chapters I will present more information that is based on this degree circle math or graphics that involve the degree circle. In the next chapter, I will explain to you about the binaural beats that are encoded into the first 18 tones of the Solfeggio scale.

The Binaural Beats

It's interesting that I always put the tones into two columns when I was working on how to display them. I guess it was just a natural inclination to separate the first 9 tones from the next 9 tones that were made with the other combinations of the numbers. Over time though, I began to put together another puzzle that I had not thought of before. In the book *Healing Codes for the Biological Apocalypse* there are several exercises that are meant to help with the development of balancing the left and right hemispheres of the brain. When I read the book and worked on those exercises, I never realized how important the left/right paradigm was with the Solfeggio tones, until one day I finally made the connection. I was reading the book *The Ancient Secret of the Flower of Life* by Drunvalo Melchizedek. He described in his book all about the right and left hemispheres of the brain and how each side works. Suddenly, I realized that the way I had been putting the tones in the left and right columns was really a significant clue. I wondered if this was a clue to listen to the tones in right and left speakers. I wondered if I had missed a clue somewhere in Numbers 7 that might have let me know about this arrangement of the tones.

During the time that I was learning about the Flower of Life and the different functions of the right and left hemispheres of the brain, I went to some of my friends' church in Danville, Virginia. The preacher started to read verses about Jesus yoke, and suddenly it was like bells were going off in my head. I went home and read the verses in Matthew 11:29-30 and Numbers 7:3 and realized that I needed to pair the tones up like two oxen yoked together. It's interesting that Jesus tells us to take his yoke, because it is easy. A yoke is a wooden cross piece that is used to connect two oxen together to pull a cart or wagon. Notice that in Numbers 7:3 there were 12 oxen pulling 6 covered wagons, so that means that the oxen were yoked together to pull the 6 covered wagons, therefore, they were paired together two by two just like the 72 Disciples of Christ.

Luke 10 (NET Bible) *1 After this the Lord appointed seventy-two others and sent them on ahead of him two by two into every town and place where he himself was about to go.*

Numbers 7:3 *And they brought their offering before the LORD, six covered wagons, and twelve oxen;*

Matthew 11:29-30 [29] *Take my yoke upon you, and learn of me; for I am meek and lowly in heart: and ye shall find rest unto your souls.* [30] *For my yoke is easy, and my burden is light.*

At some point I remembered reading about binaural beats and how if you play two different tones on the right and left speaker of headphones, then you will hear another completely separate tone. I looked up more information about binaural beats and found out that there had to be certain rules that must be followed to get a binaural beat. I applied these rules to the tones and was shocked to realize that there were only 6 binaural beats in the tones, and amazingly they came from just 12 tones that were paired together. Those twelve oxen that are yoked together are the twelve tones that produce the six binaural beats which are hidden like the six covered wagons.

The two rules of the binaural beats:

1. The frequencies of the tones have to be below 1,000 hertz to hear a binaural beat.
2. The difference between the two frequencies have to be less than or equal to 30 hertz for the binaural beat effect to occur.

In the next exercise you can find the binaural beats in the Solfeggio tones for yourself. First, the tones have to be under 1000 hertz, so that means that only the first 18 tones would qualify. Second, you have to figure out the differences between the left and the right column tones.

$$174-147=\_\_$$
$$285-258=\_\_$$
$$396-369=\_\_$$
$$471-417=\_\_$$
$$582-528=\_\_$$
$$693-639=\_\_$$
$$741-714=\_\_$$
$$852-825=\_\_$$
$$963-936=\_\_$$

The binaural beats were first discovered by Heinrich Wilheim Dove in 1839. I kind of laughed when I first read this information because the Holy Spirit is sometimes symbolized as a dove in the Bible. It didn't seem like much of a coincidence that I was trying to decode the information about these tones in Numbers 7 and had just figured out another clue that involved the binaural beats, which I found out was brought to us by a Dove. Sometimes it seems like even God has a sense of humor.

In Numbers 7:3, where it talks about the six covered wagons pulled by twelve oxen, it refers to two different clues. I always thought that this was a clue to the six Solfeggio tones that were encoded in Numbers 7, and that the twelve oxen were the first twelve tones that are to be worked out in the pattern. However, now that I had found the six binaural beats that are formed within the first 18 tones, I began to see the dualistic nature of that verse. It can be referring to both forms of the six covered wagons that can be found. This particular verse had a dual meaning, but one of the clues was kind of like a secret within a secret. The first six covered wagons were the six tones that were found in Numbers 7:12-83, but out of those six tones comes the eighteen tones which encodes the most precious six covered wagons that are found in the six binaural beats.

As you can see from figure 26, there can only be 6 binaural beats in the Solfeggio scale, and they are all found in the first 18 tones. The three middle tones go beyond the 30 hertz cap, so therefore, no binaural beat can be heard with those tones. The second 18 tones can't have binaural beats because they are over the 1,000 hertz mark. These tones could have only been uncovered by yoking the first 18 tones together to find these 6 unique tones which are just one tone. († one)

The Binaural Beats of the Solfeggio Tones

174 ——————147	174-147= 27	27 Hz
285 ——————258	285-258= 27	27 Hz
396 ——————369	396-369= 27	27 Hz
417 ——————471	471-417= 54	
528 ——————582	582-528= 54	
639 ——————693	693-639= 54	
741 ——————714	741-714= 27	27 Hz
852 ——————825	852-825= 27	27 Hz
963 ——————936	963-936= 27	27 Hz

Figure 26

The second clue to the binaural beats only could have been meant for our modern times. The first person to demonstrate a two channel audio system was Clément Ader in 1881 in Paris, France. However, our modern stereophonic technology was invented in the 1930's by Alan Blumlein a British engineer who patented stereo records, stereo films and surround sound. The first clue to find the six hidden tones that are encoded in Numbers 7:12-83 could have been found by anyone in the past, but the second clue to find the six hidden binaural tones could have only been meant for people from 1881 to now. I find that very remarkable that God put two clues in that one verse; one for the ancient Israelites and the other for the people of our time.

The number of the binaural beat is 27 hertz which I realized is a clue to many different things in the Bible. It's interesting that there are 27 books in the New Testament which could be a clue to linking the tones to Jesus Christ. Another interesting connection to the Bible is that the number 27 is a perfect cube. (3^3 = 3 × 3 × 3=27) Remember the Holy of Holies and New Jerusalem are in the shape of a cube. If you have ever played with a Rubik's Cube, then you know this cube is made of 27 cubes with 3 cubes for the width, length and the height of the cube. Rubik's cube would be an example of the 27 cubed form of the cube.

The total number of letters in the Hebrew alphabet is 27 with the 22 regular letters and the 5 final consonants. The Hebrew language is the original language of the Israelites. It's also interesting that there are 27 hyper dimensional directions in three dimensional space, and this can easily be demonstrated in a cube. Those 27 hyper dimensional directions can actually be represented by the 27 Hebrew letters. I tried to link those letters to the directions, but I have not found all of the clues to complete my diagram yet.

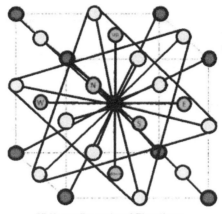

27 Hyperdimensional Directions

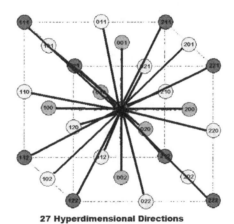

27 Hyperdimensional Directions

Figure 27

The *Sefer Yetzirah* is the Book of Creation, and it was traditionally ascribed to the patriarch Abraham according to the legends, however, scholars do not know the origin of this book. What I find interesting is that this book shows the directions of certain Hebrew letters, and so I realized that I could find those positions on the cube. Years ago I was watching the movie *Stargate,* and I saw a scene where the coordinates used by the stargate was drawn as a cube. The character Daniel draws a cube and then shows that there are 6 points on the surface of the cube. He then draws the seventh point out away from the cube for the destination. That movie showed me that the cube could be used for directions in space, so ever since I have realized that concept, I have been trying to figure out which ones of the 27 hyper dimensional directions match with their corresponding Hebrew letter. I have never been able to figure out all of the clues to how the Hebrew letters match those 27 directions on the cube, but I have found 19 of the letters as specific directions on the Holy of Holies cube. Those clues were given to me in the *Sefer Yetzirah*.

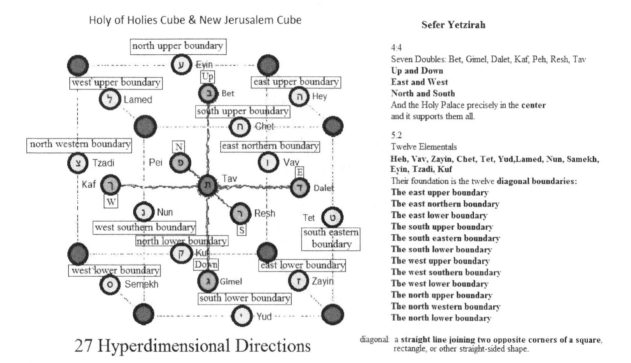

Figure 28

Time and time again the Solfeggio tones keep giving me clues to the Holy of Holies cube and the New Jerusalem cube. In my next chapter I will show even more clues to the cube.

As I was looking at the way I subtracted the right and the left tones, I realized that there was an all familiar pattern once again of counter-rotation within the tones. These tones seem to keep showing me the same clues over and over again of spirals in the counter-rotating numbers and of torsion physics. As I have shown you before in the wraparound effect of the tones and the clockwise and counterclockwise rotation of the triad tones around the degree circle, these tones are encoding counter-rotating spins and spirals. It was, therefore, not all that surprising that I also find the same pattern within the math to find the binaural beats. It's also interesting to note that only the tones that can be subtracted from the left to the right are the binaural beats. The middle tones that give the subtraction total of 54 are subtracted from the right to the left, and they do not produce the binaural beats, therefore, the right (pun intended) tones for the binaural beats are facing towards the right.

Left/Right Pattern in the Binaural Beats

174 → 147	174-147= 27	left to right
285 → 258	285-258= 27	left to right
396 → 369	396-369= 27	left to right
417 ← 471	471-417= 54	right to left
528 ← 582	582-528= 54	right to left
639 ← 693	693-639= 54	right to left
741 → 714	741-714= 27	left to right
852 → 825	852-825= 27	left to right
963 → 936	963-936= 27	left to right

Figure 29

As you can see the number 27 seems to be a very significant clue altogether, but if these clues are not enough to convince you that there is something mystical to this number, then I have more evidence. The mirror number to 27 is 72, so in other words, if you read it backwards or in a mirror it will be the number 72. The number 72 is crucial for many different reasons. First of all it is the possible number of the disciples. In certain versions of the Bible the number of disciples is seventy two, whereas other interpretations say that there were seventy disciples.

Luke 10 New English Translation (NET Bible)

The Mission of the Seventy-Two *1 After this the Lord appointed seventy-two others and sent them on ahead of him two by two into every town and place where he himself was about to go. ² He said to them, "The harvest is plentiful, but the workers are few.*

I believe that the number 72 makes more sense to me for many different reasons. First, the number 72 is a multiple of 12, and there were originally 12 apostles. Second, the number of disciples that sing the new song in the book of Revelation is 144,000, which is also a multiple of 12 and 72. Third, 72 doubled is 144, which is the number of the measurement of the walls in New Jerusalem. Fourth, the number 72 is a precession of the equinox number; because the Earth moves 1 degree in its circle wobble every 72 years.

$$72/12=6$$

$$72 \times 2 = 144$$

$$144,000/72=2000 \text{ or } 2000 \times 72 = 144000$$

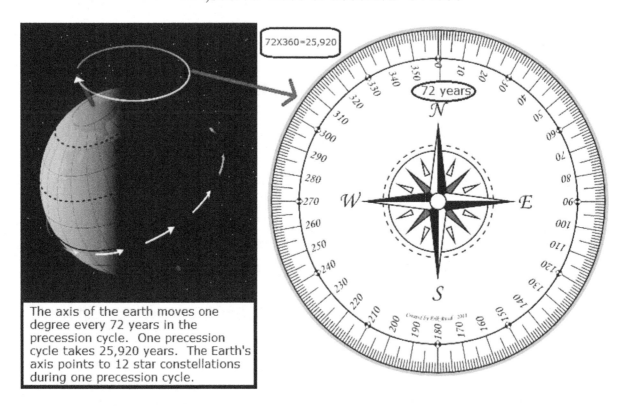

The axis of the earth moves one degree every 72 years in the precession cycle. One precession cycle takes 25,920 years. The Earth's axis points to 12 star constellations during one precession cycle.

Figure 30

The Earth has a slight wobble which traces out a huge circle over a period of 25,920 years, and this circle can be thought of as a degree circle, the Earth moves only 1 degree in this huge circle every 72 years. If you multiply that 72 year period by the 360 degrees of a circle, then you will find the number of years in a Great Year of the earth.

As you can see the mirror number of 27 is also very remarkable, and it would account for more scientific knowledge that is recorded into these very mysterious tones. As you read along in this book, I will share with you more of the knowledge to the creation of this universe that is encoded within these tones. Through the years that I have worked on research with these tones, I have been astounded time and time again by what I am finding encoded within these tones. For anyone that does not believe in God as the Creator of our universe and the earth, this information that I am finding within these tones is very significant proof of Divine design in our universe. The math behind God's Creation is completely awesome in terms of the knowledge and blueprints that are contained within the math of these tones.

As I began to think in more detail about the binaural beats within the tones and the one tone that was encoded in between the 12 tones 6 times, I started to realize that a theory that I had earlier on in my research was correct. I realized that New Jerusalem was being hinted about a lot within the tones. To reiterate the key points that I have brought up before in the earlier chapters, the 3, 6 and 9's that goes around the 15 degree interval circle in the Song of Degrees adds up to 144, which is the number for the measurement of the walls of New Jerusalem. I also kept finding the cube encoded within the tones, which is the shape of New Jerusalem. It was interesting to me to realize that New Jerusalem is made up of 12 stones for the foundations of this Holy city. My theory was that New Jerusalem is made with tones and not stones like Jerusalem in Israel. Stones can be an anagram for tones, and it seems that these tones are encoding New Jerusalem for a reason.

Revelation 21:19-20

*^{19} And the foundations of the wall of the city were garnished with all manner of precious **stones**. The first foundation was jasper; the second, sapphire; the third, a chalcedony; the fourth, an emerald;*

^{20} The fifth, sardonyx; the sixth, sardius; the seventh, chrysolyte; the eighth, beryl; the ninth, a topaz; the tenth, a chrysoprasus; the eleventh, a jacinth; the twelfth, an amethyst.

Keep in mind that most scholars believe that New Jerusalem is either in the shape of a circle or a cube. It is wise to see the connections between the degree circles' Star of David and the Holy of Holies cube as it is found within the circle at certain degrees. There is another ancient drawing called Metatron's Cube, and legend has it that the Archangel Metatron formed this cube from his soul. The story is told in the apocryphal texts of the *Second Book of Enoch*. The graphic is composed of 13 circles which can be seen as the 12 apostles around Jesus Christ in the center. It can also symbolically represent the earth in the center which points to 12 star constellations in the precession of the equinox with the circle wobble of 25,920 years. Nevertheless, I also realized that I could put these 12 tones in the 12 circles going around the binaural beat of 27 hertz in the center circle. The 12 tones in this regard might be thought of as the 12 gates going around New Jerusalem. It is also most worthy to note that you can trace out two cubes within Metatron's cube from the placement of the circles which is a hypercube. The corner of both the cubes in the hypercube is exactly in the center circle which is remarkable for the fact that there are many verses in the Bible in both the Old Testament and the New Testament that talks about the corner stone. In the New Testament it talks about the corner stone being rejected, and remember the center circle in the Metatron's cube can symbolically represent Jesus with his 12 apostles around him. In the tones that Jesus gave to Puleo, the binaural beat of 27 hertz that comes from the 12 tones would be in the center circle of the Metatron's cube, and therefore, the twelve tones circle around the one tone. In other words, Jesus Christ and the binaural beat of 27 Hz are in the same circle.

Job 38:6

Whereupon are the foundations thereof fastened? or who laid the corner stone thereof;

In the next exercise, you can find the corner stone or corner tones for yourself. Remember, 27 hertz is the tone that is found 6 times with the 12 tones. Think about how this tone is heard only when it is played with one tone in the left ear and one tone with the right ear, therefore, you want to line up the tones so that each two tones are lined up with 27 hertz n the middle. Give it a try and remember to use a pencil so that you can erase any mistakes.

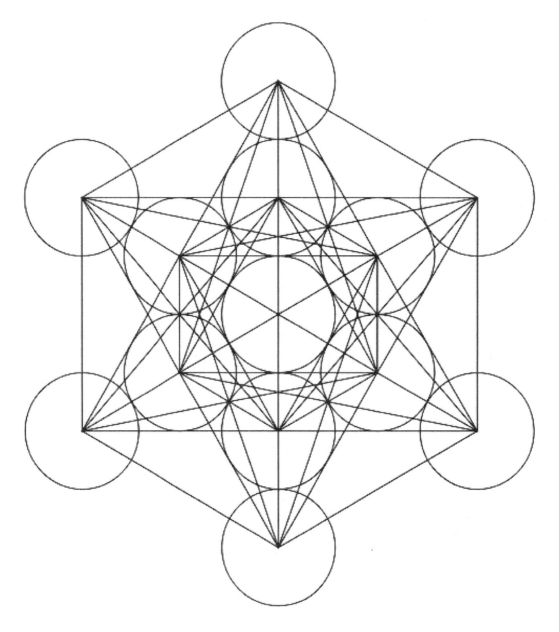

Psalm 118:22

The stone which the builders refused is become the head stone of the corner.

In Psalms 118:22, this verse talks about a corner stone that was rejected by the builders. Many biblical scholars say that the corner stone is Jesus because he was rejected as the Messiah by his own people. We can see that the middle circle in the Metatron's cube shows the cornerstone of both the cubes is in the center circle. This circle that holds the corner stone is the sure foundation in Zion. Not only is Christ in the center as the corner stone, but the 27 Hz tones is also in the center and is the corner tones. I use this in the plural, because 27 Hz shows up 6 times in the binaural beats. This is Christ's tones.

Isaiah 28:16

Therefore thus saith the Lord God, Behold, I lay in Zion for a foundation a stone, a tried stone, a precious corner stone, a sure foundation: he that believeth shall not make haste.

Now after you are done, observe Metatron's Cube again and notice that the center circle lines up with all 12 tones in a line. Also notice that the middle circle or 27 hertz is located at the corner of both of the cubes in the hypercube. The corner stone for New Jerusalem is actually the corner tones as the 6 tones that come from the 12 tones is in the center of them all. Now you have the actual corner tone to build New Jerusalem, but remember it will take 144,000 singing the new song with Jesus in the center sitting on the throne. This cube will be made by both light and sound!

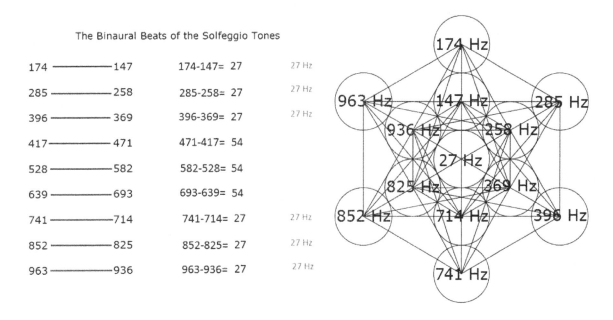

Figure 31

When you are done with the exercise, then you should have something similar to my graphic up above, although you might have arranged the tones a bit differently. I arranged these tones differently my first time around, but after studying my graphic, I realized that I needed to put the left column tones in the big cube or outer circles and the right column tones in the smaller cube or inner circles. With this arrangement the bigger number tones are in the outer circles and the smaller number tones are in the inner circles, therefore, you can subtract the tones from the outer circle to the inner circle that is attached and lined up which will give you the number 27 Hz in the center. This exercise shows us that each column in the 18 tones is a cube. I will cover more about the cube in the next chapter.

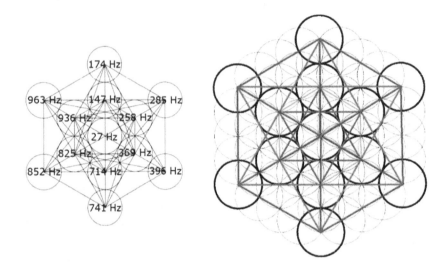

Figure 32

In figure 32, you can see that the Metatron's Cube fits perfectly inside of the Flower of Life, and that it is still easy to trace out the two cubes in both the Flower of Life and inside Metatron's Cube. They both go together. You can almost imagine the circles in the Flower of Life as being sounds or tones that are vibrating outward almost like throwing a stone into the water would do. This is always called the ripple effect as the waves of water flow outward from the impact of the stone. Likewise, sound or tones create the same ripple effect in the air as they travel outward in circles.

The one last thing that I wanted to write about with the binaural beats is how they can help the brain to work more holistic because they help to balance out the left and right hemispheres of the brain. I was watching a neuroscientist on *Ted Talks* that described how a stroke affected her brain. Jill Bolte Taylor described what it was like as a stroke took place in the left hemisphere of her brain. What is interesting is that the left hemisphere of the brain is associated with logic and reasoning, and the right hemisphere is associated with creativity and love. The two hemispheres of the brain are opposites in most cases, and Jill describes them as having almost two different personalities and says that they think differently. She describes the right hemisphere as thinking in pictures, and the left hemisphere thinks in languages. Once her left brain went offline and wasn't working properly, she began thinking right brained. She was feeling at one with the universe, and she no longer had that background chatter of her thoughts. It's so beautiful listening to her describe how her brain worked on the day of her stroke, so I highly recommend watching her on *Ted Talks*. The video is also on *You Tube*.

It was when I was watching this video that I began to realize how these tones balance out both hemispheres of the brain. In other words, most people tend to think more left brained or more right brained, but these tones played in right and left speakers with the binaural beats will make people think more whole brained. This means that they will excel in the way they think.

The binaural beat effect is caused because the two separate tones played in the right and the left ears are so close together that the brain creates a third tone, which is the difference of the two tones. This means that both hemispheres of the brain are working together to create this third tone. The left hemisphere of the brain deals with the mathematics of the two tones, and the right hemisphere deals with the rhythm of creating the third tone, therefore, when you listen to the binaural beats of the 12 tones, you are literally tuning your brain to work more balanced or whole brained.

Another clue to the purpose for the binaural beats in the Solfeggio tones is that Jesus Christ was crucified in Golgotha, which means the place of the skull. His followers of the 144,000 will have to be crucified as well, however, Jesus does not demand that they be hung on a cross and killed for their sacrifice. The binaural beats or 6 covered wagons suggest that the crucifixion of the 144,000 shall take place in their skull. The 144,000 will be sacrificing their will or ego for God's will, and so they will be literally turning their bodies into Temples just like Jesus did. These tones will help the 144,000 servants of God and assistant shepherds of Jesus Christ to make their Temple not from stones but from tones.

In the 27th chapter of Matthew, we find the true purpose of the binaural beats in many diverse ways. We know that Jesus was crucified at the place of the skull, and that he was crucified with two thieves to the right side and the left side. Christ was at the center! The 27 Hz tones is created at the center of the brain with both the right and left hemisphere working together in perfect balance, so we can see a parallel between Jesus crucifixion and the tones. The two thieves were crucified at the right and left side of Jesus, which we can see as being a parallel to the binaural tones being created by both hemispheres of the brain due to the tones that are being played in the right and the left ear.

Mathew 27

*^{33} And when they were come unto a place called Golgotha, that is to say, a place of a **skull**,*

*^{38} Then were there two thieves crucified with him, one on the **right** hand, and another on the **left**.*

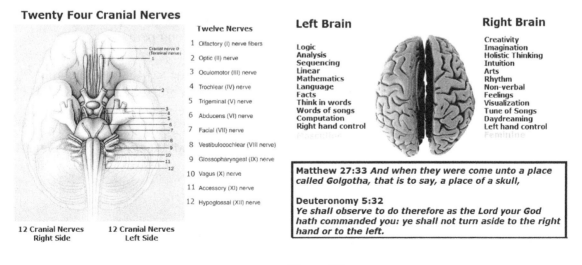

Figure 33

Edgar Cayce interpreted the book of Revelation in the Bible in a symbolic way that applied to each individual, instead of interpreting this book from a prophetic level. Revelation 4 talks about the throne of God as being in the brain of the individual that serves God and the 24 elders are the 24 cranial nerves. This chapter can be interpreted in many diverse ways, as all books of the Bible have many different layers. The throne of God also has electricity, because there is lightning that proceeds from the throne, and lightning is the same thing as electricity. The brain and the entire nervous system run on electrical impulses. There are 12 cranial nerves on the left side of the brain and 12 cranial nerves on the right side of the brain. Jesus Christ sits on the throne with the 24 elders around the throne of God. Again we can see parallels between the story of Jesus being crucified at a place of the skull in the center with the thieves to the right side and the left side, and the brain creating the third tone together with information being received from both the right and the left hemispheres of the brain. In Deuteronomy 5:32 God commanded Moses when he said "ye shall not turn aside to the right hand or to the left." This commandment is verifying that we must learn to center ourselves or balance ourselves in all that we do. In other words, don't go too far one way or the other. Let Christ center us in all that we do!

I was watching the movie *Little Buddha* one day when I heard this interesting interpretation on how to live our life. It was so simple of a statement and yet so profound when fully realized. Buddha overheard an old musician telling his students that if you tighten a string too much when trying to tune it, then it will snap, however, if you leave the string too slack, it will not play. This led to Buddha's realization that you must not go to extremes in either direction but pick the middle path. Buddha describes the middle way as following the path of moderation and therefore, not choosing to always be self indulgent in the senses or pleasure and not choosing to always take the path of self-mortification by self denial of all pleasures of this life. He believed that the middle way was the path of wisdom.

<u>Lama Norbu</u>: [Narrating] One day Siddhartha heard an old musician on a passing boat speaking to his people.

<u>Old Musician</u>: If you tighten the string too much it will snap and if you leave it too slack, it won't play.

<u>Lama Norbu</u>: [continues narrating] Suddenly, Siddhartha realized that these simple words held the great truth, and that in all these years he had been following the wrong path.

It is the same with how we use our brain. Have you ever heard someone say that they are more right brained or left brained? Creative people are said to be more right brained, and analytical people are said to be more left brained. Really the ideal would be to be more whole brained, which would describe a person that can be both creative and analytical at the same time. These tones will help you to be more whole brained as they will tune your body just right. Not too tight and not too loose.

Revelation 4

⁴ And round about the throne were four and twenty seats: and upon the seats I saw four and twenty elders sitting, clothed in white raiment; and they had on their heads crowns of gold.

⁵ And out of the throne proceeded lightnings and thunderings and voices: and there were seven lamps of fire burning before the throne, which are the seven Spirits of God.

Another example of the middle path is found in Revelation 4:5 which talks about the seven Spirits of God. Our whole universe is made of light and sound, and we can find that in the electromagnetic spectrum. There are seven types of the electromagnetic spectrum, and they all vary at different frequency or vibration rates. This is the true symbolic meaning of the seven candle stick Menorah. In the middle of the electromagnetic scale is visible light, therefore, Christ is in the middle. The EM scale and the Menorah can also take on the appearance of a balancing scale where light is at the center.

John 8:12 *Then spake Jesus again unto them, saying, I am the light of the world: he that followeth me shall not walk in darkness, but shall have the light of life.*

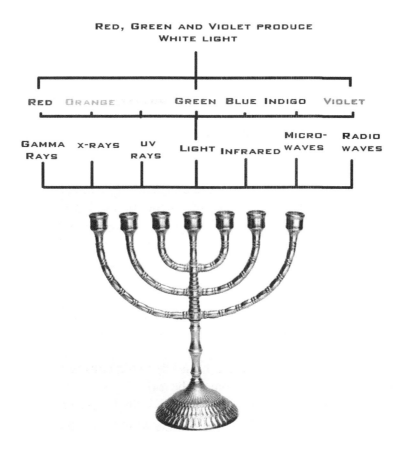

Figure 34

There is another example of the middle way or centering for balance that is in Revelation 4:3. Even though Jesus was surrounded by a rainbow on the throne, it is very clear that he was in the middle of the rainbow. The middle color of a rainbow or the seven primary colors is the color green, and an emerald is always a green gemstone.

Rev. 4:3 *And he that sat was to look upon like a jasper and a sardine stone: and there was a rainbow round about the throne, in sight like unto an emerald.*

If you have ever learned about the Buddhist or Hindu concept about seven main chakras or energy centers within the body, then you may already know that the heart chakra is in the center. According to Edgar Cayce these seven energy zones are associated with seven major endocrine glands. In the Bible, the seven candlesticks of the Menorah Lamp were located inside the Temple or Tabernacle. It is important to note that Jesus turned his body into a Temple and that his followers should do the same. From this point of view, the seven candlesticks of the Menorah would be represented as the seven energy zones within the Temple body. The heart is at the center which represents balance.

John 2:19-21

[19] Jesus answered and said unto them, Destroy this temple, and in three days I will raise it up.

[20] Then said the Jews, Forty and six years was this temple in building, and wilt thou rear it up in three days?

[21] But he spake of the temple of his body.

The Institute of Heart Math has found that the heart can influence the decisions of the brain. There are 40,000 neurons in the heart which can send pain signals and other sensations to the autonomic parts of the brain. Investigations by Heart Math have found that the heart can send messages that inhibit or facilitate electrical activity in the brain which can influence perception, decision making and emotional responses. In other words, the heart can affect the brain. The Institute of Heart Math also found that the heart generates a powerful electromagnetic field. They found that the heart generates the largest electromagnetic field in the body. The electrocardiogram (ECG) measures the electrical activity of the heart, and the institute found that the ECG is 60 times greater in amplitude than the brain waves recorded in an electroencephalogram (EEG).

Matthew 6:21

For where your treasure is, there will your heart be also.

Another critical piece of information that I have found from the pairing of the tones is found in the skip rates. I have already discussed the binaural beat of 27 Hz, but I have not discussed the number 54 which is found in the difference of the three middle tones. Of course, it goes without saying that 54 is a multiple of 27, but there is another reason for these numbers that are encoded in the skip rate of the paired tones.

$$54/27 = 2 \text{ or } 27 \times 2 = 54$$

At some point, I was researching the directional orientation of Solomon's Temple, and I came across a website that explained more about the alignment. The Temple's door faced east towards the rising sun and the Holy of Holies was facing west. There is a lot of symbolism to the Temple's alignment with the sun. We can think of the sun as being a homophone for the Son of God. Both the sun and the Son give light and the sun gives us life in this physical world, but it is only the Son of God that gives us eternal life. The person from this website looked up the azimuth of the sunrises and sunsets in Jerusalem. It turns out that the sun moves through 54 degrees from the summer solstice to the winter solstice.

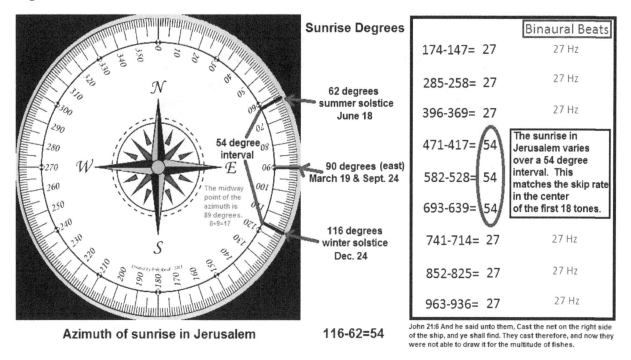

Figure 35

When I also did a graphic of the sunset's azimuth in Jerusalem, I found out that it also has a 54 degree interval from summer solstice through the winter solstice. This is when I began to see an even bigger connection between the tones and the azimuth of the sunrises and sunsets in Jerusalem.

$$54+54=\underline{}$$

If you added the numbers together, then you saw that this number matches another skip rate in the Solfeggio tones. It's interesting that these sunrises and sunsets in Jerusalem were encoded into these tones. We can see time and time again that the math of God's Creation is based on the degree circle. There is an underlying blueprint for Divine design within the mysterious tones that are found in the Bible. It is amazing!

Matthew 24:27

For as the lightning cometh out of the east, and shineth even unto the west; so shall also the coming of the Son of man be.

Zechariah 14:4

And his feet shall stand in that day upon the mount of Olives, which is before Jerusalem on the east, and the mount of Olives shall cleave in the midst thereof toward the east and toward the west, and there shall be a very great valley; and half of the mountain shall remove toward the north, and half of it toward the south.

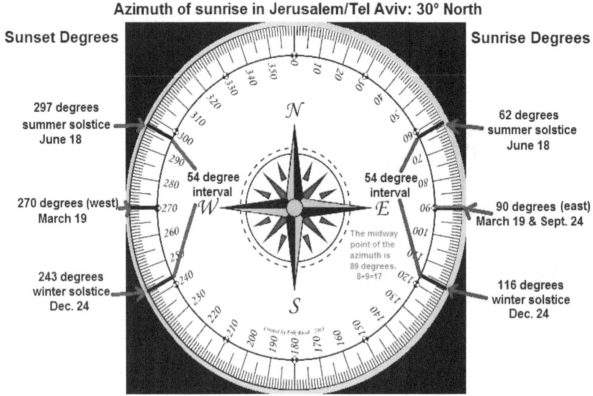

Figure 36

I also realized when I made the graphic including the azimuth of the sunsets that another Solfeggio tones skip rate was encoded. The winter solstice has an azimuth in the sunset of 243 degrees. It's also interesting that these tones belong to Jesus Christ for the new song of the 144,000, and it also records a skip rate of 243 degrees in the azimuth of the sunset on the day before Christmas. Also when I think of Jesus return to the Earth for the second coming, I think of the Son descending in the sky for all to see. The sun setting in the west is an analogy of Jesus coming back in the last days as was the rising sun is an analogy of Jesus ascension in the sky following his death. The Temple was facing east toward the rising sun, but really it was a prophecy set in stone until the real Son arose in the sky. Jesus return is said to be in Jerusalem on the Mount of Olives, and he will come down like the setting sun. The Holy of Holies was in the west side of the Temple which was facing the setting sun.

Mark 14:62

And Jesus said, I am: and ye shall see the Son of man sitting on the right hand of power, and coming in the clouds of heaven.

Azimuth of sunrise in Jerusalem/Tel Aviv: 30° North

Date	Sunrise Time	Sunrise Azimuth East	Sunset time	Sunset Azimuth West	Daylight Hours
1/1	06:55	116°	17:11	243°	10:16
10/12	06:44	116°	17:00	243°	10:16
17/12	06:49	116°	17:02	243°	10:13
24/12 winter solstice	06:53	116°	17:06	243°	10:13

At winter Solstice the sunset is at 243 degrees in Jerusalem. This is a skip rate in the Solfeggio tones.

Skip Rates in the Solfeggio Tones

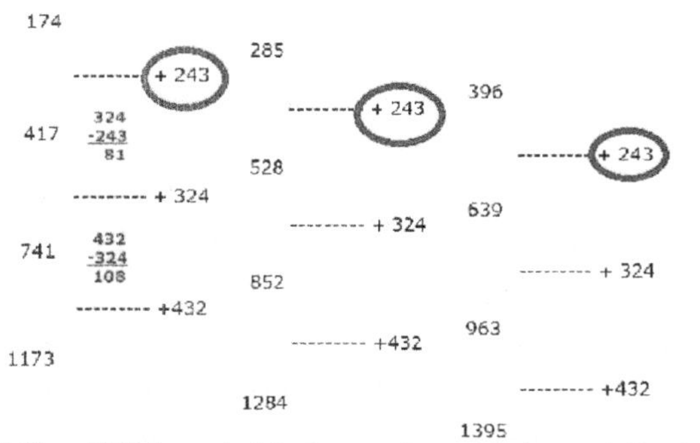

174
285 -------- +243
417   324
      -243
       81
            396 -------- +243
528
         -------- +324
                          639
741   432
      -324
      108
852
         -------- +432
                          -------- +324
1173
1284
            963
                  -------- +432
1395
                          -------- +432

Matthew 24:27 *For as the lightning cometh out of the east, and shineth even unto the west; so shall also the coming of the Son of man be.*

Figure 37

As you can see, these mysterious tones have a lot of information encoded within them, and I have found this to be the most rewarding journey in finding the purpose for these tones. It almost seemed like I am on some kind of massive treasure hunt, and I keep finding the most precious treasures hidden just beneath the layers of this new song. God's song is so beautiful beyond measure, and there is nothing else like this math that is associated with these tones. Just when I think I have found all of the gems hidden within the tones…..I find more.

In the next chapter I will talk more about the Solfeggio tones representing the Holy of Holies cube and New Jerusalem.

The Cube

I read the book *Emanation of the Solfeggio* by Dan Burisch, Sc.D and Marcia McDowell, Ph.D and was astounded to find out that you can make a cube from the first nine tones. This was early on in my research, and at that time I did not realize that there were all of these clues about the cube encoded in the degree circle of the Song of Degrees. It was only later that I started to put it all together that the binaural beats and pairing the tones together hint at forming the cube with the first 9 tones and the second 9 tones. The corner stone of 27 hertz also hints around about forming a perfect cube of 27 or a 3X3X3 cube. Mr. Burisch showed in his book that you can take the nine tones and put them into 27 squares and then layer them to form a cube to find other tones. You can read the numbers three dimensionally in a diagonal and vertical pattern in addition to the horizontal patterns of the numbers. I still really do not know what to make of the idea of finding other tones by connecting them in a three dimensional tic tac toe pattern, however, I do agree that we can make cubes from both the first 9 tones and the second 9 tones.

In the next exercise, put the first 9 tones into the first 27 squares, and put the second 9 tones into the second 27 squares. Remember to keep the triad tones together.

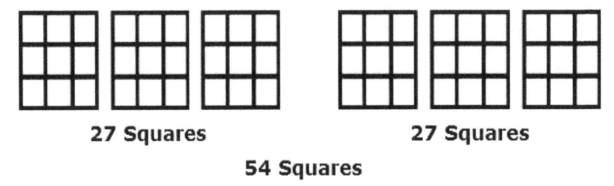

27 Squares   **27 Squares**

54 Squares

Isn't it interesting how the two skip rates in the paired tones and binaural beats show up again in making the two cubes. All of the numbers in the first 9 tones and the second 9 tones are exactly 27 numbers.

When I was a teenager my parents bought a 3-D tic tac toe game that was made of three tic tac toe boards with 9 holes on each layer for marbles to fit on top. This was an exciting game compared to the two dimensional tic tac toe which got to be boring after playing it for awhile. This game was simply more complicated due to the fact that we had to be aware of not only the horizontal connections, but we had to be watchful for opportunities to make a connection with three marbles in a diagonal and vertical pattern as well. This is exactly how Mr. Burish was trying to form the new tones by reading all of the numbers from a vertical and diagonal perspective. He found 39 new tones just from the first 9 tones that were made into a cube. I have never really understood if we are supposed to view the tones in this way or not, and I have never found a clue that we should form new tones from this method. If this clue is found in the Bible, then I have not found it so far. Suffice it to say, I was just interested in the blueprint that was being presented to us in forming the two cubes, instead of using it as a platform to find more tones.

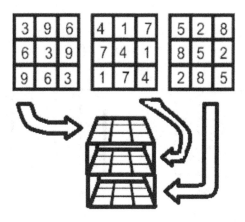

Figure 38

The graphic above shows the blueprint of how the first 9 tones form a perfect 3X3X3 cube, as each side has three squares for the length, width and the height of the cube. The first 9 tones form a blueprint of the Holy of Holies cube or the New Jerusalem blueprint of a cube. Does this mean that the tones can help to build New Jerusalem, or does it mean that the tones can put us into the Holy of Holies? The patterns and blueprints encoded within the tones are beckoning us to ask these questions.

Once we include the second 9 tones and its cube, then it becomes very clear that we are making a blueprint of a hypercube. A hypercube can look like a cube within a cube if a light is shined on a higher dimensional tesseract to form a shadow into our third dimension. Therefore, the tesseract or hypercube is a clue to a higher dimensional geometry. This new clue beckons us to explore the idea of higher dimensions beyond our own third dimension.

Remember we have found the cube within the Star of David drawn in the degree circle, and we have put the binaural beats into Metatron's cube which shows a hypercube. When we found the six tones, it was easy to see that the Star of David's vertices pointed to six of the 3, 6 & 9 tones around the degree circle. We know that if we put a dot in the center of a Star of David and start connecting the vertices together and then connect the vertices with the dot in the center, then we can find the cube. We also know that both the Holy of Holies in the Tabernacle and in Solomon's Temple were perfect cubes and that New Jerusalem's height, width and length were equal like a cube. We also know that the cube can represent the 27 hyper directional markers in three dimensional space, and that each one of those directions can be represented by Hebrew. It starts becoming clearer that the cube is a blueprint for mapping out the idea of hyper dimensional geometry, and we are being asked to figure out how this geometry works.

It is also surprising that the clue about the Temple facing east is another clue to the geometry of a cube. The cube is made up of squares joined together at a 90 degree angle, and the east direction on a compass within the degree circle is facing towards the 90 degree point in the circle. In geometry this is called a right angle which is an angle that bisects the angle formed by two halves of a straight line.

The next diagram shows the two cubes and their 9 tones positioned in the 27 squares. Both of the cubes can be put together into a hypercube configuration by putting the cube within a cube. If you focus on this graphic, you may start to see another pattern starting to emerge within the tones. I know that I did.

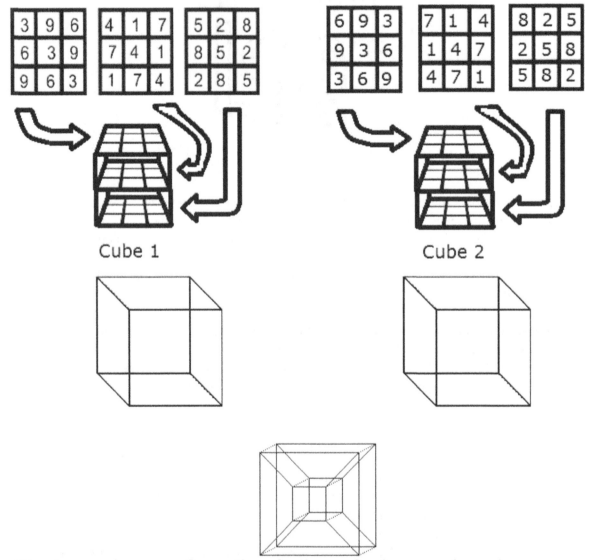

The two cubes can form the shadow of a hypercube, also known as a fourth dimensional tesseract.

Figure 39

First you can see that the 18 tones form 6 squares which can be put together to form a perfect cube, and second you can see that the tones can be mirrored from one cube to the next. In other words we can see the perfect cube represented in the 18 tones and then the shadow of a hypercube within the mirrored tones. The smaller cube within the hypercube is a mirror image of the bigger cube on the outside. It's almost like when we look into a mirror, or when we look at a reflection on the water and see that the image is backwards. A shadow is a darkened area that has the form or shape of an object or person that light can't penetrate, and since a cube within a cube is only a shadow of a fourth dimensional cube, we can compare the shadow to being like a reverse light and darkness within a negative print for a normal photo. When we view the fourth dimensional cube as a shadow, we are getting a glimpse into fourth dimensional geometry: however, we are only getting the shadow of that object, so we are not viewing this object as it really looks in every detail. It's hard to really visualize what a fourth dimensional object appearance would be, but these clues within the tones are trying to convey a fourth dimensional object of the cube in a three dimensional way.

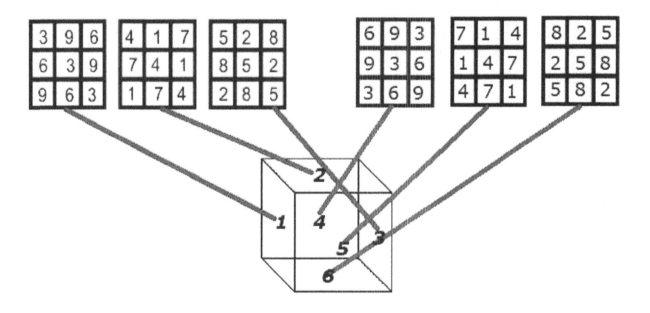

Figure 40

A tesseract is made up of eight cubes in a cross configuration, therefore, from the clue of finding the hypercube from the two cubes, or the clue to finding one cube in the six squares of the tones is also a clue to find the cross. The cross is always associated with Jesus Christ in Christianity. I must say that I never fully understood why we represent Jesus by the implement upon which he was killed. It would be similar to someone I knew dying from a gun, and I display a gun as a remembrance or memorial of their death. I think people would be offended by that idea, however, as Christians we put up the symbol of a cross to memorialize the way he died. I never fully understood why that is done until I started learning sacred geometry. It turns out that a cross of six squares can be folded up to make a cube: therefore, the cross is a symbol of the Holy of Holies cube and even the New Jerusalem cube. This is actually another clue to the cross of cubes that actually forms a tesseract, so we can see that the cube and the cross are extensively related to one another from different views of perception or from different dimensional realities. The two dimensional cross of squares can be folded up into three dimensions as a cube, and likewise, the cube can be folded out into a cross in four dimensions.

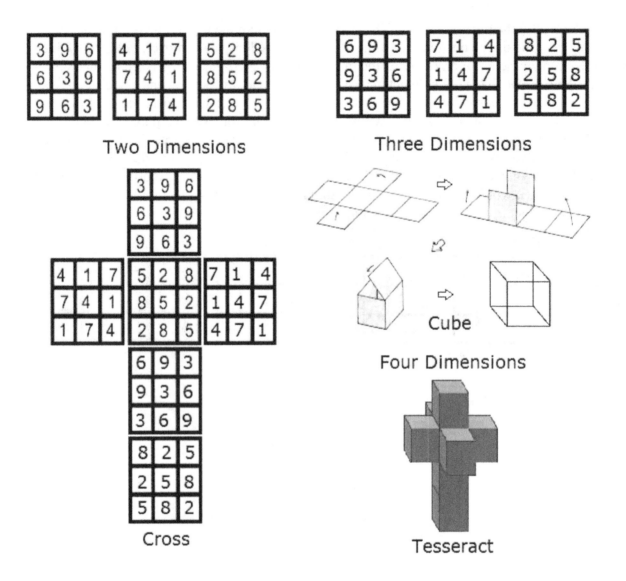

Figure 41

In this next exercise, count the vertices on the line, square, cube and hypercube. The vertex (plural- vertices) is where two lines meet at a corner or point. Notice the numeral pattern that it makes as you go up the dimensions in these shapes.

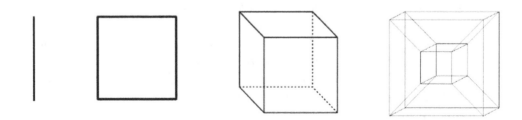

There is another clue to the cube and tesseract or hypercube in Numbers 7, which is astounding to me, considering the clue is found at the same location where the infinity pattern and binary code is encoded. The number pattern of 2, 4 & 8 in Numbers 7:7-8 also matches the pattern in the vertices of the three dimensional cube and the fourth dimensional hypercube and other higher dimensional shapes. The vertices on the three dimensional cube is 8, and the vertices on a tesseract or hypercube is 16, and the shapes going up in dimensions keep doubling their vertices to keep the pattern going along. The vertices of a cube keep doubling every time you add another dimension. The cube is made up of lines, which have 2 vertices, and from there it goes up to a square in two dimensions of length and width which has 4 vertices. It takes 6 squares to make a cube with three dimensions of length, width and height which has 8 vertices. The cube in the fourth dimension becomes a tesseract which has 16 vertices, and in the fifth dimension the cube becomes a Penteract which contains 32 vertices. The pattern continues into the higher dimensions. The Bible uses the cube of the Holy of Holies pattern and from the New Jerusalem cube pattern to show us hyper dimensional geometry.

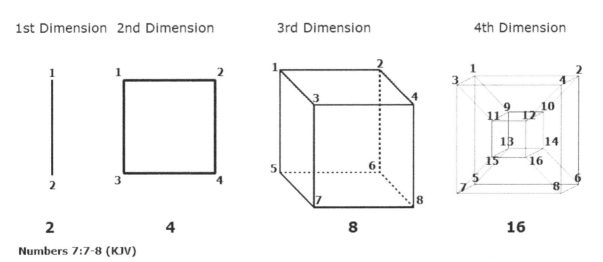

Numbers 7:7-8 (KJV)

7 **Two** wagons and **four** oxen he gave unto the sons of Gershon, according to their service:

8 And **four** wagons and **eight** oxen he gave unto the sons of Merari, according unto their service, under the hand of Ithamar the son of Aaron the priest.

2, 4, 8 ....

Figure 42

Another interesting fact about the cube is that it can be filled with six pyramids. Imagine 6 pyramids on six squares, and then imagine folding them up into a cube. Each pyramid would fit perfectly within the cube. The cube being represented in the Bible is also a clue to the Great Pyramid being a monument to the Lord. In Isaiah 19:19 it says, "In that day shall there be an altar to the LORD in the midst of the land of Egypt, and a pillar at the border thereof to the LORD." Many biblical scholars believe that the Great Pyramid is the altar to the Lord, and they find evidence in the fact that some of the measurements of the pyramid seem to be significant numbers that are also in the Bible. Another discovery that strengthens the reason why many believe the Great Pyramid is a monument to the Lord has to do with the Hebrew letters also having a numerical value as well. If we add up the numbers in the verse, its sum is the exact height of the Great Pyramid in inches, which is 5,449.

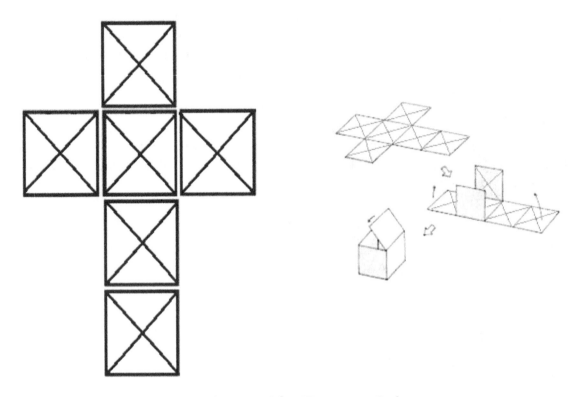

Six Pyramids Form a Cube

Figure 43

The last thing that I want to discuss is about the mirroring of the triad tones. When I was working on the cube graphics for the 18 triad tones, I automatically positioned the second column of tones in the square in a mirror sequence to the first cube. For example: the number 396 became 693 in the second cube. It just seemed to be the best way to position them in the second cube. When I mirrored them in this way, it looks as if you could flip the right side over to the left side like turning a page, and it would look the same as the left side and vice versa. We could view one cube as mirroring the other cube. In other words, the upper cube would be the first 9 tones from the left to the right, and the lower cube would be the next 9 tones in the reverse or reflection of the first 9 tones from the right to the left. It's interesting because Hebrew is written and read from the right to the left. Also, the two cubes seem to be displaying the ancient hermetic phrase of "As above, so below," however, the cube below is only a mere reflection of what is above.

There is an interesting phenomenon that is suggested when I mirrored the tones in the two cubes. It seems to suggest that both the cubes in the hypercube are counter-rotating to each other. The first cube is rotating clockwise, and the second cube is rotating counterclockwise. We have seen this information come out in numerous kinds of ways, so there must be a good reason for it to be encoded in these tones. In the next chapter, I will discuss torsion physics, and how this seems to play a role within the pattern of the tones.

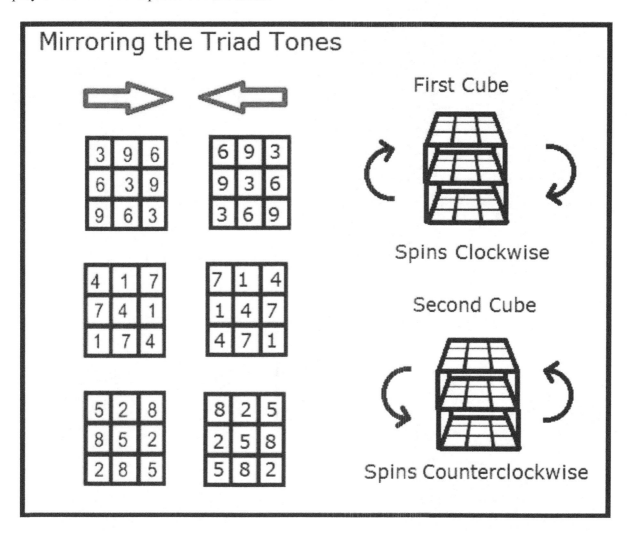

Figure 44

The clue about the corner stone and corner tones made me wonder if perhaps the hypercube could expand out from the corners rather than from the faces of the cube. In many depictions of the tesseract it is shown as a cross of cubes that extend from the middle cube at the faces of the three dimensional cube, however, all of the clues seem to point to the corners of the hypercube. The Bible keeps talking about the corner stone, and a corner stone is the first stone placed in the construction of a masonry foundation. All other stones will be set in reference to this corner stone which is placed at a 90 degree angle. I decided to see what kind of geometrical figure I could make if I expanded the cube outward at the corners rather than at the faces. The graphic it makes is interesting in that it seems to form a holey cube, which seems to be a play on words, when we consider that the Holy of Holies was cube shaped in the Temple. The diagram only shows the hypercube in three dimensions in a two dimensional image, therefore, we still could not even begin to imagine what this would look like in the fourth dimension. Once I made the graphic, I started to count the lines, faces and vertices, and some interesting numbers popped out.

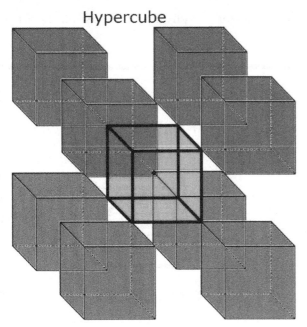

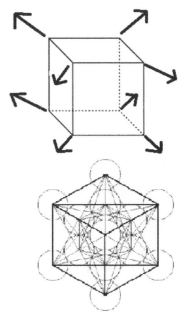

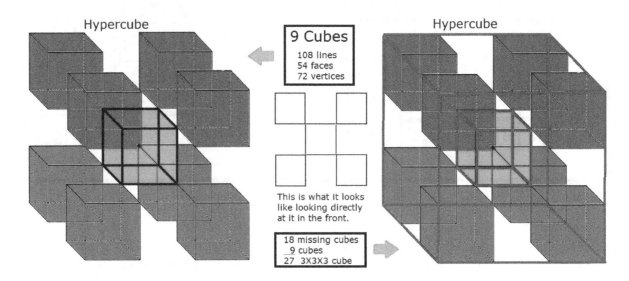

Figure 45

Notice that in the graphic above there are 108 lines in this version of the hypercube which matches a skip rate in the tones. There are 54 faces, which matches the skip rate of the pairing of the tones in the left and right columns. The 72 vertices is the mirror number for the corner tones, and it also can represent the 72 names of God, the 72 Disciples of Christ and the processional number. Also, remember it is a multiple of the number 144, which is associated with the measurements of New Jerusalem. These cubes show the outline of a big cube. There are 9 cubes in the big cube, which could represent the number of tones in each column, and there are 18 missing cubes which could symbolize the 18 tones in a set or group. Add the missing cube spaces with the cubes, and it gives the corner tones number of 27 Hz. This outline of the big cube would represent a 3X3X3 cube of 27 cubes. The big cube contains the little cube or inner cube in the middle which appears to be showing the shadow of a hypercube.

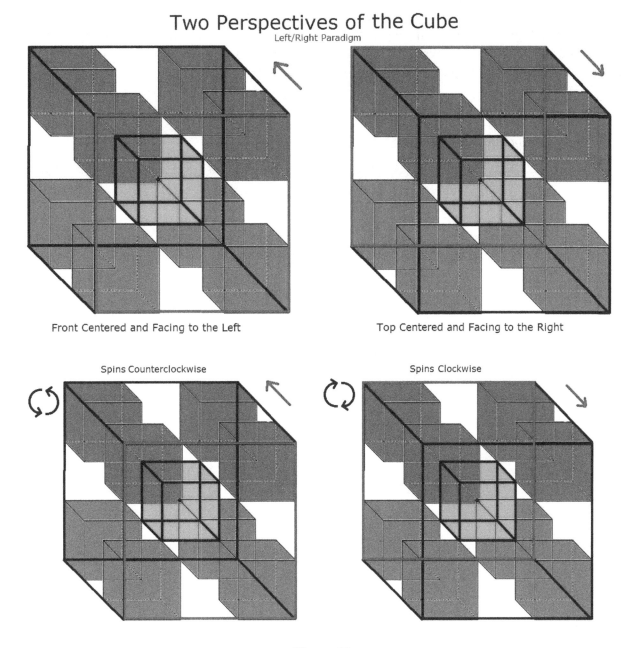

Figure 46

The big cube has two different cubes just like a Necker cube, when we re-adjust our perspective between a front centered cube facing to the left or a top centered cube facing to the right. This also seems to be showing the counter rotating spin within the hypercube. The front centered cube spins counterclockwise, and the top centered cube spins clockwise, so this also seems to be confirming the tones counter rotation as well. The two perspectives of this cube also shows the left/right paradigm that is displayed in the columns of the tones.

As you can see from this chapter, the ancient biblical measurement of cubits could be a clue to "cube it" with these tones. The Holy of Holies was cubed shape and so is the futuristic city of New Jerusalem. The city of Jerusalem in Israel has been made by stones and so were both of the Temples that once stood there. Hidden within these tones could very well be a clue that we need to make the body Temple and New Jerusalem with tones. The new song of the 144,000 may very well be a higher dimensional song with higher frequencies to raise the vibration rate of a person and the earth as well. Jesus told us that he would give us the keys to the kingdom of heaven, and those keys may very well be musical keys.

Matthew 16:19

And I will give unto thee the keys of the kingdom of heaven:

Torsion Physics and the Merkaba

I showed my wraparound graphic of the Solfeggio tones to a friend who is a sculptor, and she said that she sees the pattern as being three dimensional spirals. She believes that being a sculptor made it easier for her to see the wraparound effect in three dimensions as she sculpts in three dimensions. I realized that I had failed to see that pattern as a spiral because I was just looking at the two dimensional effects within the number's rotations. I was astounded at her perception of the tones in three dimensions, and it gave me another perspective when working with the tone's patterns. Since that time I have found numerous patterns that show spirals and counter-rotating spins as I have shown in previous chapters.

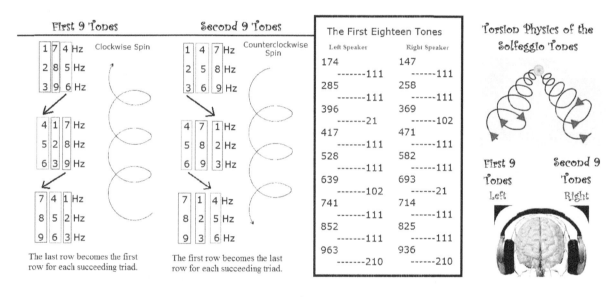

Figure 47

After I worked on a graphic showing that the pattern seems to be indicative of the tones creating spirals of energy, I realized that the left column is spinning clockwise, and the right column is spinning counterclockwise. This immediately made me think of the definition of a Merkaba or a light chariot of God. A Merkaba is defined as a light vehicle or chariot that is used to transport a person's spirit or body from one dimension to another. "Mer" means light, "Ka" means spirit and "Ba" means body, and the Merkaba means that the spirit or body is surrounded by counter-rotating fields of light. It is said to be the vehicle of wheels within wheels that Ezekiel saw. I must say that I never understood where these Jewish myths came from, or how they knew about this vehicle because the Bible doesn't talk about a Merkaba. The story of Ezekiel seeing a vehicle with wheels within wheels has been puzzling to most people that read the Bible, and there have been many people that have suggested that it was some kind of space vehicle. Perhaps this is where the legend of the Merkaba has originated.

For the first time I was starting to understand that the tones are displaying the same motion of counter-rotation of the Merkaba. Could this myth be true? Could these tones connect us with a higher dimension? It was something that I would have to think about for awhile. It made me wonder if this is how this myth got started. I was starting to see mathematical proof for the legend of the Merkaba.

The modern way to visualize the Merkaba is to look at the counter-rotating fields of light or energy as having the geometrical shape of a stella octangula, also known as a star tetrahedron. It turns out that a star tetrahedron looks like a Star of David from a two dimensional perspective.

An equilateral triangle means that all sides of the triangle are equal in length. In the next exercise count the equilateral triangles within a Star of David, a tetrahedron and a star tetrahedron.

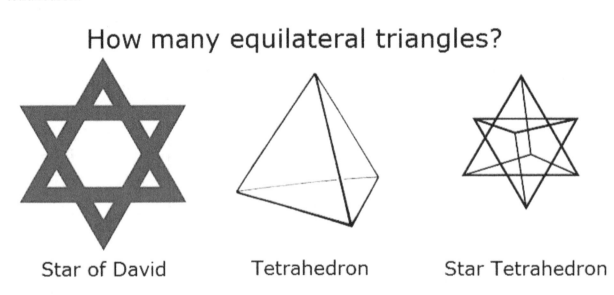

In another chapter, I will cover more about how the Bible encodes the shape of the equilateral triangle in John 21 of the Bible. I have discovered many geometrical blueprints in stories of the Bible. In the diagram below, it is interesting to note that a shadow of a star tetrahedron is a Star of David. Remember that Jesus spoke in parables, so it is wise to view all stories of the Bible to be parables. There are literal and symbolic meanings to the parables in the Bible, and as Jesus told his Apostles there are mysteries to the kingdom of God for those that understand.

Luke 8:10 *And he said, Unto you it is given to know the mysteries of the kingdom of God: but to others in parables; that seeing they might not see, and hearing they might not understand.*

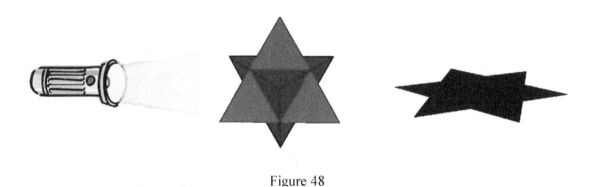

Figure 48

In the exercise that you did with counting the equilateral triangles, you should have recognized a familiar pattern that came from the numbering of the equilateral triangles. The Star of David is made of 2 equilateral triangles. The tetrahedron is made of 4 equilateral triangles, and the star tetrahedron is made of 8 equilateral triangles. It's interesting that this also fits the pattern of Numbers 7:7-8 because the process in going from a two dimensional Star of David up to a three dimensional star tetrahedron shows 2, 4 and 8 equilateral triangles. This will all start to make even more sense in my chapter on the fishing net o

f John 21.

Another remarkable fact is that the star tetrahedron can fit perfectly into a cube, and each point on its two tetrahedrons fit right into the 8 vertices of the cube. It fits quite snug actually, and so this means that this energy pattern does go along with the cube blueprints of both the Holy of Holies and the futuristic city of New Jerusalem.

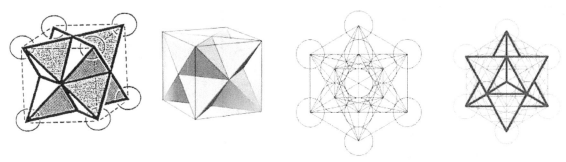

Star Tetrahedron in a Cube   Star Tetrahedron is a Metatron's Cube

Figure 49

What is interesting is that a physicist named Stan Tenen started to see that the Hebrew letters in the Bible are geometrical as well as many Bible verses. With his research he started the Meru Foundation to further study the relationships between the words in the Bible and the underlying geometrical patterns. Tenen broke the first word of the book of Genesis into parts and found that the word is actually comprised of two smaller words that mean "fire" and "six-edged thorn". The tetrahedron has six edges or sides, three are on the sides, and three are located at the base. He believed that the six-edged thorn is a tetrahedron, so he constructed a model of it and placed the "fire" or torus inside. Tenen calls this model "The Light in the Meeting Tent," and he says that it reflects perfect symmetry. He said, "When I looked through the faces of the tetrahedron at the vortex, each view displayed a different letter in the Hebrew alphabet." He then went on to say in the article, "I realized the 27 gestures that accompany the letters correspond to the 27 'preferred' pointing directions used in hyper-dimensional space." In other words the tetrahedron formed all 27 Hebrew letters which also showed the 27 directions in hyperdimensional space. Remember, the binaural beats encoded this precious number with the 12 special tones. Again we can see that there is something very special about the corner tones of 27 Hz in the binaural beats.

I read a book called *The Philosopher's Stone* by Joseph P. Farrell, and he wrote in detail about the Nazi Bell, and how it had counter-rotating drums. He also wrote about torsion physics, which I knew just a little bit about, so it really helped me to understand more about torsion. It was interesting that I was starting to connect torsion physics from a book that talked about the white powder gold that I have taken. It was when I first took this mysterious powder that I learned about these tones, and I have been set on a journey to decipher them ever since that time, despite the fact that I always hated math before. It's odd that I am now enjoying the mathematical and geometrical patterns within the tones.

An example of torsion would be when you wring out a towel to get out the excess water. In one hand you turn it towards the right, and in the other hand you turn it towards the left. The towel will start to coil or spiral as a result of the two hands rotating it in different directions. This is the very same physics that is happening within the tones. It shows torsion in the encoding of the counter-rotating spirals in the tones wraparound effect, the clockwise and counterclockwise spin in the two cubes, the left and right pattern in the binaural beats and the counter-rotation within the degree circle.

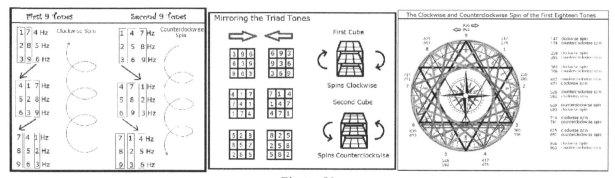

Figure 50

The counter-rotation encoded within the numbers of the tones is just like the counter-rotation with the two tetrahedrons in the star tetrahedron. One tetrahedron spins clockwise, and the other tetrahedron spins counterclockwise. I made some graphics to demonstrate how the tones cause the possible spin within the upper and lower tetrahedrons. The fact that spin is encoded into these numbers is a possible explanation of how these frequencies cause the counter-rotation of light or energy within the Merkaba.

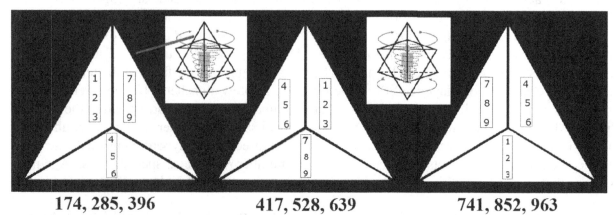

This represents the top side of a tetrahedron looking down, so the base is not seen in this graphic. The frequencies of this tetrahedron in the Merkaba appear to be turning clockwise.

Figure 51

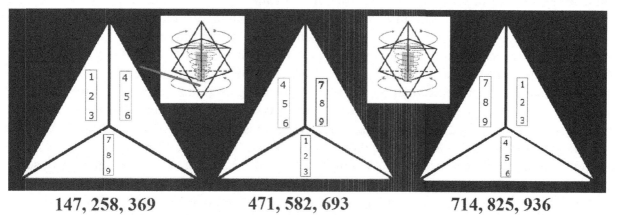

147, 258, 369   **471, 582, 693**   **714, 825, 936**

This represents the top side of a tetrahedron looking down, so the base is not seen in this graphic. The frequencies of this tetrahedron in the Merkaba appear to be turning counter clockwise.

Figure 52

Dr. Nikolai A. Kozyrev was a physicist and mathematician who did extensive research on time and torsion physics. He believed that time was the result of spiraling movement, and he also believed that the spiraling patterns in nature and life itself are the manifestation of time. Everything in the universe is spiraling from the Milky Way galaxy to our own Solar System and even right down to the microscopic DNA in our body. Our sun is moving around the galaxy in circles while the galaxy itself is moving through the universe, and the earth is moving around the sun in circles. These circles become spirals because our galaxy is moving through space and dragging the sun and Earth along with it as it goes. A circle in motion becomes a spiral. Torsion is a spiraling motion that occurs within the fabric of space and time. We can compare the act of wringing out a dish cloth to the torsion that occurs in the fabric of space, which according to Dr. Kozyrev causes time. The time pattern that Dr. Kozyrev discovered unfolds differently depending upon the degree of spiraling, folding and pleating that enters a system due to the amount of torsion it is experiencing.

Dr. Kozyrev did experiments with a gyroscope moving in a clockwise and counterclockwise position, and he found that the weight would change based on the angles of the rotation, the rotor's radius, weight of the gyroscope, the spin of either clockwise or counterclockwise and the velocity of the gyroscope. It is not only time that is created by these spirals of motion, but the spirals under different circumstances have the ability to create change in the mass of an object.

This becomes even more exciting when we apply these results to these mysterious tones which show the patterns of torsion. Could these tones be representing the fourth measurement of time? Is the counter-rotation in the tones showing us the concept of how time unfolds in space due to torsion and spirals?

It's interesting to note that the earth is spinning counterclockwise as are seven of the planets in our Solar System. There are two planets that are spinning clockwise in our Solar System and those are Venus and Uranus. What I find fascinating about this is that Venus is the morning star and is associated with Jesus Christ. In June 6, 2012, we had a Venus transit occur, and I was interested in learning more about this celestial event, so I looked it up on the internet and found out that these events occur every 243 years in what is called a Venus Transit cycle. I was astonished, because 243 is a skip rate in the tones, and I also remembered that Jesus compared himself to the morning star which is the planet Venus. As I was writing about torsion and the movements of spirals in our universe, I started to think about the movements of our planets, and that was when I remembered that Venus spins in the opposite direction of the earth. I looked up more information about Venus rotation and found something even more amazing. I found out that a day on Venus lasts a little more than 243 earth days. I find it very remarkable that the skip rate of 243 in the Solfeggio tones is found twice in the transit cycle and in its days, however, keep in mind that the 243 cycle and the days are both based on earth, as the Venus transit is viewed from the earth and the days on Venus is compared to earth days. I would dismiss this as a mere coincidence if it wasn't for the fact that Jesus compares himself to the morning star or Venus. This seems really significant when we take into account that Venus spins backwards when compared to the Earth's spin.

Revelation 22:16

*I Jesus have sent mine angel to testify unto you these things in the churches. I am the root and the offspring of David, and the bright and **morning star**.*

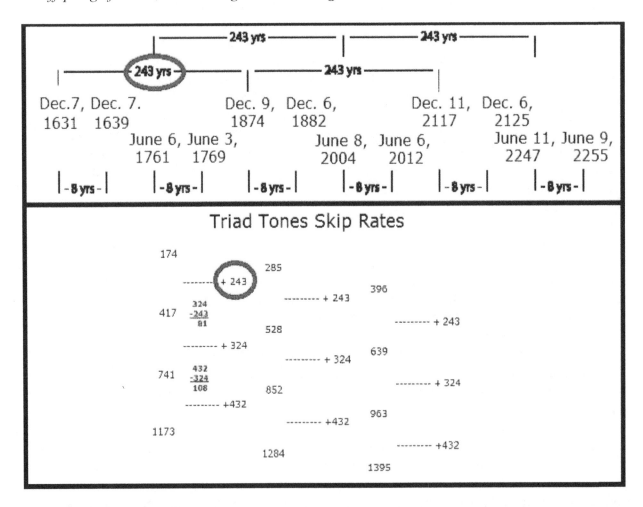

Figure 53

Why does the earth spin counterclockwise and Venus spin clockwise? Out of the nine planets seven spin counterclockwise and two spin clockwise. What is peculiar is that the Solfeggio tones seem to also hint around about the morning star (Venus), and the 243 number comes up from the earth's point of view, therefore, when we compare the earth and Venus we can see that the earth spins counterclockwise as opposed to Venus spinning clockwise. This appears to be another clue to the counter-rotation that happens in the torsion field.

Venus is sometimes called the sister planet of earth or earth's twin because the earth and Venus are about the same size and mass, and they have very similar compositions. The earth and Venus are also located next to one another. Another clue to counter-rotation can be found with the sun's motion on the earth as opposed to Venus. On Venus the sun rises in the west and sets in the east, and on the earth the sun rises in the east and sets in the west. On the earth, the sun appears to go from the right to the left on a compass, and from Venus the sun appears to go from left to the right on the compass.

Another interesting thing about the clockwise spin and the counterclockwise spin of the 18 tones is that the spiral makes a fish or vesica picis. Jesus Christ symbol is the fish, but it is also interesting that the Flower of Life makes fish symbols or vesica picis. The Flower of Life is thought to be the underlying energy pattern that is throughout the universe. We can see that the counter-rotation of spirals created from the tones pattern may be showing us evidence for the Flower of Life.

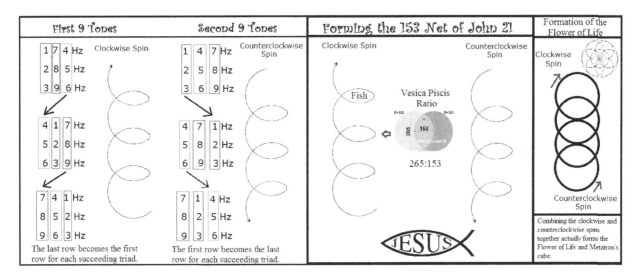

Figure 54

Now we have to ask ourselves why there are so many encoded messages in the tones about torsion physics, and what does this mean for us? If time is a consequence of the spiraling motion in the universe and torsion is the cause of time, then we must conclude that not only does the Solfeggio tones encode a cube of length, width and height, but it also includes the measurement of time. A cube can't spin without time, and motion can't occur without time.

Fortunately we still have a little bit of time to figure out what this all means before the end times cease.

Binary Code and Trinary Code

One of the more surprising discoveries that I have made in the Solfeggio tones is to realize that both binary and trinary code are encoded within the tones. I had previously thought that binary code was a more modern invention, although I found out it was discovered by Gottfried Leibniz in 1679. It seems reasonable upon this discovery to conclude that they were known in ancient times as well.

The main skip rate in the Solfeggio tones is 111, and this number is significant in many diverse ways. Remember the number pattern of 2, 4 and 8, which was presented in Numbers 7:7-8? It turns out that this is the same pattern as binary bytes, and with this pattern we can count the numeral value of each binary number. Over and over again we can see that the book of Numbers is actually about numbers. It not only teaches us about the tones' frequency numbers but about binary and trianry code as well.

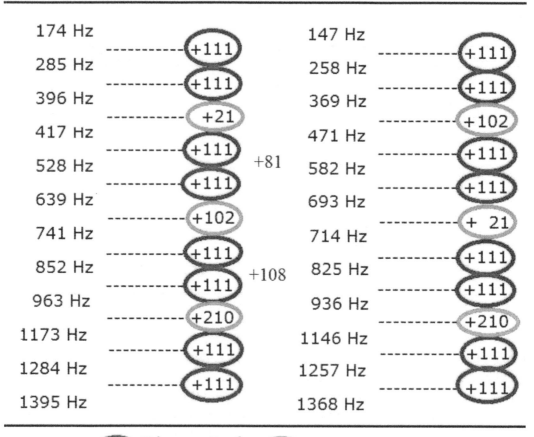

Figure 55

As you can see from the binary code graphic, the 111 skip rate keeps repeating throughout the tones, and the very spacing of these numbers and frequencies seems to be implying that there is a connection between binary code and the tones. This clue has really been hard for me to understand, but after a great deal of time, I believe that I have figured out what this clue might mean, although I can't be sure. Not only does binary code work in our modern day computers, but it is also used in electrical engineering as well. I have studied electricity and plasma quite extensively, and I can tell you that I believe that this connection has to do with the electricity within our body. I have a friend that listens to the Solfeggio tones quite a bit, and she told me that she feels energy when she listens to them. I had never really thought about that aspect of the tones, but they do pulse energy or electricity through the body. Perhaps the tones provide a tune up for our body and are healing to the listener.

Binary code is used in electrical engineering to show what circuits are off and on. The number 1 denotes +5V or "high" voltage and the number 0 denotes as 0V or "low." Actually, the voltages are the binary, so therefore, binary is a symbolic mathematical interpretation of what the circuits do with the voltage levels. Humans interpret the voltages as binary numbers because it is easier to understand.

All binary circuits are just switches in electrical circuits. Here is an example of storing a number in binary on a circuit board. If we wanted to store the number 7 in binary code, and we have 8 switches, we would use the binary number of 111 to store this number. All we do is set the switches of 0, 1 and 2 to 5V denoted by 1 and switches 3, 4,5,6,7 and 8 to 0V denoted as 0. This stores the number 111 in binary code. In other words, switches 0, 1 and 2 would be set to on and switches 3, 4,5,6,7 and 8 would be set to off.

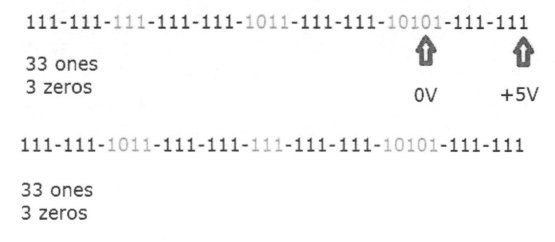

Figure 56

I decided to string the binary code of the skip rates together, and I also translated the trinary code into binary code as well. When I counted the ones and zeros, I realized that there are 33 ones in the binary code of the skip rates of each column. This number is usually recognized by Christians as representing the number of years that Jesus lived on the earth, but it is also recognized as having to do with the Mason's number of thirty three degrees within their hierarchy system. It is the highest that a Mason can go in their organization. There are also 3 zeros, which denote there is no or low electrical charge, so therefore, we have 33 high voltage charges and 3 low voltage. If we put these binary strings together of each column, then there are 66 high voltage ones and 6 low voltage zeros. There are 66 books of the Bible in the King James Version. If we add all of the bits together, then there are 72 bits for both columns. This seems quite significant, since 72 could represent Jesus disciples and the Precession of the Equinox movement of 1 degree every 72 years, and we also know that 72 is a multiple of 144.

In computer programming binary code can represent on/off, true/false, yes/no, positive/negative etc. Therefore binary represents 2 states, and trinary (ternary) represents 3 states. Trinary code could represent a third choice like yes, no and maybe or positive, negative and neutral. Binary codes are used to encode data, and the binary code signal is a series of electrical pulses that represent numbers, characters and operations to be performed by computers.

Figure 57

The graphic below shows how to count in binary code. You label each 1 and 0 from the left to the right in a pattern in which you double the number from 1 and each number afterwards. (Example: 1,2,4,8,16,32,64, 128, 256, 512, 1024…,) You then add up the numbers that correspond to the number 1 and skip the numbers that correspond to the number 0. It's interesting that labeling the binary numbers is done from the right to the left. This reminds me of how Hebrew is written and read, which is from the right to the left. Again we can see that the number pattern presented in Numbers 7:7-8 comes in quite handy when counting numbers in the binary code system.

COUNTING IN BINARY CODE

1 1 1 1 1 1 1
64 32 16 8 4 2 1

Count from the left to right and each digit doubles.

1+2+4+8+16+32+64=127

Add up the number for only the one's in binary code. Zeros are not counted.

Numbers 7:7-8
7 **Two** wagons and **four** oxen he gave unto the sons of Gershon, according to their service:
8 And **four** wagons and **eight** oxen he gave unto the sons of Merari, according unto their service, under the hand of Ithamar the son of Aaron the priest.

Figure 58

Using the graphic above as an example, the next exercise is to find the sum for the skip rate number of 111. Label the number 111 with the same pattern as above and then add those numbers together to come up with the number that is represented by 111 in the binary number system.

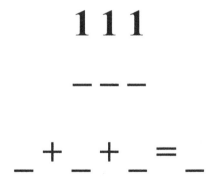

If you labeled the ones correctly and counted correctly, you should have gotten the number seven. The number seven seems to be God's favorite number, as the Creation took seven days with one day of rest. There are also seven Spirits of God, and there is the seven candlesticks Menorah lamp that was kept in the Tabernacle and the Temple. It's interesting that the 111 skip rates in God's tones also add up to the number seven in binary code.

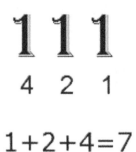

1+2+4=7

Figure 59

I read in a book called *Programmable Logic Controllers: Hardware and Programming*, and it talks quite a lot about binary code. I read the first chapter, and I realized that the next step that I should take with the Solfeggio tones was to convert the tones into binary code since the skip rates of the tones encodes binary and trinary (ternary) codes. In this chapter it explained about converting from analog to digital, which means to convert a variable or analog electrical signal to a binary value. Since the Solfeggio tones are electromagnetic frequencies, I realized that perhaps the binary code hints in the skip rates was trying to show that the tones could be converted into binary code and perhaps even trinary code as well. I decided to convert all 24 tones into binary code to see if there was any kind of pattern that I could discern from the list of 1's and the 0's. There isn't any kind of pattern that I could discern. Unfortunately, I don't know how to use this information, because I am not a computer programmer or an electrical engineer.

24 Solfeggio Tones in Binary Code

174	10101110	147	10010011
285	100011101	258	100000010
396	110001100	369	101110001
417	110100001	471	111010111
528	1000010000	582	1001000110
639	1001111111	693	1010110101
741	1011100101	714	1011001010
852	1101010100	825	1100111001
963	1111000011	936	1110101000
1173	10010010101	1146	10001111010
1284	10100000100	1257	10011101001
1395	10101110011	1368	10101011000

Figure 60

It turns out that binary code is also a pattern found throughout nature. It is the numbering system that occurs with mitosis, which is the splitting that occurs with microscopic cells in our body. The cells start splitting from one into two and as each cell splits the number of cells keeps doubling in number.

Binary is also found in the family tree pattern or genealogy because if you go backwards through your ancestry each generation doubles. My step dad was the first one who pointed this pattern out to me. With the binary pattern it is possible to count the number of past generations, so therefore, this hint in the book of Numbers could also be the key to counting past generations. Everyone has two parents, four grandparents and eight great grandparents, and it will continue to double all the way back as far as you can go.

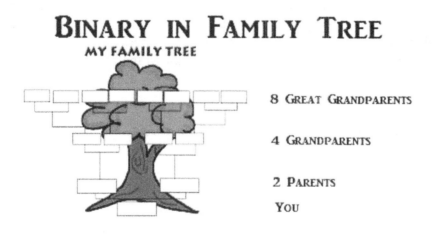

Figure 61

I found another interesting discovery when I watched a documentary on fractals. They displayed the Cantor Ternary Set, which was one of the early patterns for fractals. Cantor drew a line and then erased the middle third of the line which made two lines. He continued to eliminate the half of the lines by taking out the third of it in the middle. This pattern can continue on into infinity. I noticed that the pattern this fractal makes has the same binary numbers that we use for counting in binary. Koch's snowflake is made with erasing a third of the line in the center and then adding triangle lines in the center which also follows the pattern of binary.

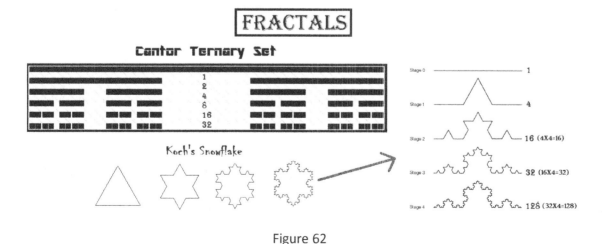

Figure 62

As you can see from the fractals graphic, these fractals are created through a binary numbering process. Nature mostly consists of irregular shapes and not the perfect shapes of Euclidean geometry; through the discovery of fractal geometry, the shapes become more irregular like the jagged edges of the coastlines or the mountain peaks. Fractal geometry more closely mimics nature in the world around us through repetition of specific shapes over and over again.

I was studying about bits, bytes and words in binary code, and so I decided to see how this would look in the skip rates. Each column has 24 bits with just the binary code of 111 because there are 24 ones in the eight 111 numbers of each column, and this matches the 24 tones. Each column of just the binary code of 111 has 3 bytes and 1 word with 1 byte. I translated the trinary skip rates into binary, and then I stringed all of the binary code in the skip rates together, so that I could distinguish how many bits, bytes and words are in the binary code. Each column has 36 bits, which together both columns would have 72 bits altogether. This seems quite significant since 72 could represent Jesus disciples and the Precession of the Equinox movement of 1 degree every 72 years, and we also know that 72 is a multiple of 144. Both columns of skip rates in binary and trinary also has 9 bytes of data.

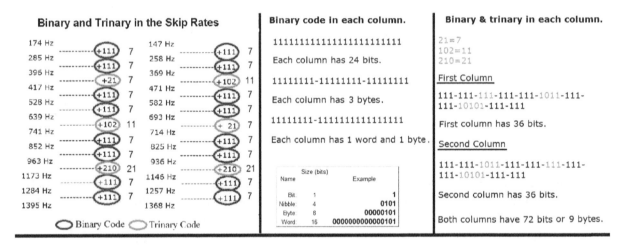

Figure 63

It should also be noted that binary code is the choice of languages for transmitting information to extraterrestrial civilizations in the universe; therefore, binary code could be considered a universal language as well as math and pictures. Binary messages have been sent in the Pioneer 10 spacecraft in 1972 and the Pioneer 11 spacecraft in 1973 as well as through a transmission over the Arecibo radio telescope in Puerto Rico on November 16, 1974.

I started researching about binary code and music, and amazingly, I ended up finding links about binary music. I had never heard of such a thing, so I continued to research the topic, and I found an online PDF paper called *Using Binary Numbers in Music* by Vi Hart of Stony Brook University. The paper explains that composers can use binary code to construct the rhythm of a musical composition by using the 1's to place the notes and using the 0's for rest. The author of the paper used a 4/4 measure in which he assigned eighth notes to bits. In computer science eight bits makes a byte, so he divided the binary code into groups of four, which is half a byte and used the method of assigning notes to ones and rests to zeros. I must say that I know very little about music, so I only understand the mathematics in the article. He goes on to say that composing music in binary code is a great way to hide secret messages. What interests me about binary music is that I previously thought that binary code was only encoding other information within the mathematics of the tones; however, I now realize that binary code can be used to formulate the rhythm of the song itself. The ones and zeros of the tones converted to binary code may somehow form the construct of how to fit the notes and rests into the song.

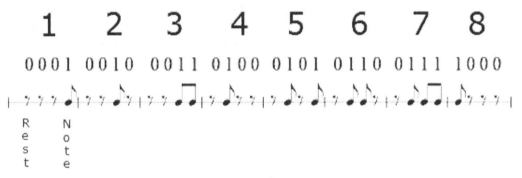

Figure 64

Perhaps binary music could play a part in the formation of how the tones are played, or perhaps the skip rates are only to be played in binary code in between the tones themselves. The binary code could be there to only encode how the rhythm of the song should go, or maybe it is only there for the mathematical clues to the tones.

I believe there is a reason the binary code is encoded into the skip rates, and I can't help but wonder how much information could be encoded into this message within these tones. It is obvious to me that there is much more encoded into these tones that I may never find. We do not merely just have the tones for a higher frequency song, but we also have many mathematical, geometrical and scientific blueprints embedded within the structure of the song. Perhaps the 144,000 will only recognize its value in terms of the new song; however, I am enjoying finding all of the encoded information that adds to the power and awe of how these tones work. Binary code might very well display the rhythm of the song in terms of rest and notes, or it could just serve as a repository of additional data about God's creation and how it works, nevertheless, the number 111 or seven is God's favorite number, so perhaps it serves as a clue to the authorship of the song.

The Net

Now that you have learned the tones, it would be wise to ask this question. What is the reason for the tones? Well, there is another clue in Numbers 7 that shows us part of what these tones mean. The clue is so subtle that most people would miss this one. I just happened to be reading Numbers 7:17 when the numbering caught my eye as well as the verse number.

Before I show you the clue, let's look at the fishing story of John 21. If you have ever read the story, then you know the apostles were fishing and not catching any fish. Jesus appears along the bank the third time after his death and offers them some advice. He tells them to throw the net on the right side, and when they did as he told them, they caught 153 fish. This story or parable has a much deeper meaning to what some believe is a simple fishing story. I will be teaching the math and geometry that is encoded into this one story.

First, let's work out the clue in Numbers 7:17.

Numbers 7:17 (KJV)

[17] And for a sacrifice of peace offerings, two oxen, five rams, five he goats, five lambs of the first year: this was the offering of Nahshon the son of Amminadab.

In this next exercise we are going to add the numbers of verse seventeen.

$$2+5+5+5=\underline{}$$

This is a simple addition exercise to show what one of the purposes is for the tones. Did you happen to notice that the answer matches the verse number? I did. Okay, so you may be asking yourself this question. What does this number mean? Good question! Well, this number is related to the fishing net with 153 fish.

Here is another exercise.

$$153/9=\underline{}$$

$$1+2+3+4+5+6+7+8+9+10+11+12+13+14+15+16+17=\underline{}$$

Did you get the same answer for the division problem? Did the addition problem clue you into John 21? Now you know what this number has to do with the John 21 story.

This fishing net is very important to Jesus, because this is God's net. Jesus said that he was teaching the apostles to be fishers of men. This clue should be applied to John 21, which means the apostles were not catching mere fish. They were catching men and women and teaching them the Word of God.

Matthew 13:47 *Again, the kingdom of heaven is like unto a net, that was cast into the sea, and gathered of every kind:*

The first time I read the John 21 fishing story, I took it very literal and thought that it was just another story that authenticated the fact that Jesus Christ was alive after his death. At some point I actually decided to research the number 153 on the internet, and to my surprise I found out that there were many really significant reasons why that number was brought up in this story. Many times the Bible puts obvious hints right in front of our face, and yet we fail to notice them. There is a reason why people do not recognize the math and science that is encoded into the Bible, and that reason is because we are simply not taught to read the Bible at this level of interpretation. Science and religion have always been at odds with one another, but it doesn't have to be this way. Spirituality and science should be able to coexist together because they complement each other beautifully. Both science and religions explain the world around us and how it came to be, so there is no use in arguing for which viewpoint is right or wrong, instead we should seek to combine the two together. Science says that the universe began in the big bang, and most religions say that God made the universe from nothing. There is no contradiction in these two theories because the big bang only explains how the universe started in an explosion, and it does not seek to explain who caused that big bang. Religion explains who caused that explosion, whereas science just explains the big bang itself.

Upon researching the number 153, I learned that the fish symbol that was used to represent Jesus Christ in early Christianity has a ratio of 265:153. The body of the fish is in the shape of a vesica piscis, which is made by the intersection of two circles interlinked together. The John 21 story is about catching 153 fish in a net, so it seems quite appropriate that the fish symbol has a ratio that contains the number 153.

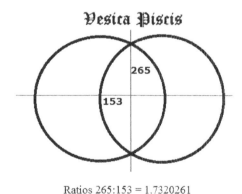

Ratios 265:153 = 1.7320261

Figure 65

The next thing I researched was about the number 153 being a triangular number. A triangular number is a number that can form a triangle. If you take 153 circles or dots and line them up with each row having one more circle added to each horizontal row and stack them downward, then you will end up with a perfect triangle. This triangle will have 17 dots or circles on each side of the perimeter. It is a perfect equilateral triangle and the vertex should be at a 60 degree angle. The person that made the 153 triangle for Wikipedia did not space out the circles on the base of the left triangle below, so this one is not an equilateral triangle, but the 153 triangle in the image on the right is an equilateral triangle with 60 degree angles on the vertices. The triangle on the left does show that there are 153 circles used to make the 153 triangle.

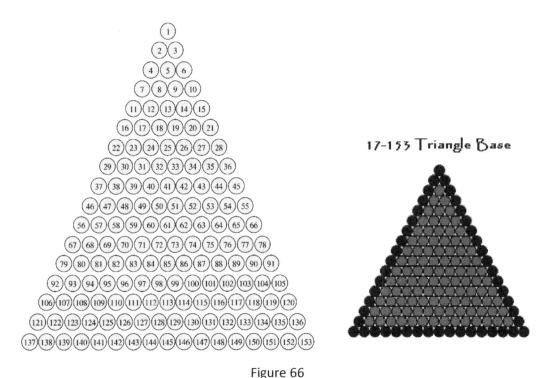

Figure 66

As I pointed out earlier, the perimeter of each side contains 17 circles, and as I showed before, this number is closely associated with the number 153 in two ways.

$$17 \times 9 = 153$$

$$1+2+3+4+5+6+7+8+9+10+11+12+13+14+15+16+17=153$$

It's interesting that the 153 triangle has a perimeter on each side that is exactly 17 circles due to the fact that 17 is a divisor into 153 and that the first 17 numbers add up to 153. You can see that the 153 triangle is perfect in every way. This is why the parable fishing story in John 21 is so special. If we look beyond the literal fishing story in John 21, we can see that Jesus Christ encoded some math lessons for those that have eyes to see and ears to hear. This story is actually showing us a blueprint for the fishing net, and as this chapter continues to progress, you will be astonished with all of the information that is encoded in this little story. The unfortunate part of all of this is that most Christian churches are not teaching this parable from a scientific and mathematical level, and therefore, most people are ignorant to a much greater story that lies just below the surface of the text and the Sea of Tiberius. Hidden with the number 153 is a powerful message that is just waiting to be discovered by the reader. I like to put myself into each one of the stories of the Bible because in a sense, we are all the characters in the Bible, and each story is speaking individually to each and every one of us who are reading its words. In Matthew 4:19, Jesus said to the Apostles *"Follow me, and I will make you fishers of men."* You can be one of those Apostles that Jesus was speaking to that very day, and you can learn to be a fisher of men as well as learn how to make the net. In this story Jesus is directly and personally speaking to you. Are you listening?

To continue our lessons to unravel the clues to the information that this geometrical net contains, we must continue to look deeper into the number 153. I also found out that the number 153 is a hexagonal number as well. This means that if you line up 153 dots into a hexagonal pattern that it will make a perfect hexagon. This is the next big clue to showing us a blueprint of the net.

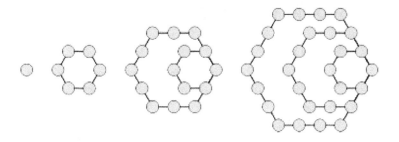

1, 6, 15, 28, 45, 66, 91, 120, 153…

http://en.wikipedia.org/wiki/190_(number)

Figure 67

We see the clue of the hexagon being presented to us. Isn't it interesting that this is the same pattern that can be found in the face of the water? The hexagon contains both the Star of David and the Holy of Holies cube.

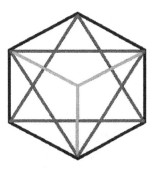

Figure 68

You can easily fit a Star of David into a hexagon by forming two triangles when drawing lines to 3 vertices for each one. This stood out to me as being a major clue in the 153 hexagon and the

153 triangle because the triangle is used to make the Jewish Star of David. In the Star of David a triangle is pointing up and another triangle is pointing down. These 2 triangles are interlocked together to form a 6 pointed star pattern, and both triangles are equilateral triangles with a 60 degree angle at each vertex. The triangle pointing up represents the masculine energy, and the triangle pointing down represents the feminine energy so in this way the Star of David is very similar to the Yin/Yang symbol. This star also represents the ancient *Hermetic* concept of "As above, so below."

I have found this same yin/yang, masculine/feminine and positive/negative pattern in the tones as well. It turns out that if you assign the 3, 6 and 9 patterns into a formula, you can find these same patterns within the tones themselves.

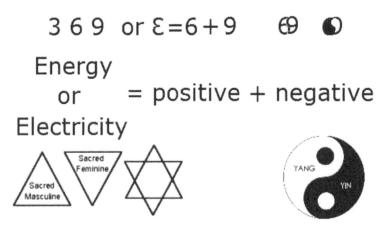

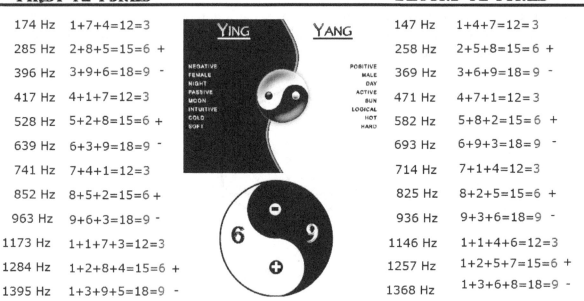

Figure 69

Notice that I have assigned the positive symbol beside every 6 and the negative sign beside every 9. I matched up the 6 and 9 to the yin/yang symbol, and it fits quite perfectly together. The number six is masculine and the number nine is femi*nine*, so these tones each have a set of qualities to them. Also you may have noticed that some of the tones are neither positive nor negative. These are the neutral tones, and they are spaced in between the positive and negative tones as a sort of gap. These tones closely resemble the atoms because they have positive, negative and neutral tones, and the atom has a positive proton, a negative electron and a neutral neutron. It is also important to note that electrical polarity is present in every electrical circuit. In a direct current circuit, like a car battery, one pole is negative and the other pole is positive, but in alternating current circuits the two poles alternate between negative and positive.

Now getting back to triangular numbers, I found out that there is an interesting number pattern that shows how to find all of the triangular numbers. We are not taught this number pattern in school, but we are taught this number pattern in the Bible. If you start adding the numbers together in succession, then you will find that all numbers added together will add up to triangular numbers. It is very interesting to note that all triangles have 3 sides and 3 vertices, and this goes along with the trinity that Christian religions teach. There is the Father, Holy Spirit (some say Mother) and the Son, so the 153 triangle represents all three. There are 2 obvious numbers in the Bible that are triangular numbers, and one of these 2 numbers may surprise you. The 153 triangular number is used to represent Jesus Christ's fishing net, and the 666 triangular number represents Satan's net or trap. I was shocked when I first realized that 666 is also a triangular number. If you add the first 36 numbers together, then you will get the number of 666, which is also the number of the beast. You can look at the triangular numbers chart below which shows how it all works out. I also found some other interesting numbers, which I bolded to make them stand out. If you go down 9 rows from the 153 number, then you find the mirror number of 153 which is 351. Jesus net number perfectly mirrors itself in the triangular numbers just as water mirrors us in visual reflections and in our emotions. The other funny thing is the 9 connection to those numbers and the spacing of 9 in between them on the chart (1+5+3=9 or 3+5+1=9). This number chart shows just how special this number is and why it is the number associated with Jesus' fishing net.

All sums are triangular numbers!

1+2=**3**

1+2+3=6

1+2+3+4=10

1+2+3+4+5=**15**

1+2+3+4+5+6=21

1+2+3+4+5+6+7=28

1+2+3+4+5+6+7+8=36

1+2+3+4+5+6+7+8+9=45

1+2+3+4+5+6+7+8+9+10=55

1+2+3+4+5+6+7+8+9+10+11=66

1+2+3+4+5+6+7+8+9+10+11+12=78

1+2+3+4+5+6+7+8+9+10+11+12+13=91

1+2+3+4+5+6+7+8+9+10+11+12+13+14=105

1+2+3+4+5+6+7+8+9+10+11+12+13+14+15=120

1+2+3+4+5+6+7+8+9+10+11+12+13+14+15+16=136

1+2+3+4+5+6+7+8+9+10+11+12+13+14+15+16+17=**153**

1+2+3+4+5+6+7+8+9+10+11+12+13+14+15+16+17+18=171

1+2+3+4+5+6+7+8+9+10+11+12+13+14+15+16+17+18+19=190

1+2+3+4+5+6+7+8+9+10+11+12+13+14+15+16+17+18+19+20=210

1+2+3+4+5+6+7+8+9+10+11+12+13+14+15+16+17+18+19+20+21=231

1+2+3+4+5+6+7+8+9+10+11+12+13+14+15+16+17+18+19+20+21+22=253

1+2+3+4+5+6+7+8+9+10+11+12+13+14+15+16+17+18+19+20+21+22+23=276

1+2+3+4+5+6+7+8+9+10+11+12+13+14+15+16+17+18+19+20+21+22+23+24=300

1+2+3+4+5+6+7+8+9+10+11+12+13+14+15+16+17+18+19+20+21+22+23+24+25=325

1+2+3+4+5+6+7+8+9+10+11+12+13+14+15+16+17+18+19+20+21+22+23+24+25+26=**351**

1+2+3+4+5+6+7+8+9+10+11+12+13+14+15+16+17+18+19+20+21+22+23+24+25+26+27=378

1+2+3+4+5+6+7+8+9+10+11+12+13+14+15+16+17+18+19+20+21+22+23+24+25+26+27+28=406

1+2+3+4+5+6+7+8+9+10+11+12+13+14+15+16+17+18+19+20+21+22+23+24+25+26+27+28+29=435

1+2+3+4+5+6+7+8+9+10+11+12+13+14+15+16+17+18+19+20+21+22+23+24+25+26+27+28+29+30=465

1+2+3+4+5+6+7+8+9+10+11+12+13+14+15+16+17+18+19+20+21+22+23+24+25+26+27+28+29+30+31=496

1+2+3+4+5+6+7+8+9+10+11+12+13+14+15+16+17+18+19+20+21+22+23+24+25+26+27+28+29+30+31+32=528

1+2+3+4+5+6+7+8+9+10+11+12+13+14+15+16+17+18+19+20+21+22+23+24+25+26+27+28+29+30+31+32+33=561

1+2+3+4+5+6+7+8+9+10+11+12+13+14+15+16+17+18+19+20+21+22+23+24+25+26+27+28+29+30+31+32+33+34=595

1+2+3+4+5+6+7+8+9+10+11+12+13+14+15+16+17+18+19+20+21+22+23+24+25+26+27+28+29+30+31+32+33+34+35=630

1+2+3+4+5+6+7+8+9+10+11+12+13+14+15+16+17+18+19+20+21+22+23+24+25+26+27+28+29+30+31+32+33+34+35+36=666

The chart above shows the first 36 triangular numbers.

Figure 70

I also found out that there is a special relationship between the number 153 and 666. Only one website I found tried to explain this relationship, but at first I was unable to understand what the person was showing on their blog. It took me a few days to completely understand how this relationship works out. I discovered that the numbers of 153 and 666 were mentioned in the Bible to also display the mathematical anomaly that occurs between these 2 triangular numbers.

When I first started to explore the connection between the number 153 and 666, I decided to work out the perimeter formula on both the 153 and 666 triangles. To use the perimeter formula, I had to add the sides of the triangle (i.e. A+B+C=). The 153 triangle has 17 circles on each side, so I added them together and got the number 51 (i.e. 17+17+17=51). It's interesting that the number 51 also divides into the number 153, so that was definitely a fascinating correlation. I then decided to work on the perimeter formula on the 666 triangle, and I found out that the sum of its perimeter does not divide into 666, so the 153 triangle is more perfect than the 666 triangle. I added the numbers of the perimeter and got the number 108 (i.e. 36+36+36=108), which interestingly enough also seems to be a significant number in many different religions and is a skip rate in the Solfeggio tones. There are 108 beads on Hindu and Buddhist malas or rosaries. The most significant fact about this number is that the sun's diameter is 108 times the Earth's diameter. The number 108, and all of its multiples are found throughout the universe, but I am not going to go into detail about the 108 number. Anyway, I divided 666 by 108 and got the number 6.166666666666667, so it does not divide evenly like the 153 triangle and 666 is not a hexagonal number either.

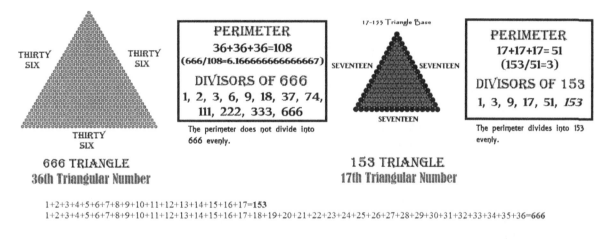

Figure 71

Now remember the tones that were discovered on the 15 degree intervals of a circle in the Song of Degrees are pointed to by the vertices on a Star of David which consist of two equilateral triangles. Also the infinity pattern has each triad tone traced out in an equilateral triangle as well. The 153 triangle and the 666 triangle are both equilateral triangles, but only one is perfect in every way. Only the 153 triangle is perfect in that its perimeter adds up to the number 51, which divides into 153 perfectly; therefore, this is the reason why John 21 points this number out as being the net of Jesus.

A few days later, I realized what the article on a blog was trying to explain about the relationship between the 153 triangle and the 666 triangle. If you count the circles or dots going around both triangles and then add those sums together, you will get the number 153, and only the perimeter sums of these 2 triangles will make the 153 number. This is astounding to me considering the belief among most Christians is that this number represents evil. The number 666 is not evil, but the Bible does say that we can identify the beast with this number. In this case, the number 666 is only being used to find the identity of the beast or antichrist, so it is being used like a name is used to identify a person.

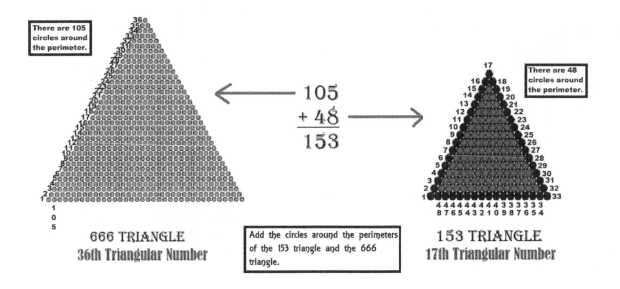

Figure 72

You should be able to see by now that the first 17 verses of John 21 actually contain an encyclopedia amount of information. The key to unlocking that information is to thoroughly research about the number 153, and to find that within that number are vast amounts of geometrical blueprints that were designed by God in the making of this universe. If the Christian religion actually taught the multi-perspective aspects of the fishing story in John 21, then they would be teaching it from a mathematical, geometrical and scientific perspective. You could actually use this story to teach students in school about mathematics, geometry and the physics of energy. The multi-layered information in this one parable alone could probably fill a volume of an encyclopedia, so we can see that this simple fishing story is in all actuality a very complex blueprint to the universe. The Bible is truly an encyclopedia galactica of data that contains the knowledge of the universe.

One thing that I noticed at some point in my research is that the equilateral triangle can be divided evenly into 4 equilateral triangles. The amazing thing about this is that when we do divide an equilateral triangle into 4 triangles, then we can now bring this triangle into three dimensions. We can literally raise it up into a tetrahedron shape. A tetrahedron is a three dimensional shape that has four sides made up of equilateral triangles.

Now you can see why I put the tones on tetrahedrons in a previous chapter. A star tetrahedron fits perfectly into the Holy of Holies cube, and it is said to be the shape of a Merkaba. The blueprint of John 21 is actually helping us to understand the blueprint within the tones energetic pattern. As you can see, the fishing net of John 21 is helping us to put together the blueprint of the tones within the 153 net, and this is why Numbers 7:17 gives us a hint to look at the story of John 21. That verse is a clever clue to show us that these tones are associated with the fishing net, and its clues actually circle us back to the clues that we found within the tones. We can finally see that the tones and the net are the same thing from our comparison of the sacred geometry within the tones and within the fishing story. Not only is John 21 teaching us how to fish, but it is telling us to do it with the tones. We must sing to catch the fish, and much in the same way that a make believe mermaid sings to catch the fish in the sea.

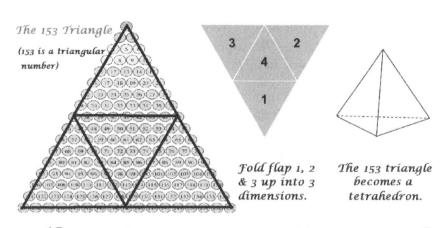

Fold flap 1, 2 & 3 up into 3 dimensions.

The 153 triangle becomes a tetrahedron.

Two tetrahedrons form a Merkaba. One is pointing up and one down, and it looks like a two dimensional Star of David from the side.

The #153 Connetion to the Merkaba

Figure 73

As you can see from the graphic above, we can fold flaps 1, 2 and 3 upwards and make a tetrahedron. Now remember 153 is also a hexagonal number, and within that hexagon we can make a Star of David which contains 2 triangles. If we carry that template into the third dimension, then the two dimensional Star of David would actually be a star tetrahedron. It's interesting that in spiritual teachings the shape of a Merkaba or light chariot is in the shape of a star tetrahedron. As you may recall this is actually an energy pattern of light in which each tetrahedron spins in counter rotation to the other, which is the same pattern we have seen within the tones. The star tetrahedron is said by some to be the underlying energy of all objects in our universe, so this is where our lesson starts to cross over into the science of physics. Richard C. Hoagland has found that there is a star tetrahedron energy pattern in the earth. He found that the base of each tetrahedron is located at 19.5 degrees on the north and south latitudes.

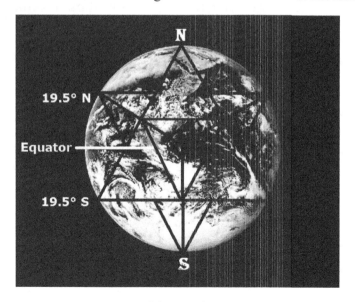

Figure 74

At 19.6 degrees north there is the largest shield volcano on the earth at Mauna-Kea volcano on the island of Hawaii. A shield volcano is usually built almost entirely of fluid lava flows, and it resembles the shape of a warrior's shield. The Mayan ruins of Teotihuacan near Mexico City has a latitude and longitude of 19°41'33"N 98°50'37.68"W, which is very close to this 19.5 degree zone, so perhaps the ancient people were trying to mark out this tetrahedron energy zone.

The underlying energy pattern of the universe is based upon the hexagon shape, and we can see this in the water (snowflake) on a microscopic level, but on a macroscopic level we can see that the energy pattern of all objects in this universe is based upon the star tetrahedron and the hexagonal patterns. The John 21 story is basically describing the energetic patterns of the three dimensional universe. It is astounding to think that this level of the Bible has been hidden from our perspective for thousands of years by religions that sought to control this information and to hide it from the masses. All the while the answers to the universe were hidden in plain sight within the Bible, and those keys could only be understood for those that "have eyes to see and ears to hear," as Jesus would say. It was only a matter of learning to shift our consciousness into new and higher levels or perspectives to unlock the keys to the mysteries of this universe. Reading the Bible from the level of science and math is a new way to read this ancient book.

Before I continue with the number 153, I want to say that I did not discover all of this information on my own. The Holy Spirit has been an intricate part of all of my discoveries on this learning path, and without this instruction I could have never understood the higher meanings contained within the Bible. I am merely a curious student, as everyone else, but at some point a student becomes a teacher, and I love to share what I have learned with anyone that wants to learn also. The Holy Spirit is the best teacher of these mysteries, and I hope that each person reading this book has been able to learn in this way.

I also learned a lot of information from the net as well. I'm not talking about the fishing net though; I learned much knowledge from the internet. We are now living in a time that knowledge can easily be shared from around the world and looking up information on the internet is like having all of the world's libraries at your fingertips. It certainly makes me think of the prophetic times of the last days that is talked about in Daniel 12:4, when it says " *But thou, O Daniel, shut up the words, and seal the book, even to the time of the end: many shall run to and fro, and **knowledge shall be increased**".*

Now to continue, the hexagon is associated with a very ancient symbol called the Flower of Life, and this mysterious symbol can be found in the ancient Egyptian, Assyrian, Greek and Jewish cultures. The centerpiece of the Flower of Life is called a Seed of Life, and it consists of 7 circles intersecting one another to form the vesica piscis or fish symbol over and over again until it fits into a hexagon shape. The Seed of Life diagram below depicts the 6 days of creation.

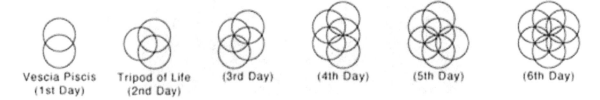

Figure 75

The tones create the Flower of Life pattern by creating counter-rotation within its energy patterns, and this is easily demonstrated by the tones wraparound effect which creates three dimensional spirals. The clockwise spin of the first 9 tones and the counterclockwise spin of the second 9 tones create interconnecting circles and the Vesica Piscis formation. We can clearly see from the diagram below how it is the combination of both spins put together that is forming the net. The two columns of tones played in the right and left speakers are combined together by both hemispheres of the brain to create the corner tones, but likewise, both frequencies in space are also put together to weave the circles in the fishing net.

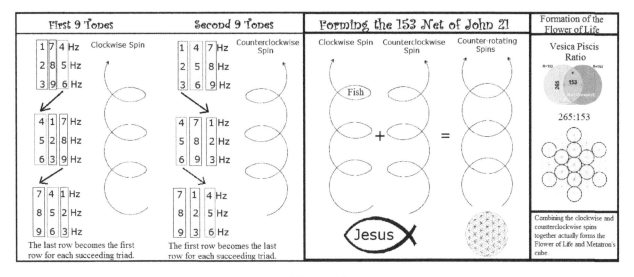

Figure 76

We can see the tones are not only moving in circular patterns together, but that those circles are also moving in spirals to create the Flower of Life. In the figure above, I've shown the circles moving in a line to easily demonstrate the concept, however, those circles would actually be moving in spirals to create the circular Flower of Life pattern. The actual Flower of Life builds upon the Seed of Life in the center and extends outward into 3 layers of seeds, and then it is completed by putting a circle around the exterior with 6 points of the hexagon touching the circle's edge. The diagram is below.

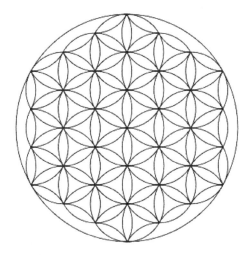

User:Life of Riley – Wikipedia

Figure 77

There are other blueprints hidden within the Vesica Piscis and the Flower of Life which also encodes the 153 triangle. You can make two triangles inside of the Vesica Piscis that resemble a diamond pattern, and from those two triangles you can add two more to make a big triangle made of four.

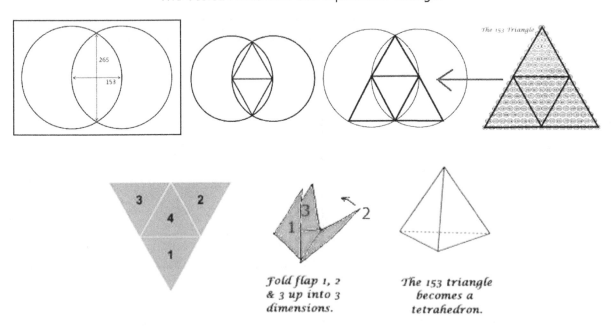

Figure 78

From this pattern, you can then take the triangle from two dimensions into three dimensions by folding up the flaps to make a tetrahedron pattern. Therefore, the pattern being presented to us in the tones makes two counter-rotated motions that would seem to invisibly draw out the patterns of the Vesica Piscis and the Flower of Life if you were to model these motions on a computer. If we took the models being presented to us in the tones into a three dimensional model, then those circles would become spheres, and those triangles would become tetrahedrons. This seems to be the blueprints being presented from the counter-rotation within the tones.

If you haven't already noticed the Vesica Piscis also forms the pattern that goes on with cell division, also known as mitosis. The single cell divides into 2, and those two cells divide into 4, and this process continues along in a progression of 1, 2, 4, 8, 16, 32, 64 and on into the billions. This is another clue from Numbers 7:7-8 again.

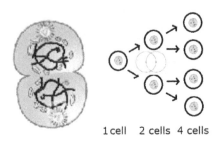

Figure 79

One day I realized that there were a lot of fish symbols within the Flower of Life, so I thought I should count the fish and see how many there are. There were 90 small fish inside the Flower of Life, and so I gradually began to shift my perspective to see bigger fish within the net also. Eventually, I saw a graphic on the internet that combined the Flower of Life with Metatron's cube, and I realized that I needed to include the cube and count all of the fish on the outer edge. Once I did that the fish number began to climb to 150 fish. I got to a point where I was stuck on finding the 3 fish that must be there somewhere, and I got frustrated. It was just so close to count 150 fish and to not be able to find the 3 fish anywhere. One day it dawned on me that the 3 fish are made up by the 6 points around the hexagon. I went fishing around to catch some fish, and by the time I had finished, I had finally caught the 153 fish within the net, and I didn't even have to go in the water to catch them.

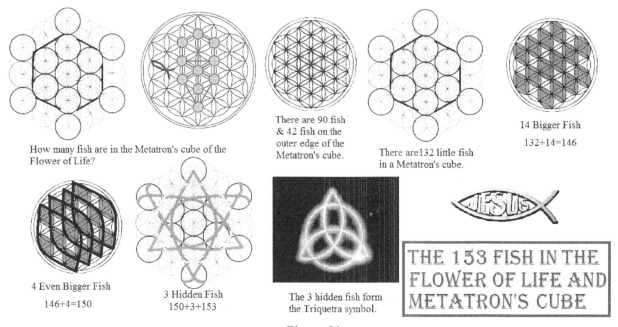

Figure 80

I drew the last 3 big fish out, and it made 3 intersecting fish, and I knew that somehow this looked very familiar to me, but I couldn't remember where I had seen this image before. I looked for a long time before I finally found this symbol, and I found out that it was called the Triquetra. The 3 fish are similar to the Triquetra but not quite the same. I learned that the Triquetra originally referred to the triangle, but now it had become the shape of three Vesica Piscis. This symbol is also used by Christians to represent the trinity of the Father, Son and the Holy Spirit. I believe the three fish represent the Father, the Holy Spirit and the Son of God.

The symbol that I found in the center of the net is very similar to the Triquetra, but the symbol that I drew out seems to look a lot like the Star of David with two triangles. If you look closely at the drawing above, you will see a Star of David in the three fish.

There is another interesting factor to the Flower of Life within the ring. It is interesting to note that the 6 points where it touches the outer ring or circle is also the same area of the degree circle where a Star of David is drawn. This shows a connection between the Flower of Life and the

Star of David as well as the equilateral triangles. Also, within the Flower of Life, you can trace out 7 small Star of David symbols.

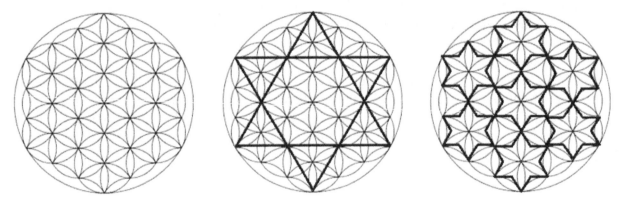

Revelation 1:20

The mystery of the seven stars which thou sawest in my right hand, and the seven golden candlesticks. The seven stars are the angels of the seven churches: and the seven candlesticks which thou sawest are the seven churches.

Figure 81

In the figure above, you can see the seven stars in the Flower of Life as seven Star of David symbols and a big Star of David which touches the ring or circle of the pattern. I left out the lines within the seven Star of David symbols to show how beautifully the stars fit into the pattern. Now you know the mystery of the seven stars that are the angles in the Flower of Life.

In Isaiah 19:19, it says "*In that day shall there be an altar to the LORD in the midst of the land of Egypt, and a pillar at the border thereof to the LORD*". As I showed before, this verse is referring to the Great Pyramid among the pyramids of Giza in Egypt. I will now show you further evidence that will tie the Great Pyramid into the Bible and specifically into the John 21 fishing story.

List of facts that I have found about the Great Pyramid:

1. The slope of the Great Pyramid is **51** degrees. (51X3=153)
2. The Grand Gallery in the Great Pyramid is **153 feet** long.
3. The main entrance inside the Great Pyramid is at the **17th** level of blocks. (17X9=153 & 1+2+3+4+5+6+7+8+9+10+11+12+13+14+15+16+17=153)
4. The **153rd** course of masonry from the ground, on the outside of the Great Pyramid, is 360 feet above the ground. (360 degrees of a circle)
5. Inside the Great Pyramid, from the King's Chamber floor up to the summit platform there are **153** courses of masonry.

As you can see the number 153 is encoded all throughout the Great Pyramid in many different ways. The Great Pyramid has 4 equilateral triangles on its sides, and the base is a perfect square. Each side of the Great Pyramid is clearly representative of the 153 triangle because the mathematical clues offer evidence that the Great Pyramid or monument to the Lord was encoded with the John 21 story.

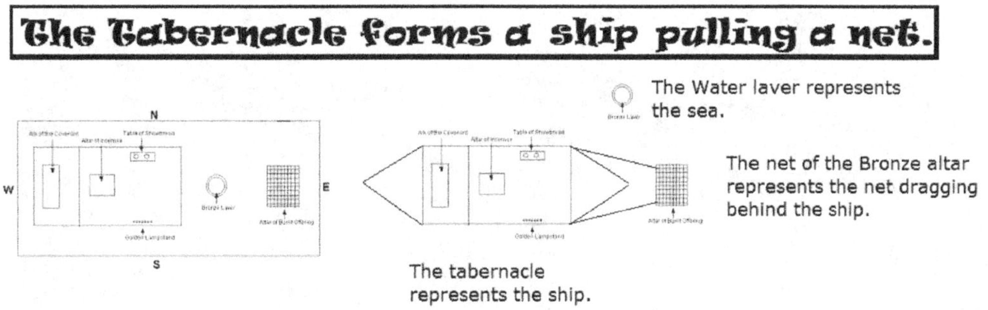

The Tabernacle forms a ship pulling a net.

The Water laver represents the sea.

The net of the Bronze altar represents the net dragging behind the ship.

The tabernacle represents the ship.

Figure 82

I realized at some point that the Tabernacle and Temple also encoded the fishing story of John 21. The first clue can be found in Exodus 27:5 where it says *"And thou shalt put it under the compass of the altar beneath, that the net may be even to the midst of the altar"*. The net on the Bronze Altar is meant to symbolize the fishing net in John 21. The Bronze Water Laver is also in the courtyard outside of the Tabernacle, and it represents the water or sea where the Apostles are fishing. The Tabernacle also represents a star map. The Table of Shewbread and the 7 candlestick Menorah represents the Pisces constellation with the two fish, so we can see the symbolism of the fish that are being caught in the net. In John 21:8, the verse says *"And the other disciples came in a little ship; (for they were not far from land, but as it were two hundred cubits,) dragging the net with fishes."* It's interesting to note that the Bronze Altar with the net is located outside of the Tabernacle, and therefore, we can see the Tabernacle as representing the ship, and the Bronze Altar represents the fishing net. It all fits in beautifully! The Holy of Holies is cube shaped, and therefore, it represents the Star of David and the star tetrahedron in a three dimensional configuration. This cube shows the 153 triangle and the 153 hexagon from a two dimensional perspective. I got creative and added 2 of the 153 triangles on each end of the Tabernacle to make it look more like a ship with the bow and the stern.

The Tabernacle had its door facing east towards the rising sun, and that is also prophetic of Jesus Christ ascending or rising in the sky after his death. In John 21:6, Jesus says *"Cast the net on the right side of the ship, and ye shall find. They cast therefore, and now they were not able to draw it for the multitude of fishes."* We can see that the net is on the right side of the Tabernacle because the east side of a compass is always on the right side. In this interpretation or perspective of the Tabernacle pattern, we can see that the net was cast out on the right side of the ship. You can clearly see that the John 21 fishing story was embedded into the pattern of the Tabernacle, and it shows the ship dragging the net towards the west. The ship is sailing towards the setting sun or should I say the setting Son. This clearly represents the second coming of Jesus Christ to claim his bride during the harvest or rapture.

Now that we have covered that the equilateral 153 triangle and the 153 hexagon are woven all into God's pattern of this three dimensional universe, I will show you that God put His mark on the 6th planet in our Solar System. It is certainly no coincidence that NASA has photographed a big hexagon on the north pole of Saturn. God made the universe in 6 days, and He rested on the 7th day, so it is quite interesting that God marked the 6th planet with the 6 sided hexagon symbol that represents the Holy of Holies cube and the Star of David simultaneously. I also find it quite interesting that the Jewish Sabbath is on Saturday, because Saturday is named after Saturn.

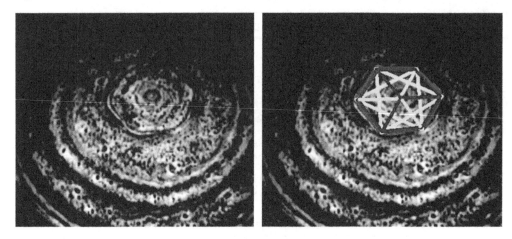

Figure 83

Surprisingly, the 153 number is also associated with chemistry too. I discovered that in the alchemical process of making the Philosopher's Stone there is a step that is called "The Net", which is a copper-antimony alloy, named for its crystalline "net" like surface. The main element used in this step is Antimony, which has an atomic number of 51. It seems somewhat clever that the alchemist called this step "The Net" considering the fact that they used this name because 153 is divisible by 51 and the John 21 story is all about fishing with a net and catching 153 fish. It became even more interesting when I started to look for all of the metals that were used in the building of the Tabernacle and the Temple in the periodic table and discovered that the four elements could form a triangle that points directly to the 51st element of Antimony. Bronze was an alloy made up of copper and tin in the biblical times, because zinc was not known at those times.

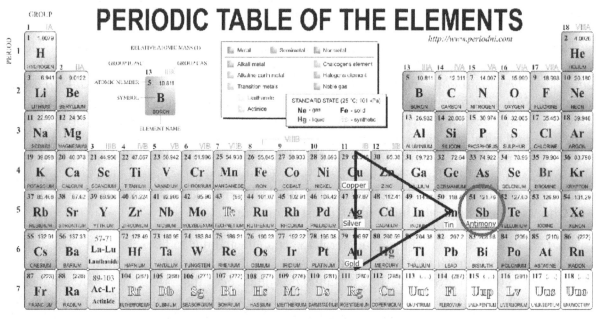

Figure 84

Exodus 25

³ And this is the offering which ye shall take of them; gold, and silver, and brass,

⁸ And let them make me a sanctuary; that I may dwell among them.

⁹ According to all that I shew thee, after the pattern of the tabernacle, and the pattern of all the instruments thereof, even so shall ye make it.

This is the 2nd encoded story of the 153 fish in the net that is included in the Tabernacle pattern. The Philosopher's Stone is the white powder gold that was used in the shewbread that the high priest ate in the Tabernacle. It was used to tune the high priest's body for worship in the Tabernacle or the Temple. In the 1970's a farmer named David Hudson rediscovered white powder gold in Arizona. He applied for a patent of his discovery, but to comply with the patent requirement he had to do more research test to provide information of the weight and other measurements. When they heated the substance, they found that the mass of the powder was reduced, and they didn't know why some of the mass had disappeared. Hal Puthoff is the director of the Institute for Advanced studies, and he had determined that when matter reacts in two dimensions, it should theoretically lose four-ninths of its gravitational weight, which was the amount of mass that was lost in the heating experiment with white powder gold. The result of their experiments have shown that white powder gold is really exotic matter which is capable of bending space/time and keeping a wormhole open for travel. A wormhole is mostly depicted in physicist models as being like a net, so isn't it interesting that "The Net" process of making the Philosopher's Stone actually leads to making a net of another kind.

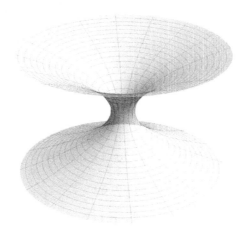

AllenMcC. – Wikipedia

Figure 85

Another topic worth discussing at this point is the subject of near death experiences or NDE's. There have been many people who have died only to be revived back to life with the modern medical technology that we have of our time. There are quite a few people that have described their souls leaving their bodies after they died, and then they feel attracted towards or are pulled into a whirling mass of darkness that seems oddly similar to a black hole. Once they have entered the hole, they begin to travel very quickly through a tunnel towards a light at the end of the tunnel. This tunnel would be considered a traversable wormhole from a physics perspective. Also from this perspective the Holy of Holies would be a wormhole, and Holy would be a homophone of holey, because the tunnel or wormhole is a hole that goes from one dimension to another dimension.

The picture Bible code discoveries that were found in the Bible by Dean Coomb has a picture of the net. It is interesting to me that one of the pictures found shows the fishing boat and the net of John 21, and it also cleverly hints at a wormhole connection to the net due to two pictures that are overlapping together. The one picture shows a boat with the net thrown into the sea, and the other one shows a prophetess with sun glasses on. The boat overlaps with the throat of the prophetess, which makes it an interesting parallel that the physicist call the opening to a wormhole a mouth and the tunnel they call a throat.

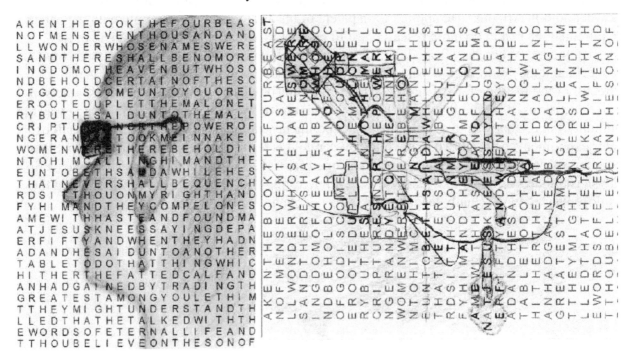

Found by Dean Coombs

Figure 86

As you can see in the overlapping pictures of the prophetess and the boat with the net, the boat has been positioned just inside the mouth, and it is getting ready to go down through the throat. There is an analogy being made between the wormholes throat and mouth and the prophetess mouth and throat.

There is a pyramid structure in the background, and it is being mirrored in the water. The base of the pyramid is 17 letters, and the height of the pyramid contains 9 letters (17X9=153), so this is perhaps a clue to the Great Pyramid in Egypt. I decided to measure the angle of the pyramid, and it was around the 50 degree mark, so perhaps it is meant to be 51 degrees. This is Dean Coombs drawing of the picture of the pyramid, so I would think the shading of the letters forming a pyramid should be at a 51 degree angle to further show the Great Pyramid connection

(51X3=153). The boat or ship says "I AM YESHUA," which is Jesus' name in Hebrew. A net has been thrown in between the boat that is 9 letters long, and the base of the pyramid which is 17 letters long; therefore, we can multiply the 9 and 17 to get the amount of fish that is in the net. The net says NETENA, which is "NET" reading it forward from left to right, and it says "A NET" reading it in reverse from right to left.

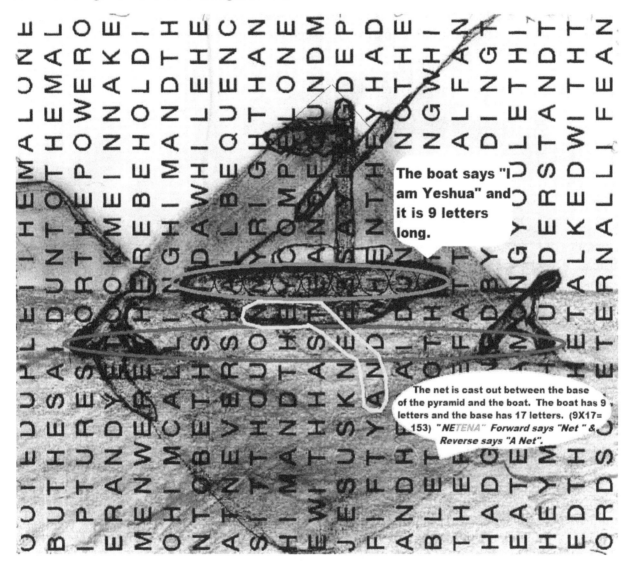

Figure 87

There is perhaps one last clue to the net of 153 fish in Revelation 21:17. Again, this clue is so subtle that it would not alert anyone to the net or the tones, unless they had eyes to see and ears to hear this clue. At the seventeenth verse we are told that the walls of New Jerusalem are 144 cubits, and this information was also found in the degree circle with the Song of Degrees. We found a two dimensional graphic of the cube of New Jerusalem within the circle. We saw how the tones were pointed to by the vertices of the Star of David, and so we did cube it to make the Holy of Holies. We learned that 144 was the measure of an angle of a decagon, which is the geometrical shape of DNA from the top looking down. It is indeed the measure of an angle of man. There is one more clue encoded into this one verse.

Revelation 21:17 (KJV)

[17] And he measured the wall thereof, an hundred and forty and four cubits, according to the measure of a man, that is, of the angel.

I'm sure you know what that one clue is now that you know what the number 17 has to do with the net. We seem to be shown a comparison between the number 144 and 153, so let's decipher what this clue means.

Here is another math problem for you to do:

$$153-144=\_$$

$$1+4+4=\_$$

$$1+5+3=\_$$

The tones are spaced apart in columns of nine, so this seems to be a valid clue to using the tones instead of stones to make New Jerusalem. There is more encoded into this clue than what it seems like at first glance. The first tone in the Solfeggio tones is located in between these two numbers.

144-145-146-**147**-148-149-150-151-152-153

Here is another mathematical exercise:

$$147-144=\_$$

$$153-147=\_$$

We must decide if this is a coincidence or not. Is Revelation 21:17 pointing us to the first tone?

There are three numbers that come forth from these mathematical numbers, and all three are the numbers of the underlying pattern within the tones of 3, 6 and 9. The spacing between 144, 147 and 153 is 3 and then 6. In the book, *Healing Codes for the Biological Apocalypse* there was a chart about the numbers 3 and 6 to show how it is related to the number 153.

Here is another exercise to help you see what is so special about the three and the six which are multiples of nine. Remember to use the Pythagorean mathematical skein to reduce the number to a single digit, and then add the numbers together for the sum.

$$1X3=\quad 1X6=$$

$$2X3=\quad 2X6=$$

$$3X3=\quad 3X6=$$

$$4X3=\quad 4X6=$$

5X3=   5X6=

6X3=   6X6=

7X3=   7X6=

8X3=   8X6=

9X3=   9X6=

10X3=   10X6=

11X3=   11X6=

12X3=   12X6=

13X3=   13X6=

14X3=   14X6=

15X3=   15X6=

16X3=   16X6=

17X3=   17X6=

18X3=   18X6=

19X3=   19X6=

20X3=   20X6=

21X3=   21X6=

22X3=   22X6=

23X3=   23X6=

24X3=   24X6=

25X3=   25X6=

26X3=   26X6=

You should have gotten the same answer for both if you reduced the number to a single digit on each multiplication problem. You are probably asking yourself why we had to multiply 3 and 6 all the way down to number 26 to get this answer. It is well known that God's main name in Hebrew is Yud Hey Vav Hey. Every Hebrew letter is also a number, so if you add up the number to God's name you get the sum of 26.

$$10+5+6+5=26$$

Figure 88

The chart below shows multiples of the numbers 3 and 6 all the way down to the number 26. It turns out that the numbers 3 and 6 are linked with the net, and we also see this with the tones. Another interesting pattern emerges that also shows two of the tones. Notice that the multiples of 3 show the repeating tone of 369 Hz, and the multiples of 6 show the repeating tone of 639 Hz. Notice that the 3 and 6 change places with one another from the left to the right column.

Multiples of Three and Six Using Pythagorean Skein

Multiples of 3	Multiples of 6
1X3= 3	1X6= 6
2X3= 6	2X6=12- 3
3X3= 9	3X6=18- 9
4X3=12- 3	4X6=24- 6
5X3=15- 6	5X6=30- 3
6X3=18- 9	6X6=36- 9
7X3=21- 3	7X6=42- 6
8X3=24- 6	8X6=48- 3
9X3=27- 9	9X6=54- 9
10X3=30-3	10X6=60- 6
11X3=33-6	11X6=66- 3
12X3=36-9	12X6=72- 9
13X3=39-3	13X6=78- 6
14X3=42-6	14X6=84- 3
15X3=45-9	15X6=90- 9
16X3=48-3	16X6=96- 6
17X3=51-6	17X6=102-3
18X3=54-9	18X6=108-9
19X3=57-3	19X6=114-6
20X3=60-6	20X6=120-3
21X3=63-9	21X6=126-9
22X3=66-3	22X6=132-6
23X3=69-6	23X6=138-3
24X3=72-9	24X6=144-9
25X3=75-3	25X6=150-6
26X3=78-6	26X6=156-3
153	153

Figure 89

I have one more thing to add before I close this chapter. There are 2 Solfeggio tones in the first 1000 triangular numbers, and I just recently found that clue. In my chart on the triangular numbers I highlighted the number 528 in green. I recognized that this was the middle tone in the first 9 Solfeggio tones, but later on I decided to check and see if there were anymore tones that were triangular in the triad tones and found one more. It turns out that 528 Hz and 741 Hz are both triangular numbers, and they are both located in the first 9 tones.

1, 3, 6, 10, 15, 21, 28, 36, 45, 55, 66, 78, 91, 105, 120, 136, 153, 171, 190, 210, 231, 253, 276, 300, 325, 351, 378, 406, 435, 465, 496, 528, 561, 595, 630, 666, 703, 741, 780, 820, 861, 903, 946, 990......

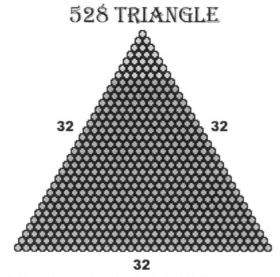

Figure 90

The number 528 is the 32nd triangular number, the number 741 is the 38th triangular number, 528 Hz is the 5th tone and 741 is the 7th tone in the first 9 tones. This shows us that the equilateral triangle is associated with the tones. When I looked at both of these triangular numbers, I found that there is another pattern being displayed that seems to be a clue to the tones being grouped together in 18 tones.

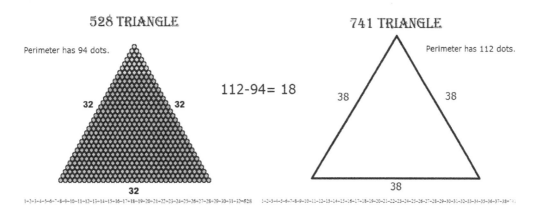

Figure 91

I have shown you all of the hidden meanings within the John 21 story, so now what seemed to be a simple fishing story has become a story filled with mathematical and geometrical clues to the mysteries of our universe. This story is really a highly entertaining parable, which at the literal level seems magical and like a fishing tale, but at a symbolic level it is filled with the evidence to the energetic pattern of everything in God's Creation. How could so much information be packed into a story that has merely 17 verses? I am astounded at the amount of information that is squeezed into such a small story.

In this world we poke fun at every man's fishing story because usually the fish they caught ends up gaining in size every time the fisherman tells his tale. The fish he caught could have been a minnow, but by the time he tells his fishing tale over and over again, it becomes the size of a whale. It becomes a whale of a tale. However, in the case of the fishing story of John 21, every time I read the story I would find more and more information, so what seemed like a simple fishing tale became a quite complex encyclopedia of information. The 153 fish in the net became the biggest catch that I ever caught, and I hope you enjoyed this whale of a tale for yourself.

Science of the Song of Degrees

When I first started to study about these tones, I had no idea where this journey was going to take me. I've always believed in God and Jesus, but I have never felt comfortable with the Christian religion, and therefore, I have never joined a church. I have found that most Christians are very judgmental, and that disturbs me so much. I feel it goes against everything that Jesus taught when he was here.

As a Christian, I feel that Jesus' words are simple from a moral perspective. For example: when Jesus says we should love one another, he doesn't put any limits on that love. He doesn't say love only your own race, love only your own gender, love only your own nationality, love only heterosexuals, or love only people of your own religion. It's simple and bold……..love one another. Generally, love means so much more than we can ever fully define. If you look up the word love in a dictionary, it will explain the many different variations of love. In the Webster's dictionary it explains that love is "unselfish, loyal and benevolent concern for the good of another." That is the core of love, but it isn't all that love is or should be. In 1 Corinthians 13, this verse attempts to describe love by our behavior.

1 Corinthians 13 New King James Version (NKJV)

[4] Love suffers long and is kind; love does not envy; love does not parade itself, is not puffed up; [5] does not behave rudely, does not seek its own, is not provoked, thinks no evil; [6] does not rejoice in iniquity, but rejoices in the truth; [7] bears all things, believes all things, hopes all things, endures all things. [8] Love never fails.

The older Bibles actually say charity instead of love. Paul wrote this book, but what Paul does not say is that in this world we are stuck with imperfect love. This would be true if we had unconditional love in this world, but we don't. Jesus words were simple….love one another, but he doesn't tell us how to love one another…..he shows us. Jesus showed us that love is about preaching the Word of God, feeding us when we are hungry (bread and fish parable) and helping or healing the sick. These were the things that Jesus did.

Paul told us that "Love never fails," but the truth is that it does. There are many people that have gone through heartache because love failed. The kind of love that Paul talks about is perfect love, but unfortunately we are not living in a perfect fairytale world. If we had perfect love in the world right now, then we wouldn't have wars, hunger or even poverty.

All Christians and everyone else in this world show us imperfect love. Sometimes we show perfect love and other times imperfect love, and this has been the kind of love that I've encountered in this world. The truth is that love does fail us at times, and at other times love heals us. It's neither black nor white but usually shades of grey. Love gets messy down here. Love is complicated! It means one thing to one person and something else to the next.

During the time of writing this book, I had a friend accuse me of many things and judge me. She ended the friendship we had. If love were perfect, I'm sure this would not have even happened, but love has never been perfect here.

The reason that I have explained about the moral rules in the Bible is to show that in an imperfect world truth is hard to find. For example, the parable or story about people wanting to stone a woman for adultery shows us imperfect love. Those people had forgotten Jesus three most crucial moral rules.

Matthew 7 (KJV)
7 Judge not, that ye be not judged.
² For with what judgment ye judge, ye shall be judged: and with what measure ye mete, it shall be measured to you again.

John 13:34-35 (KJV)

³⁴ A new commandment I give unto you, That ye love one another; as I have loved you, that ye also love one another.

³⁵ By this shall all men know that ye are my disciples, if ye have love one to another.

Matthew 6:15

But if ye forgive not men their trespasses, neither will your Father forgive your trespasses.

They weren't showing her love. They were judging her, and they didn't forgive her sin either. Jesus told them, "He that is without sin among you, let him first cast a stone at her." No one could. What is interesting here is that those people thought that they were doing right because the wages of sin are death. They took God's Word literally, and they were willing to be her accuser and executioner. They were doing this to her for their love of God. They forgot their love of her.

The problem is that humans have different ideas of what love is or what judgment means. Humans have different perspectives on the Word of God. We have 3 different religions that all read the first 5 books of the Bible, but all disagree on what the words of God mean. There are thousands of Christian denominations all around the world because Christians can't agree with one another on verses in the Bible.

This is why my ministry is not involved with morals, and why I delight in learning and teaching about the math and science in the Bible. This is why I desire to learn and study these tones. I do not desire to cast stones, but I do desire to cast tones for the atonement. Tones will not hurt anyone. The math and science in these tones are truthful and do not lie. Math can't be disputed from one perspective to the next. If I hold up 4 fingers to show how many newspapers I want to buy in any country around the world, most will know what I mean despite the language barriers. Four fingers means that I want to buy four, and everyone will count my fingers the same. There is no confusion! In math two plus two will always be four, and no one can dispute this fact. This is truth! There are no diverse perspectives in math. Likewise, if I throw up a ball to someone in America, they will know that it is going to come down, and that they need to catch it when it does. No matter what countries I do this experiment of throwing up a ball in the air, people will know that the ball is going to come down and that someone needs to catch it. This is science…..this is the law of gravity. The law of gravity is the same all over the earth, and everyone knows how it works. There is no debate as to whether gravity exists or not. There are no different perspectives on gravity; so for example, you can't say we have gravity in America, while Africa has no gravity. This would be ludicrous! As you can see math and science shows truth, and no one can dispute this on our earth.

Astronomy

I realized after I decoded the clue in the book of Joshua, that figuring out the rotations of the compass was also a key to deciphering something very fascinating about our Solar System. It seems that the Sumerian's invention of the 360 degrees of a circle encodes much more than we have ever been taught. This system encodes perhaps a hidden mathematical reality that goes beyond measuring the degrees on a compass to find where we are. In fact, the knowledge that it encodes shows a far superior mathematical system that not only shows a pattern to our universe, but it shows evidence for Divine design. It blew my mind when I realized what all is encoded in the degree math.

As I worked out the rotations of a compass all the way to the seventh rotation, I began to see some numbers that I recognized. After I looked up the numbers I was recognizing, I was astonished to see how this circular pattern of degrees is embedded into everything around us. We just were never taught how this mathematical system is encoded throughout God's Creation. After the third rotation, I found the radius of the moon, and after the sixth rotation I found the diameter of the moon. I thought, "How can this be?"

Psalm 8:3

When I consider thy heavens, the work of thy fingers, the moon and the stars, which thou hast ordained;

Remember the exercise where you figured out the math in seven rotations of the compass? It turns out that the third rotation and the sixth rotation became pretty interesting markers for not only the Church or followers of Christ, but it is also a marker for the 144,000. It's interesting that we tried to complete the 36 tones to bring the rotation up to the 7th; however, we found that the rotation of the 36 tones only went up to the 6th rotation. The third and the sixth rotation are also clues to the number of tones we can find in the six rotations with the seventh rotation being a rest day. The moon represents Christ's followers because it represents an analogy for his people. The moon reflects the light of the sun, but the followers reflect the light of the Son. We can see that this is a hidden message for the 144,000. The message about the moon is a comparison to Christ's followers reflecting his light for all to see. It's somewhat poetic that the Song of Degrees encodes a beautiful analogy for those that have eyes to see and ears to hear what God and the Son of God has put so strikingly before our eyes. We are the moon, and our light shines just as bright. The followers of the Son reflect his light, but we have to remember that the moon shines the brightest during the darkness of the night sky. Perhaps we must shine the light when it is the darkest of times; we must reflect His Light when the Son isn't here, as the moon shines its brightness when the sun is hidden behind the Earth.

Rotations of the Compass (1-7)

1. 0-360

2. 360-720

3. 720-1080   *1st 18 Tones*   (moon radius 1080 miles)

4. 1080-1440 (multiple of 144- Rev. 21:17 1440/144=10)

5. 1440-1800

6. 1800-2160 (Diameter of the moon 2160 miles- 144,000 marker) *2nd 18 Tones*

Also, notice that 1080 miles is a multiple of 108, which is a skip rate within the tones (108X10=1080), so therefore, these tones are associated with the moon. The 144,000 followers of Christ are being compared to the moon in the new song.

Song of Solomon 6 (KJV)

6 Whither is thy beloved gone, O thou fairest among women? whither is thy beloved turned aside? that we may seek him with thee.

[10] Who is she that looketh forth as the morning, fair as the moon, clear as the sun, and terrible as an army with banners?

There is also a Precession of the Equinox connection to the number 2160. Every age last exactly 2,160 years (25,920/12=2160). Is it a mere coincidence that the moon has a diameter of 2,160 miles and that every age lasts 2,160 years? It seems rather interesting that the degree circle is actually showing us a mathematical pattern to the earth and the moon. The Song of Degrees is much, much more than just a song. It appears to show the underlying mathematical patterns to our universe.

Genesis 1:14

"Let there be lights in the firmament of the heavens to divide the day from the night; and let them be for signs."

At the time of writing this book, we just went through the last blood moon in a lunar tetrad cycle in September, which consisted of 4 blood moons in 2014 and 2015. These lunar eclipses all happened on the Jewish Holidays of Passover and Sukkot (Feast of Tabernacles). The last three blood moon tetrads happened during significant times for the Jewish people. In 1493-1494, just after the Spanish Inquisition took place, and around the time that the Jews were expelled from Spain, a blood moon tetrad took place. Columbus had just discovered America in 1492, and the United States of America has the largest population of Jews outside of Israel. The next blood moon tetrad happened in 1949-1950, which is just after Israel became a nation again in May 14,

1948. In 1967-1968 the next blood moon tetrad occurred during the time of the six day war in 1967, and this coincided with Israel getting the Holy city of Jerusalem back. By the way, my birthday is May 14, 1967, so I was born exactly 19 years after Israel became a nation and during the year that Israel took Jerusalem back.

Everyone was wondering what this last blood moon tetrad would coincide with for the Jews, and there were many that believed they will soon build the third Temple or that Israel will soon be in a war. When it comes to the third Temple being built, I believe that Jesus Christ was the third Temple, because he said "Destroy this temple, and in three days I will raise it up."

John 2

^{20} Then said the Jews, Forty and six years was this temple in building, and wilt thou rear it up in three days?

^{21} But he spake of the temple of his body.

^{22} When therefore he was risen from the dead, his disciples remembered that he had said this unto them; and they believed the scripture, and the word which Jesus had said.

Although the last blood moon tetrad may mean that the Jewish Temple will soon be rebuilt in Jerusalem, I believe that this blood moon tetrad is a sign that Jesus will soon return, and that the 144,000 will transform their bodies into Temples just like Jesus did. Like I said before, the moon represents the followers of Christ, but also the blood moon represents the bloodline of Israel which has spread all over the world. The 144,000 will come out of the twelve tribes of Israel.

Joel 2:31

The sun shall be turned into darkness, and the moon into blood, before the great and terrible day of the Lord come.

Now if we continue the rotations of the compass on the degree circle, we can also find numbers that show the diameter of the sun. I worked out the tones pattern to 180 tones and found that the 24th rotation coincides with a number that is a multiple of the sun's diameter. The sun's diameter is 864,000, and the 24th rotation on the compass is 8280-8640. (8640/864,000=100). If we were to continue the cycle, then it would take 2400 rotations on the degree circle or compass to find the diameter of the sun. (864,000/360= 2400 or 2040-2400 cycle). Isn't it interesting that both the sun and the moon are encoded into the rotations of the compass or degree circle? Remember this is the same degree circle that encodes the Song of Degrees from Psalms 120-134 in the tones that we found. This degree circle math probably has all of God's Creation encoded with mathematical numbers that are found throughout our Solar System and throughout the universe.

Rotations of the Compass (8-28)

8. 2520-2880

9. 2880-3240 *3rd 18 Tones*

10. 3240-3600

11. 3600-3960 (72 tones) *4th 18 Tones* 2 rotations?

12. 3960-4320

13. 4320-4680

14. 4680-5040 *5th 18 Tones*

15. 5040-5400

16. 5400-5760

17. 5760-6120 *6th 18 Tones*

18. 6120-6480

19. 6480-6840

20. 6840-7200 *7th 18 Tones*

21. 7200-7560

22. 7560-7920

23. 7920-8280 (144 Tones) *8th 18 Tones*

24. 8280-8640 (Diameter of the Sun 864,000 miles- Son of God marker) 153

25. 8640-9000 *9th 18 Tones* 2 Rotations?

26. 9000-9360

27. 9360-9720

28. 9720-10080 *10th 18 Tones*   Gate (180 tones- 180 degrees of a triangle)

The 153rd tone is also in the 24th rotation of the compass, so since this is a multiple of the sun's diameter, I call it the "Son of God marker". There are 24 elders going around the throne of God, so this all seems symbolic of Jesus' throne, and his net filled with 153 fish. It's also interesting that the number 144,000 comes in at the 400th rotation of the compass (144,000/360=400). We can clearly see that the Joshua 6:4 verse is clearly telling us that the Song of Degrees is to be found in the rotations of the compass. Only the 36 tones were used to bring down the walls of Jericho, so perhaps only the 36 tones will tear down the wall that we have between us and God to reconnect us to our Father.

Joshua 6:4 *And seven priests shall bear before the ark seven trumpets of rams' horns: and the seventh day ye shall compass the city seven times, and the priests shall blow with the trumpets.*

Anatomy and Biology

Astronomy is not the only information that is encoded within the Song of Degrees in the degree circle math but perhaps anatomy as well. The seven trumpets are comparable to the seven lamps Menorah or the seven spirits of God but in the body temple, which is a requirement for the 144,000, these seven trumpets are the seven chakras or energy zones within the body. Edgar Cayce called them the seven special Endocrine glands of the body. These glands or energy zones must be tuned up like we tune up a musical instrument. I did some research and found out that the word chakra in Sanskrit means "wheel", and a wheel is round like a circle; so therefore, I tried to match up the rotations of the compass with these wheels in the body. In the graphic below I did not include the tones for the seventh chakra, as I had not worked out the rotations of the compass beyond the sixth rotations of the first 36 tones at that time. Nevertheless, it is only the first 36 tones that will allow you to break down that wall within your body.

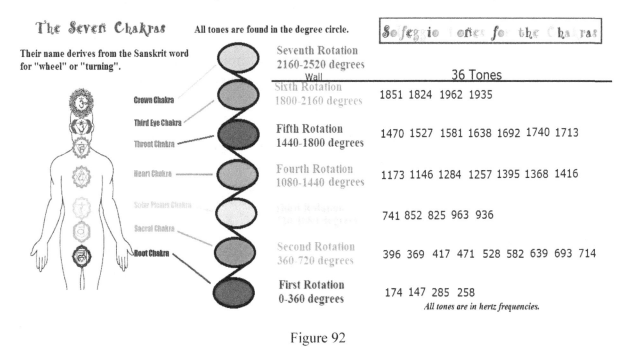

Figure 92

There is another clue to the degree circle and the wall in Daniel 5 of the Bible. At this point, I also must explain about the Picture Bible Code that was discovered by Dean Coomb after he found a clue in Daniel 5. Mr. Coomb has found actual pictures encoded into the Bible, and surprisingly some of these pictures have an animated sequence related to them which allows us to play an animated gif. In other words, there is actual video encoded into the Bible.

Belshazzar the king saw a man write a message on the wall in his palace. He was perplexed to what the message said and after no one else could interpret the message, he asked Daniel to interpret it for him. Mr. Coomb discovered a clue when looking for Bible code within the message on the wall in this story. The writing on the wall said, "Mene, Mene, Tekel, Upharsin." It turns out that this message was written with 15 Hebrew letters, which seems to be a comparison to the 15 chapters of the Song of Degrees. The letters arranged in a pattern of three rows of five letters gives the Bible code that can be read in the three middle letters. It simply says, "To go around." Mr. Coomb had to figure out what he needed to go around. It turns out that *Mene*, *tekel*, and *peres* were ancient round Babylonian coins; so therefore, he must go around the Hebrew letters by tracing a circle around these coins. Mr Coomb also discovered that these same three letters in Aramaic say "a shekel", and chapter 5 of Daniel was originally written in Aramaic. The Hebrew word shekel means weighing, and therefore, the shekel coins also displayed the weight of the metal used for the coins. Mr. Coomb wrote on his website that the code says to "go around the shekel"; so therefore, the encoded prophecy is read by reading in circles.

Daniel 5: 5, 25

⁵ In the same hour came forth fingers of a man's hand, and wrote over against the candlestick upon the plaister of the wall of the king's palace: and the king saw the part of the hand that wrote.

²⁵ And this is the writing that was written, MENE, MENE, TEKEL, UPHARSIN.

It's interesting that this code that was written in 15 Hebrew letters has a parallel to the tones that are written in the 15 degree intervals within the 360 degree circle. While Mr. Coomb has been finding picture Bible codes by reading in circles, I have been finding tones while reading in circles.

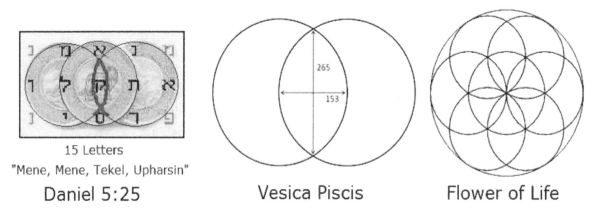

Figure 93

The graphic above shows the message that was found within the writing on the wall, and this message also has the image of the vesica piscis, the Flower of Life and the symbol of Jesus Christ with the fish in the middle. The two vesica piscis beside the fish has a ratio of 265:153 which perhaps is a signature by the author of the message. The vesica piscis is more than just geometry because it encodes the process of cells dividing and the underlying energy process that takes place within our universe.

Mr. Coomb also reads these circles either clockwise or counterclockwise, which is also the way that the tones can be read. As we can see, the pictures that are being found embedded within the words in the Bible are also displaying the same blueprints of the Creation which we are also finding within the tones.

Plasma

The circular pattern found within the Song of Degrees and the spiral pattern found within the tones shows the motion of everything within the universe, from the spiraling of galaxies to the circular orbits of planets in our Solar System, and right down to even the microscopic level of our DNA spiraling to the electrons traveling in circles around the nucleus of an atom. These blueprints within the tones are actually describing a process that goes on within the fourth state of matter which we call plasma. Plasma makes up about 99% of the universe. According to an article in the New Journal of Physics from August 14, 2007, dust inside of plasma forms into crystal shapes and spirals just like in our DNA. This dust convection within plasma is theorized to form a torroidal pattern which rotates clockwise in the upper torroidal vortex and counterclockwise in the lower torroidal vortex. It seems interesting to me that dust makes spiral patterns within the plasma that make the same formations that we can see within the tones. It's also rather fascinating to realize that dust makes crystallized patterns, which a crystal is mostly in the form of hexagons. The hexagon shape is the same shape as the Star of David and the Holy of Holies cube in two dimensions, so we can see that dust in plasma is making these same shapes that the ancient people regarded as being highly important.

The wind and ocean currents of the earth also rotate in the same formation as the tones, and it's also quite surprising to realize that the air and the ocean currents travel clockwise in the northern hemisphere and counterclockwise in the southern hemisphere. How is it that these tones that were encoded into the Bible keep displaying this same rotational pattern over and over again? Is it a mere coincidence that this pattern is the same one all over the universe? It seems as if God made the whole universe in this pattern, and so the mathematical patterns within the tones are displaying His very handiwork in the making of the creation.

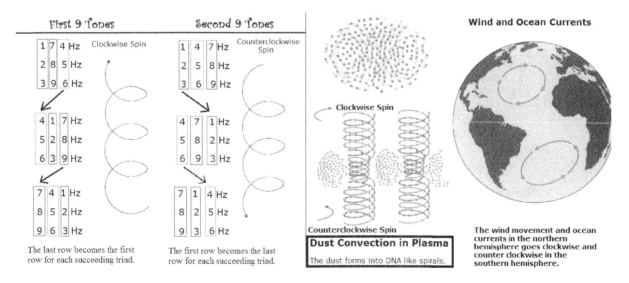

Figure 94

DNA and Fibonacci Spiral

It's quite interesting that the spiral formation within the tones is also pointing to the structure of our DNA helix, which is found throughout the microscopic cells within our bodies. I first found evidence of the DNA early on in my research within the tones. I divided the skip rates by three and got a sequence of prime numbers except for one. Once I looked at the 34 number, I knew that it was a Fibonacci number. That was when I also noticed that the skip rate of 21 is a Fibonacci number too. I looked up those two numbers together and found out that the DNA is 34 angstroms long by 21 angstroms wide for each full cycle of its double helix spiral. I wasn't sure if it was a coincidence or not, but I still kept the information. In a separate mathematical project, I decided to take the 21 and 102 in the skip rate of the 9 main tones and subtract, add, multiply and divide them. Other than the 81 skip rate, I didn't really see any numbers that were significant, so I decided to divide those numbers by the number 3, and all kinds of interesting numbers popped out. The seventh tone was made by one computation and a number that looked to be close to Phi, so I checked it out and found out that it was really close to Phi. It turned out that this number that approximates Phi was only off by 0.0010137, so I made a note about it being close to Phi but didn't think anymore about this discovery. I was really kind of disappointed that the number wasn't Phi. Then years later I started to look at these computations again and realized that this number was very significant. It turns out that the number 1.6190476 is the ratio of the Fibonacci numbers of 21 and 34. Therefore, it turns out that the Fibonacci numbers of 21 and 34 are encoded in two different ways, and since these numbers are the length and width of DNA, I believe this encodes the measurement of the DNA. It also shows that the ratio of the Fibonacci numbers of 21 and 34 approximates Phi or the golden spiral. This is very significant because the Fibonacci numbers are found all throughout nature. It also is very interesting to note that the New Jerusalem measurement for the walls of Jerusalem is 144 cubits, and this number is also in the Fibonacci sequence of numbers and is associated with the golden spiral (0, 1, 1, 2, 3, 5, 8, 13, **21, 34**, 55, 89, **144**....).

Skip Rates Divided by Three & Math Patterns in 102 and 21

111/3=37
111/3=37
21/3=7
111/3=37
111/3=37
102/3=34
111/3=37
111/3=37

102-21=81/3=27 Binaural beat
102+21=123/3=41
102X21=2142/3=714 7th tone
102/21=4.8571428/3=1.6190476   Ratio of 21 & 34
　　　　　　　　　　　　　　　　and approximates Phi

Fibonacci Numbers

0, 1, 1, 2, 3, 5, 8, 13, 21, 34, 55, 89, 144....

Ratio of 21 &34   Phi
1.6190476 - 1.6180339-=0.0010137

The numbers 34 and 21 are numbers in the Fibonacci series, and their ratio 1.6190476 closely approximates Phi. (1.6180339)

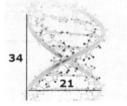

DNA measures 34 angstroms long by 21 angstroms wide for each full cycle of its double helix spiral.

Figure 95

In addition to the spiral in the tones and the numbers 21 and 34 encoded into the tones, I also found that mirroring the numbers and subtracting them from one another brings out the number 297. I briefly mentioned this in another chapter. I didn't think that there would be anything special about that number when I looked it up, however; I found out that it is the 9th decagonal number, and the cross section view of DNA is in the shape of a decagon. To make this even more interesting the outside angle of the decagon is 144 degrees, so therefore, this number ties in with New Jerusalem as well. Perhaps this information is showing us that the tones will tune up or affect our DNA somehow.

As you can see the Fibonacci numbers of 21, 34 and 144 keep popping up throughout the tones or Song of Degrees and so does the spiral. The DNA helix has two strands coiled up or spiraled together to look like a spiral staircase. We can see many blueprints for the DNA within these magical or mystical numbers that are encoded throughout the Bible in many diverse ways. This is proof from God to His creation that He is the maker of everything from the spiraling galaxies to the spiraling DNA throughout our body. Dust in plasma spirals just like our DNA, and the Lord God told us that He made us from the dust of the ground, so these tones prove that He designed us not just from the atoms, but that He designed us from His Word. Sound is the very essence of who we are, and as we see from the tones that the blueprints for this world are based on them.

Genesis 2:7 *And the LORD God formed man of the dust of the ground, and breathed into his nostrils the breath of life; and man became a living soul.*

Cross-sectional View of DNA

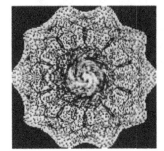

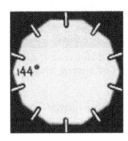

Mirror Tones

693-396=(297)
936-639=297
963-369=594

714-417=297
741-147=594
471-174=297

825-528=297
852-258=594
582-285=297

The number 297 is the 9th decagonal number 1, 10, 27, 52, 85, 126, 175, 232, 297.

The angles on a decagon is 144 degrees. The cross-sectional view from the top of the DNA double helix forms a decagon.

Figure 96

The fact that Fibonacci numbers are encoded within the Solfeggio tones is very clear, but why is this in the tones instead of Phi? It turns out that Fibonacci approximates Phi. It is very close to the Phi ratio, and another interesting fact is that it is found throughout nature. The Fibonacci numbers and the Fibonacci spiral are found in plants and in animals. The Fibonacci numbers are found in the reproduction of rabbits and honey bees, and it is also found in many flowers, seeds and plants. In fact, Fibonacci numbers are found all throughout the Earth and the Fibonacci spiral, which is very close to the Golden spiral of Phi, is found in our DNA. All of these clues that I have found encoded within the tones is definitely pointing to the blueprint for our DNA and for nature. God has encoded so much into these tones that form the blueprints of all of nature and even the measurements of everything in the universe. These blueprints are in the form of mostly circles and spirals, which we can then trace out any geometrical shape within the degree circle.

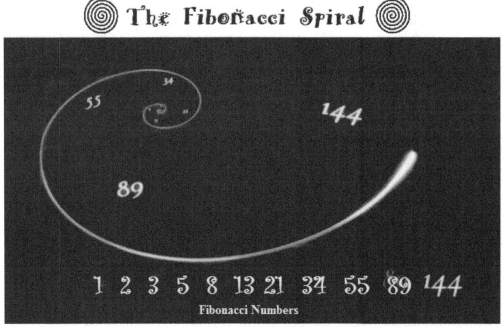

Figure 97

Here is an analogy of the spiral: if you have ever been to the show Walt Disney World's Carousel of Progress, you may remember that the place was circular and that the audience seats revolve around six stages that are in a circle. Now let's picture ourselves revolving around the stages, only now you start to go up at an angle at the same time, so therefore, you are still revolving in a circle, but you are moving upwards at the same time. You are now moving in spirals instead of circles, as long as you continue to move upwards and circular at the same time.

Many people do not realize that we are moving in spirals all the time, although the earth moves in ellipses around the sun and not circular, which means we are moving in elliptical spirals. This is due to the fact that the earth moves around the sun in elliptical orbits, but the sun is moving around the galaxy in an elliptical orbit around the center of the Milky Way Galaxy as well. The galaxy is moving through the universe and is also dragging us along for the ride. If you can picture this in your head, then you would see the earth moving in orbit around the sun, and the sun moving in orbit around the galaxy, and then the galaxy moving through the universe. We would appear to be moving in elliptical spirals from all of the earth's different movements. This is the circle or ellipse in motion, and since everything in this universe is in motion, then we are traveling in spirals. As dust moves in spirals inside of plasma, all matter is moving in spirals throughout the plasma universe. As I pointed out in a previous chapter, Dr. Kozyrev believed that the spiraling motion of torsion is also what causes time. It's interesting that the tones are hinting around about Fibonacci numbers and spirals, and that Revelation 21 is also pointing out the Fibonacci numbers of 21 and 144. Could there be a connection between the spiral and New Jerusalem?

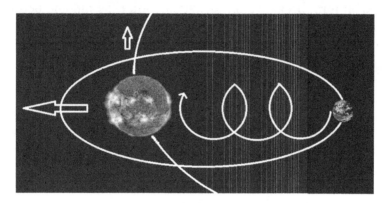

Figure 98

Atoms

The tones are also hinting around about positive, negative and neutral charges within the tones themselves. I briefly wrote about this in another chapter. Out of the first 24 tones there are 8 neutral tones, 8 positive tones and 8 negative tones. It's interesting to note that Jesus name in Greek gematria adds up to 888. The throne of God has 24 elders around and the throne has Jesus Christ in the middle. The tones seem to be mimicking atoms because they have the same kind of charges as particles in the atoms do. In the atom the neutrons are neutral, the protons are positive and the electrons are negative, and likewise, in the triad tones the 1, 4 & 7 tones are neutral, the 2, 5 & 8 tones are positive and the 3, 6 & 9 tones are negative.

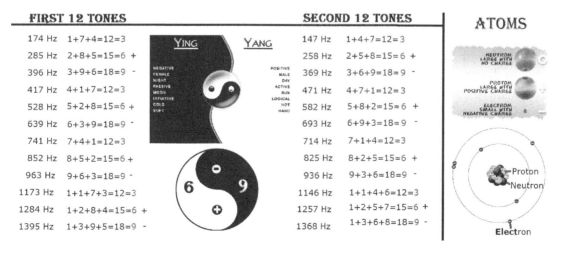

Figure 99

Out of the first 18 tones there are 6 neutral tones, 6 positive tones and 6 negative tones. The first 18 tones seem to be mimicking the pattern of man in this fallen state of physical beings. Of course, it goes without saying that the mark of the beast has the number of 666 as the identifier. It also should be noted that physical beings are carbon based life forms, which means that we could not exist without the element of carbon. Even though carbon is not the most common element in our body, carbon is the best element for bonding, and it's one of the elements that is present in our DNA. So without carbon's bonding abilities to create long carbon chains and rings there would be no DNA. Carbon has 6 protons, 6 neutrons and 6 electrons, so therefore, it has the literal name of 666, and it is the reason we are in this physical form. God made Adam, but Adam in his physical form became a physical being after the fall and became filled with atoms, and one of those major atoms for human beings on this earth is carbon. Although the beast will use that number in some form, it probably also represents human beings in the physical form. Only physical beings buy and sell, and spiritual beings do not.

Remember when I showed you the connection between the number 153 of John 21:11 and the number 666 of Revelation 13:18? They both are triangular numbers, and the addition of the perimeters of each triangle added together is 153. The 153 triangle has 17 circles on each side with 48 total circles for the perimeter, and the 666 triangle has 36 circles on each side with 105 total circles for the perimeter. The addition of 105 and 48 makes 153, so we can see a special relationship between these two triangles. The symbolic representation of the 153 triangle appears to be an identifier of Jesus Christ, and the symbolic representation of the 666 triangle appears to be an identifier for the beast or Satan. Many people believe that the beast or antichrist will have a name that adds up to 666 in gematria; however, I believe that the mark will be the 666 triangle. The triangle was sewn on the clothes of certain prisoners in concentration camps, and the Star of David was the symbol on the clothes of the Jews in concentration camps. This seems to be prophetic of the seal of the beast being the 666 triangle. There is much controversy now over a possible carbon tax due to the fact that global warming is causing an increase in carbon dioxide in our atmosphere. The thought is that we need to clean the air by reducing the carbon dioxide, and in order to do that on a global scale we need a tax to fund this project. If this ever comes to fruition, then everything we buy or sale will have this carbon tax associated with its cost. This could be another possibility with the mark of the beast being the carbon tax, and the encoded 666 would have to do with the amount of electrons, protons and neutrons which are 666. Although this is merely speculative at this point, I must point out that the number 666 is not evil, and it will only be used to identify the beast.

In the case of the tones in the 24 tone pattern, we see an 888 pattern that is associated with Jesus Christ, but in the 18 tone pattern we see the pattern of 666. These tones seem to be displaying duality of positive and negative but also a duality of the tree of knowledge of good and evil. Both the negative and the positive get represented within these tones, as they do in the atoms that make our physical bodies, so what is going on with these tones, and why are they used in the Song of Degrees?

As you can see from the graphic below, the first 24 tones contain 8 positive, 8 negative and 8 neutral tones, and the 111 skip rate also adds up to 888 for each column. The 111 total for both columns is 1776, and if you are an American, then you will recognize this number as being the founding year for America becoming a nation. America has the second largest population of Jews in the world.

First 12 Solfeggio Tones	Second 12 Solfeggio Tones
174 Hz ---------(+111) 1	147 Hz ---------(+111) 9
285 Hz ---------(+111) 2	258 Hz ---------(+111) 10
396 Hz ---------- +21	369 Hz ---------- +102
417 Hz ---------(+111) 3	471 Hz ---------(+111) 11
528 Hz ---------(+111) 4	582 Hz ---------(+111) 12
639 Hz ---------- +102	693 Hz ---------- + 21
741 Hz ---------(+111) 5	714 Hz ---------(+111) 13
852 Hz ---------(+111) 6	825 Hz ---------(+111) 14
963 Hz ---------- +210	936 Hz ---------- +210
1173 Hz ---------(+111) 7	1146 Hz ---------(+111) 15
1284 Hz ---------(+111) 8	1257 Hz ---------(+111) 16
1395 Hz	1368 Hz

111 X 16= 1776   888 X 2 = 1776
Jesus name in Greek letters adds up to 888.

FIRST 12 TONES		**SECOND 12 TONES**	
174 Hz	1+7+4=12=3	147 Hz	1+4+7=12= 3
285 Hz	2+8+5=15=6 +	258 Hz	2+5+8=15=6 +
396 Hz	3+9+6=18=9 -	369 Hz	3+6+9=18=9 -
417 Hz	4+1+7=12=3	471 Hz	4+7+1=12=3
528 Hz	5+2+8=15=6 +	582 Hz	5+8+2=15=6 +
639 Hz	6+3+9=18=9 -	693 Hz	6+9+3=18=9 -
741 Hz	7+4+1=12=3	714 Hz	7+1+4=12=3
852 Hz	8+5+2=15=6 +	825 Hz	8+2+5=15=6 +
963 Hz	9+6+3=18=9 -	936 Hz	9+3+6=18=9 -
1173 Hz	1+1+7+3=12=3	1146 Hz	1+1+4+6=12=3
1284 Hz	1+2+8+4=15=6 +	1257 Hz	1+2+5+7=15=6 +
1395 Hz	1+3+9+5=18=9 -	1368 Hz	1+3+6+8=18=9 -

Eight Positive, Negative & Neutral Tones
888

Figure 100

Electricity

Well, an interesting pattern emerges when we understand the underlying science behind the description of the throne of God in Revelation 4. It turns out that there is an electrical connection involved with the throne of God. In Revelation 4:5, we learn that lightning emanated from the throne of God, and lightning is electricity.

Revelation 4:5 *And out of the throne proceeded lightnings and thunderings and voices: and there were seven lamps of fire burning before the throne, which are the seven Spirits of God.*

There are actually many references to electricity in the Bible, but I am not going to cover them all in this book. If you would like to learn more about the electrical connections in the Bible, you can read my books *The Blueprints of God* or *Is God Plasma?* I go into extensive explanations in my plasma book because plasma is the fourth state of matter and lightning/electricity is plasma.

I will briefly explain about electricity and its connections with the tones. If you have ever used a battery or have ever charged a car battery, then you know in regular batteries there is a positive and negative side and on the car battery a negative and positive pole. Electricity flows from the negative to the positive in a battery. These tones are actually displaying an electrical quality to them with the positive tones representing the positive charge, the negative tones representing the negative charge, and the neutral tones seem to represent the ground wire.

When listening to the tones, you may feel a lot of energy rushing through your body, and this is the reason why you feel the energy pulsing. The human body has a nervous system which is connected to the brain. This is actually an electrical system, so you can think of the nerves as being like copper wires that are transporting electricity throughout the body. Anytime you feel something, your fingertips will transport an electrical signal to the brain to interpret that information. If you feel something that is too hot, then the brain will decode that electrical impulse and send back another electrical pulse through the nerves to tell your hand to let go of the hot object, so that you don't get burnt.

These tones literally increase the electricity or energy within the body, and after you have listened to them for awhile, you will start to hear a humming sound. I briefly talked about hearing this sound after taking the ancient white powder gold, but after listening to the tones for awhile, I also realized that they have the same affect on the body. The humming sound can sound like the wind or buzzing bees. It can also sound like the hum of a transformer or electricity.

In the story of Numbers 21, we learn that the fiery serpent on the pole brings healing to the Israelite people who had been bitten by snakes. This story is another example of electricity. If you have ever watched lightning, then you may recall that it zig zags back and forth in the sky, and that it looks like fire. This is why it is called the fiery serpent in the Bible.

Numbers 21:8-9

⁸ And the LORD said unto Moses, Make thee a fiery serpent, and set it upon a pole: and it shall come to pass, that every one that is bitten, when he looketh upon it, shall live.

⁹ And Moses made a serpent of brass, and put it upon a pole, and it came to pass, that if a serpent had bitten any man, when he beheld the serpent of brass, he lived.

Notice that this story is given after Numbers 7 which gave us the encoded tones. If you are a keen student, then reading the story should trigger some information about these tones. Remember the fiery serpent was made of brass, and brass is made with copper and zinc, although in the ancient biblical days it was made with copper and tin. This is an example of electricity for those that have eyes to see and ears to hear. If you wrap a copper wire around a pole and bring a magnet near it, then you too can make the fiery serpent of electricity. Likewise, if you play the tones in order, you are generating negative and positive charges, which cause the electricity to flow throughout your body. You are raising the fiery serpent on a pole, and the pole is the spinal cord which connects to your brain. The 24 cranial nerves will carry these pulses of electricity to your brain; so therefore, you are crucifying yourself in Golgotha the place of the skull. I mentioned this in an earlier chapter to make you aware that the 144,000 will not be crucified like Jesus, for them this process will take place in their skull. They will be sacrificing their will for God's will. This is how the 144,000 will follow the same pattern as Jesus but in a different way with the new song.

Numbers 7:10-13

¹⁰ And the children of Israel set forward, and pitched in Oboth.

¹¹ And they journeyed from Oboth, and pitched at Ijeabarim, in the wilderness which is before Moab, toward the sunrising.

¹² From thence they removed, and pitched in the valley of Zared

¹³ From thence they removed, and pitched on the other side of Arnon, which is in the wilderness that cometh out of the coasts of the Amorites: for Arnon is the border of Moab, between Moab and the Amorites.

In verses 10 through 13 of Numbers 21, we can see that after the Israelites get healed by the fiery serpent on the pole, then they start pitching in four places. Pitching tents is one way to read this story, but encoded just below the surface of the story is another interpretation. In music the pitch of a note means how high or low a note is playing. For example, the first note or tone of 147 Hz means that the sound waves are vibrating at 147 times a second.

Is there any clue as to how we pitch with the tones? Well, I think that we pitch from low to high, and here is the reason why:

John 3:14 (KJV) *And as Moses lifted up the serpent in the wilderness, even so must the Son of man be lifted up:*

Jesus tells us that Moses lifted up the serpent in the wilderness, so therefore, we are told to go up with the tones as well. By the way, serpent is an anagram in this verse because as soon as we are lifted up in the harvest or rapture, we leave our sins behind.

Serpent or repents

Numbers 21:17 *Then Israel sang this song, Spring up, O well; sing ye unto it:*

After the Israelites raised the fiery serpent on the pole and pitched four times, they then sang a song in verse seventeen. The verse number 17 is a clear clue to the 153 fishing net, as I have pointed out before. This verse, as well as Numbers 7:17, tells us that this fishing net is made with a song. This new song will form the net of the harvest.

The Israelites are often called the elect, and it is also interesting that elect is the first syllable of **elect**ricity. The name Israelite also sounds like "is real light", and lightning or electricity is made of light. In the middle of the word elec**tri**city is tri, which usually denotes three, and the first 18 tones are **tri**ad tones, and the symbols made from those tones are **tri**angles. The tones are grouped together in threes made of positive, negative and neutral, so we can see that electricity needs three states of positive charge, negative charge and a ground or neutral charge to light up.

If we look at the blueprint for the throne of God, we find out that there are 24 elders surrounding the throne of God. Likewise, there are 24 tones to complete the skip rate pattern. We also find that there are seraphim singing "Holy, Holy, Holy" around the throne of God, and the word *Holy* in English gematria adds up to sixty. A Star of David has two triangles, and each equilateral triangle has 3 vertices with angles of 60 degrees each, and we know that the Star of David is one of the shapes associated with the tones. There are actually four Star of David symbols within the 15 degree interval circle, and that makes 24 points going around the circle. This appears to match the four beasts that are mentioned as going around the throne of God. In fact, it seems as if the throne of God blueprint given in Revelation 4 is also the same blueprint that is in the tones of Number 7 and the Song of Degrees. Both blueprints appear to be very similar to one another, so therefore, we have to ask ourselves if the prophecy about the throne of God is somehow related to the prophecy about the new song of the 144,000.

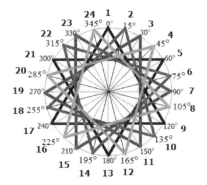

Revelation 4

4 And round about the throne were four and twenty seats: and upon the seats I saw four and twenty elders sitting, clothed in white raiment; and they had on their heads crowns of gold.

8 And the four beasts had each of them six wings about him; and they were full of eyes within: and they rest not day and night, saying, Holy, holy, holy, Lord God Almighty, which was, and is, and is to come.

There are 4 Star of David symbols around a 15 degree circle of 24 points.

English Gematria

A	B	C	D	E	F	G	H	I	J	K	L	M
1	2	3	4	5	6	7	8	9	10	11	12	13

N	O	P	Q	R	S	T	U	V	W	X	Y	Z
14	15	16	17	18	19	20	21	22	23	24	25	26

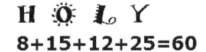

8+15+12+25=60

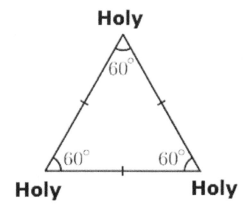

Figure 101

I also realized at one point that the four beasts could be an anagram for beats because beats in music means a basic unit of time or a pulse, which could also be related to the tempo or rhythm of the song. If this is to be the case, then perhaps we have another clue to the tones. With this clue, I surmise that perhaps the tones are grouped up in segments of 4 groups with a pause in the middle. I do not know if this is correct or not, but this could be another clue to follow in the new song. Basically, everyone that is trying to learn these tones needs to experiment with different ways of perceiving this information because there are many different methods to interpret the data about these tones. The four beats could represent the rhythm or the grouping of the twenty four tones, or it could just be simply referring to the geometry within the tones with the four Star of David symbols within the degree circle.

In the next graphic, I grouped up the four beasts from the top to the bottom, however, this is just one method of grouping that can come from just one perspective. There could be many other ways to group these tones into four, so I am only showing one method. Notice that the first 3 groups correspond to land based creatures of the lion, calf and man, but the last group is of an air based creature. This could be a clue to the last 3 tones in each column being a part of another group because they are different then the triad tones. Perhaps it means to fly away into another grouping of 18 tones.

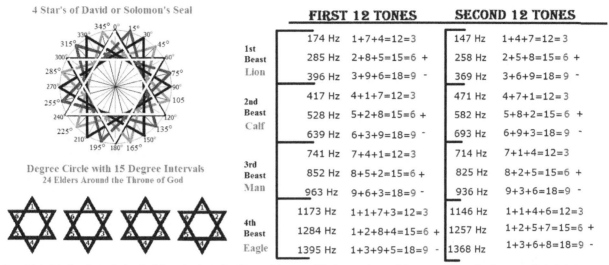

Rev. 4:8 *And the **four beasts** had each of them **six wings** about him; and they were full of eyes within: and they rest not day and night, saying, **Holy, holy, holy**, Lord God Almighty, which was, and is, and is to come.* **(4X6=24)**

Figure 102

Not only is the reference to lightning proof that the throne of God is somehow related to electricity, but the 4 beasts surrounding the throne with 6 wings could also be a reference to 4 Seraphim Angels. In Isaiah 6:2, we are told that the Seraphim had six wings, and that it flies. The root of Seraphim comes from either the Hebrew verb of *seraph*, which means "to burn," or either it comes from the Hebrew noun of *seraph*, which means "a fiery or flying serpent." The fiery serpent is none other than lightning in the sky or electricity, so here we have another clue that the lightning that was being produced by the throne of God is electricity.

Isaiah 6:2

Above it stood the seraphims: each one had six wings; with twain he covered his face, and with twain he covered his feet, and with twain he did fly.

This covers all of the science that has been found encoded into these mysterious tones. The next chapter is going to be about other mathematical clues that are encoded within the tones. I will cover some more of the geometry that I have found within the tones.

Number Patterns and Geometry

Through the years I have found numerous kinds of mathematical patterns and geometrical shapes encoded into these tones, and I have shared many of them already, so this chapter is for all of the other encoded information that I found hidden away within these mysterious tones of the Bible. Just when I think that I found everything that I could ever find within these tones, I find one more and one more and one more. It has me wondering just how much information could be found within the different layers of these tones. It has felt much like I am on some kind of a treasure hunt to find the gems that are hidden under the top layer of these tones, and so I keep digging and digging to find more hidden treasures within this song.

I decided to see what would happen if I plotted the first 18 tones within the same degree circle, so I had to keep going around the circle three times. It was very hard to keep track on the second and third rotations because I couldn't read the degrees, as they are labeled due to remembering to double each rotation by 360 degrees. After I finished plotting them on just one degree circle, I wanted to connect the dots to see if it made any kind of interesting pattern, and it did. I didn't know what shape this could be because it didn't make any kind of shape that I knew. I asked a friend what she thought it could be, and she thought it might be a three dimensional buckyball. I compared the two shapes, but I wasn't totally convinced. I went on Google to look for all kinds of three dimensional shapes, and at first I couldn't really find anything that resembled this shape. Then out of the blue, I saw an image that looked very close to the shape that the first 18 tones made within the degree circle. Someone had found a dodecahedron hidden within the pattern for the Metatron's cube, and when I looked up the words dodecahedron in Metatron's cube, I found a lot of websites that had this same information. Even though I had studied about Metatron's cube before, I had never seen this or didn't remember about this shape. I found a Metatron's cube graphic on the internet and managed to trace out the dodecahedron myself by following the same pattern that others had done. I couldn't figure out how to trace the pattern onto the 18 tones degree circle, however, I'm sure you will be able to see that the outer shape looks just like the dodecahedron that I found within the 18 tones.

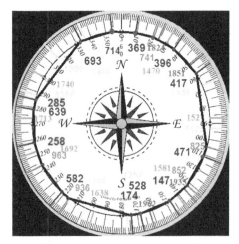

18 Tones Plotted on the Degree Circle

The First Eighteen Tones

Left Speaker	Right Speaker
174	147
------111	------111
285	258
------111	------111
396	369
------21	------102
417	471
------111	------111
528	582
------111	------111
639	693
------102	------21
741	714
------111	------111
852	825
------111	------111
963	936
------210	------210

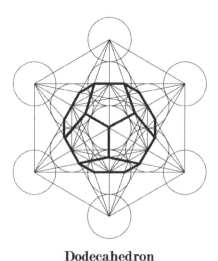

Dodecahedron

Figure 103

What astonished me was that I had heard of this shape before, and I was really sure that I had remembered that the shape for the spacecraft in the book *Contact* by Carl Sagan is a dodecahedron. I looked it up and was right. The dodecahedron was used for the spacecraft that traveled through the wormholes. It seemed like such a synchronicity that these mysterious tones encoded into the Bible show a dodecahedron in the first 18 tones, and that Mr. Sagan chose that spacecraft shape to be encoded into the message by extraterrestrials which were received from the radio telescopes in his book. What a weird coincidence!

I kept getting the number 37 which popped up everywhere in the math of the tones, but I did not know what it meant until I searched about the number on the internet. Further evaluation of the number "37" connection within the Solfeggio tones revealed that the number 37 is a very special prime number, and even though I had found that the number 37 was a multiple within the tones and within the skip rates. I had never even thought to research the number until just recently.

The Number 37 in the Skip Rates

111 111 **21** 111 111 102 111 111
/3 /3 /3 /3 /3 /3 /3 /3
37 37 7 37 37 **34** 37 37

Skip Rate Numbers divided by three.

The number 37 is a very special prime number.

$$37 \times 6 = 222$$

MATH OF THE TRIAD NUMBERS

FIRST 12 SOLFEGGIO TONES				SECOND 12 SOLFEGGIO TONES BINARY # 14			
444	555	666	1284	888	1110	1332	2541
174	285	396	1173	147	258	369	1146
417	528	639	1284	174	285	396	1173
+741	+852	+963	+1395	417	528	639	1257
1332	1665	1998	3852	471	582	693	1284
				714	825	936	1368
1332/3=444	1665/3=555	1998/3=666	3852/3=1284	+741	+852	+963	+1395
				2664	3330	3996	7623
				2664/3=888	3330/3=1110	3996/3=1332	7623/3=2541

(All numbers are divisible by 3 in Solfeggio math.)

THE NUMBER 37

37 × 3 = 111 / 3   37 × 12 = 444 / 3   37 × 21 = 777 / 3   37 × 30 = 1110 / 3
37 × 6 = 222 / 6   37 × 15 = 555 / 6   37 × 24 = 888 / 6   37 × 33 = 1221 / 6
37 × 9 = 333 / 9   37 × 18 = 666 / 9   37 × 27 = 999 / 9   37 × 36 = 1332 / 9

Figure 104

The prime numbers of 37 and 73 are unique among primes, and they have many interesting characteristics that distinguish them from all the rest. Here is a list of some special connections with the number 37 and 73;

- Sum of Genesis 1.1 = 2701   37 x 73=2701
- 37 and 73 are mirror numbers
- 37 and 73 are the 12th and 21st prime numbers respectively
- 12 and 21 are mirror numbers
- 12^2 (144) and 21^2 (441) are also mirror numbers
- 37 and 73 are star numbers
- 37 is a centered hexagonal number and is a hexagon in the 73 star
- The 73rd triangular number is 2701. (37 x 73=2701)
- The 37th triangular number is 703. (37 x 19=703)
- 703 is the 37th triangular number and 703 is the 19th hexagonal number. (37 x 19=703)

I found out through many websites that the number 37 is encoded in the first verse of the Bible which is Genesis 1:1. Hebrew letters are also numbers, and this verse in Hebrew Gematria adds up to 2701. It's remarkable that 37 actually divides into the sum of Genesis 1:1. It turns out that 37 X 73 is equal to 2701. What is truly surprising is that 37 and 73 are mirror numbers, which means if you read the number 73 from the right to the left as Hebrew is read, you would read it as 37.

הארץ	ואת	השמים	את	אלהים	ברא	בראשית
the earth	and	the heaven	(untranslated)	God	created	In the beginning
296	407	395	401	86	203	913

Genesis 1:1 *In the beginning God created the heaven and the earth.*

296+407+395+401+86+203+913= 2701   37 X 73 = 2701

Figure 105

I found out that both 37 and 73 are both prime numbers, and 37 is the 12th prime number, whereas 73 is the 21st prime number. The 12th and 21st prime number spots are also mirror numbers as well, so we can find patterns within the patterns. The numbers 12 and 21 multiplied by themselves are 144 (12X12=144) and 441 (21X21+441), which are also mirror numbers. The number 144 is mentioned in Revelation 21:17 as being the measurements in cubits of the wall around New Jerusalem, and the number 441 has been said to be the tone that is emitted by the King's chamber in the Great Pyramid. It's like the number 37 has extensive patterns related to God's Creation.

I've often felt like learning about these tones is a lot like hacking the universe because it seems as if these tones are the fabric of space-time itself, since the whole universe is made of sound and light. These tones are almost like a programming language for the whole universe and very much like the programming languages of our modern day computers. I feel like I have been given a peak behind the curtain, and I can see the Wizard pulling the levers. I feel very privileged that God has allowed me to learn about the science and math that is encoded into the Bible and to show me how his song works with these very special tones.

PRIME NUMBERS

2	3	5	7	11	13	17
19	23	29	31	37	41	43
47	53	59	61	67	71	73
79	83	89	97	101	103	107
109	113	127	131	137	139	149
151	157	163	167	173	179	181
191	193	197	199	211	223	227
229	233	239	241	251	257	263
269	271	277	281	283	293	307
311	313	317	331	337	347	349

37 12TH   73 21ST

MIRROR NUMBERS

37 & 73

12 & 21

Figure 106

The numbers 37 and 73 are also star numbers, which means that you can form a perfect Star of David from 37 or 73 dots or circles. This links these numbers to the Jewish or Israelite symbol of the Star of David, which is really the pattern for God's Spirit upon the face of water and the electromagnetic field of energy. The ancient Star of David denotes the frozen pattern of water or snowflakes which are in a hexagon pattern and the ancient Flower of Life as well as Metatron's cube can also be traced out to form this star pattern.

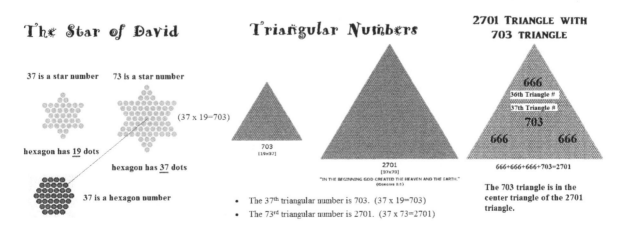

Figure 107

Remember when I discussed about how the number 153 and 666 are both triangular numbers? I worked out the pattern of the triangular numbers, but I stopped at the 36th triangular number, which was the 666 triangular number. Well, it turns out that the 37th triangular number is also very important. The 37th triangular number is 703 and the 73rd triangular number is 2701, which is the number equivalent of Genesis 1:1. If you make the 2701 triangle, and then divide it into four equilateral triangles, like I did with the 153 triangle, then you will find that the 703 triangle is in the middle, and it is surrounded by 3 of the 666 triangles.

The number 888 and 666 are repeating numbers that keep coming up within these tones. It's as if the number 666 represents the physical man because it represents carbon based life forms, and the number 888 represents Jesus Christ, but it also represents man that has transformed or ascended. The number 666 comes up in both the negative and the positive numbers, which shows a connection between duality in the Tree of Knowledge of Good and Evil and being in the physical world. As I mentioned before, the number 666 could represent the atom of carbon, which has 6 protons, 6 neutrons and 6 electrons. The numbers of 666 and 888 represent the physical world and the spiritual world which are together in this world. We each have a physical body and a spiritual (soul) body; so therefore, these tones reflect this duality in the fallen human race.

Genesis 2:17

But of the tree of the knowledge of good and evil, thou shalt not eat of it: for in the day that thou eatest thereof thou shalt surely die.

It goes without saying that a physical human being dies, but a spiritual human being does not die. We can see that duality only occurs in the physical world as not only are we carbon based beings, but everything we do here can be perceived as good or evil. I learned this aspect of our world a long time ago from a book I read called *Ascension*. This book had the teachings of the Ishayas, which is an ancient order of monks, who claim to be following the original teachings of Jesus Christ. One of the teachings in the book demonstrated how one event can seem good to many and yet evil to others. I will not give their same example, but I will give one of my own.

On Thanksgiving Day in America, we celebrate by having a feast to eat, and most Americans either choose to eat ham or turkey on this day. It's a wonderful day to spend time with family and friends and is often accompanied with prayer to God and of giving thanks for all of the blessings or good things in our lives. From this perspective it is a really good day for humans, however, from the perspective of pigs or turkeys, this day seems really evil. If you have ever really seen a turkey house, then you may know that the turkeys are raised in a rectangular building together. They never have the freedom that you and I get to enjoy. Their entire lives are spent in bondage within a prison, and at the end of their lives, they will be slaughtered for food. In most cases the turkeys are raised in crowded houses, and they do not have much room to roam. If we look at Thanksgiving Day from this perspective, then it would certainly seem evil. I don't know of very many humans who would enjoy a life like the turkeys have in farm factories. The Tree of Knowledge of Good and Evil can only be caused from the lowering of our vibrations to become physical beings of flesh. In this weird place after the fall of mankind, we experience pain and pleasure and good and evil, so this is the life of duality.

First 12 Solfeggio Tones	Second 12 Solfeggio Tones	Neutral Tones
174 Hz ---------- +111) 1 285 Hz ---------- +111) 2 396 Hz ---------- +21 417 Hz ---------- +111) 3 528 Hz ---------- +111) 4 639 Hz ---------- +102 741 Hz ---------- +111) 5 852 Hz ---------- +111) 6 963 Hz ---------- +210 1173 Hz ---------- +111) 7 1284 Hz ---------- +111) 8 1395 Hz	147 Hz ---------- +111) 9 258 Hz ---------- +111) 10 369 Hz ---------- +102 471 Hz ---------- +111) 11 582 Hz ---------- +111) 12 693 Hz ---------- + 21 714 Hz ---------- +111) 13 825 Hz ---------- +111) 14 936 Hz ---------- +210 1146 Hz ---------- +111) 15 1257 Hz ---------- +111) 16 1368 Hz	**Triad Numbers** 147 174 417 471 714 **+741** **2664** **3 X 888=2664**
111 X 8 =888	**111 X 8 =888**	

Jesus name in Greek letters adds up to 888.
111 X 16= 1776   888 X 2 = 1776   3 X 888=2664

Figure 108

In the graphic above, you can see that Jesus number of 888 is found in the skip rates of 111 and in the 1, 4 & 7 tones which are the neutral tones. This seems to imply that the neutral tones represent Jesus Christ because Jesus overcame the physical world of good and evil, and now he is in the spiritual world and is neutral.

FIRST 12 TONES

						SECOND 12 TONES	
174 Hz	1+7+4=12=3	The addition of the neutral tones are both a multiple of 666 and 888. The addition of the negative and positive tones are a multiple of 666.				147 Hz	1+4+7=12=3
285 Hz	2+8+5=15=6 +					258 Hz	2+5+8=15=6 +
396 Hz	3+9+6=18=9 -	Neutral Tones 888 & 666	Negative Tones 666	Positive Tones 666		369 Hz	3+6+9=18=9 -
417 Hz	4+1+7=12=3	147	369	258		471 Hz	4+7+1=12=3
528 Hz	5+2+8=15=6 +	174 417	396 639	285 528		582 Hz	5+8+2=15=6 +
639 Hz	6+3+9=18=9 -	471 714	693 936	582 825		693 Hz	6+9+3=18=9 -
741 Hz	7+4+1=12=3	+741 2664	+963 3996	+852 3330		714 Hz	7+1+4=12=3
852 Hz	8+5+2=15=6 +					825 Hz	8+2+5=15=6 +
963 Hz	9+6+3=18=9 -	2664/3=888 2664/666=4 666X4=2664	3996/666=6 666X6=3996	3330/666=5 666X5=3330		936 Hz	9+3+6=18=9 -
1173 Hz	1+1+7+3=12=3					1146 Hz	1+1+4+6=12=3
1284 Hz	1+2+8+4=15=6 -	2664+3996+3330=9990 9990/666=15				1257 Hz	1+2+5+7=15=6
1395 Hz	1+3+9+5=18=9					1368 Hz	1+3+6+8=18=9

Figure 109

In this next graphic, we can see that the negative, positive and neutral tones are divisible by 666, so we are seeing a visible musical pattern to the physical earth after the fall occurred. Jesus' number of 888 shows that we can overcome and one day become neutral as well. Neutral is neither good nor evil, which is the state that Adam and Eve were in before the fall. They knew neither good nor evil because there was no duality.

```
First 12 Solfeggio Tones      Second 12 Solfeggio Tones

174 Hz                         147 Hz
        ------(+111) 1               ------(+111) 9
285 Hz                         258 Hz
        ------(+111) 2               ------(+111) 10         111 X 8 = 888
396 Hz                         369 Hz
        ------(+21)                  ------(+102)            111 X 16 = 1776
417 Hz                         471 Hz
        ------(+111) 3               ------(+111) 11         888 X 2 = 1776
528 Hz                         582 Hz
        ------(+111) 4               ------(+111) 12
639 Hz                         693 Hz
        ------(+102)                 ------(+21)                   21
741 Hz                         714 Hz                              102
        ------(+111) 5               ------(+111) 13                210
852 Hz                         825 Hz                              102
        ------(+111) 6               ------(+111) 14                 21
963 Hz                         936 Hz                             +210
        ------(+210)                 ------(+210)                   666
1173 Hz                        1146 Hz
        ------(+111) 7               ------(+111) 15
1284 Hz                        1257 Hz
        ------(+111) 8               ------(+111) 16
1395 Hz                        1368 Hz
```

Red Skip Rate Numbers 888
Blue Skip Rate Numbers 666

Jesus name in Greek letters adds up to 888. The beast or antichrist in the book of Revelations has the number of 666.

Figure 110

In this graphic, you can see duality again with Jesus representing the number 888 in the 111 skip rates, and the beast representing the number 666 in the 21, 102 and 210 skip rates. We can think of 666 as representing the physical man, and 888 representing the ascended spiritual man. The number 8 is also the number of infinity, which is the promise of God by the way of Christ to an eternal or everlasting life.

The trinary numbers only add up to 666 if we add them in the 24 tones pattern, however, I discovered that there is one other trinary number that I have found hidden within the tones. The number 222 keeps coming up in many different ways as well, so when I considered that number and added it to the 6 trinary numbers found in the skip rates, then the magical number of 888 popped up again. The number 222 is the number 26 in trinary code, and this is a special number related to God's main name. God's name of Yud Hey Vav Hey adds up to 26 and so does the number 222, and the number 222 is a multiple of the special prime number of 37. The number 222 fits into 666 three times and fits into 888 four times. The number 222 represents God, so therefore, we are being given a special message when we include 222 into our addition of the trinary numbers. We are carbon based lifeforms of 666, but we can become spiritual beings of 888, but only if we become at one with God. Adding the 222 trinary number to the skip rate shows us an example of what happens when we include God into our lives.

The Number 37 in the Skip Rates

Trinary Code

```
111 111  21 111 111 102 111 111
/3  /3  /3  /3  /3  /3  /3  /3
 37  37   7  37  37  34  37  37
```

Skip Rate Numbers divided by three.

The number 37 is a very special prime number.

$$37 \times 6 = 222$$

Numbers one to twenty-seven in standard ternary

Ternary	1	2	10	11	12	20	21	22	100
Binary	1	10	11	100	101	110	111	1000	1001
Decimal	1	2	3	4	5	6	7	8	9
Ternary	101	102	110	111	112	120	121	122	200
Binary	1010	1011	1100	1101	1110	1111	10000	10001	10010
Decimal	10	11	12	13	14	15	16	17	18
Ternary	201	202	210	211	212	220	221	222	1000
Binary	10011	10100	10101	10110	10111	11000	11001	11010	11011
Decimal	19	20	21	22	23	24	25	26	27

The addition of all trinary numbers found encoded in the Solfeggio tones add up to 888, which is Jesus number in Greek gematria.

12+21+102+120+201+210+222=

888

222-102=120
222-210=12

21 = 7	12 = 5
102 = 11	120 = 15
210 = 21	201 = 19

222 = 26

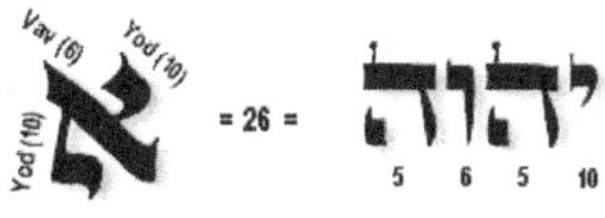

א = 26 = יהוה

God's Name in Hebrew

Figure 111

In the next graphic, it shows that the 3, 6 & 9 tones have a relationship with the number 666 and that the trinary skip rates that follow the 3, 6 & 9 numbers also reflect the 666 number. As I have shown before, the 6 & 9 numbers look a lot like the Chinese yin and yang symbol, so therefore, I believe they reflect the duality of positive and negative and feminine and masculine. The 3 turned backwards looks like an E to reflect that all energy in our universe is created through the interaction between positive and negative charges. Notice that adding all of the 3, 6 & 9 triad tones together gives a sum that also reflects those numbers. The sum of 3,996 is also a 3, 6 & 9 number, so we can see that there is a special relationship within these particular triad numbers. Tesla said that these numbers are the key to this universe, but remember we are living in a lower dimension of the universe after the fall of Adam and Eve.

The 3, 6 and 9 numbers represent the fiery serpent the most because hidden within these numbers alone is the very pattern of negative, positive and neutral. This is the very essence of how electricity works, so it seems quite fitting that 666 is related to the electricity that is created in our lower dimensional universe of matter. In the first creation of Genesis 1, we can see that the man and woman created were not given a name, however, in the creation story of Genesis 2, we can see that the man was named Adam, and that the woman was named Eve. It is only in a physical universe of matter that we have atoms, so therefore, Adam is made of the atom. Shadows and darkness are also another consequence of being physical because physical objects block the light of God and cast forth the darkness of shadows, therefore, we see the light of day become the evening or eve. Adam represents the atoms of a physical human, and Eve represents the evening of night or darkness as all physical beings block the light and cause dark shadows to form. If we can find the blueprints within the song of this life and develop the patterns for the new song, then perhaps we can increase our vibration level to a point where we are no longer seen and no longer naked in God's eyes. At this point we are no longer like Adam and Eve after the fall in that we will be spirits again, which are no longer made of atoms, and no longer cast the shadows for the darkness of the eve.

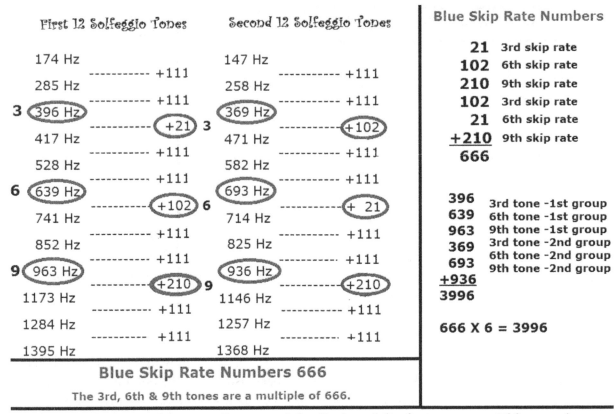

"If you only knew the magnificence of the 3, 6 and 9, then you would have a key to the universe." -Nikola Tesla

Figure 112

Not only do these tones have a special relationship with the numbers 666 and 888 of the Bible, but the 111 number is also a reoccurring theme throughout them as well. All of these numbers are divisible by the unique prime number of 37 too which is related to the first verse in the Bible. One night I had a dream where I was trying to understand the connections between the number 111 and the tones which I had to figure out. I was also shown a connection between the number 111 and Stonehenge. I told a friend about my dream, and she told me that she also had a dream about the number 111 on the very same night. That seemed much more than a coincidence to me, so I was highly interested in what her dream was about so that we could compare notes. Here is what she wrote about in her dream:

We were hiking somewhere in the mountains, and we saw a waterfall. You said "let's build it here." Suddenly I had a set of plans. (I drafted for years in my first job, and I still dream about blueprints). I was going over the drawings that looked like those compass drawings you make. Every time I tried to sum up to get the foundation numbers, it kept coming up as 111. I said ...this won't work, and you said "use these" and handed me a chisel and hammer. That was when the waterfall started making a sound that made the ground vibrate, and that startled me awake.

After she told me her dream, we began to call 111 the foundation number. It turned out after I looked for specific number patterns related to the number 111, I actually found them, and none of that would have happened without my dream or her dream about this magical number. When

I added up all of the tones in the 36 tones of the first and second eighteen tones, I found out that the sum was divisible by 111, and when I added up all of the skip rates, I also found out that they were divisible by the number 111 too. It seems that the number 111 is the foundation number for the Solfeggio tones, and therefore, not just a skip rate number of the tones themselves.

The First Eighteen Tones		The Second Eighteen Tones	
174	1173	147	1146
-------111	-------111	------111	-----111
285	1284	258	1257
-------111	-------111	------111	-----111
396	1395	369	1368
-------21	-------21	------102	-----102
417	1416	471	1470
-------111	-------111	------111	-----111
528	1527	582	1581
-------111	-------111	------111	-----111
639	1638	693	1692
-------102	-------102	------21	-----21
741	1740	714	1713
-------111	-------111	------111	-----111
852	1851	825	1824
-------111	-------111	------111	-----111
963	1962	936	1935
-------210	-------210	------210	-----210

The Number 111

The number 111 is found in the skip rates 24 times. The sum of the 36 tones and the 36 skip rates are divisible by the number 111.

Sum of the tones.   **Sum of the skip rates.**

37,962   3996

37,962/111=342   3996/111=36

Sum of the tones and skip rates.

37,962 + 3996 = 41,958

41,958/111=378

Jesus name in Greek gematria adds up to 888.

Jesus (Ιησους) = 888   888/111=8

Figure 113

I also found out that the name of the first Hebrew letter Aleph, which is also the number one, has a connection to the number 111. It turns out that the name for the letter Aleph adds up to 111 in Hebrew Gematria, which also hints around at the trinity. The a-tone-ment of the tones can also be broken apart to make at-one-ment, so therefore, we can see that the goal is to be at one with Christ or to act in unison with Christ. We are one.

Pey=80, Lamed=30, and Aleph=1

Figure 114

At the time of writing this book I was re-reading the dream that my friend had, and the hammer and chisel part stood out to me, so I looked up about their use in construction. I found out that the chisel is used to break stone for the walls in a construction which is set on the foundation. The chisel splits the stone when hit by the hammer. This is exactly what I did when I looked for the number 111 in the tones. Not only is 111 in the skip rates of the tones, but I could divide up the sum of the tones with the number 111. I symbolically used a chisel and hammer to split the tones apart and to see the 111 hidden within the tones. I believe the foundation number of 111 shows that this underlying number is what makes the foundation to build upon. I decided to plot out the 111 interval pattern into the degree circle, and to my surprise I found the corner tones of 27 Hz. I had to rotate around the compass three times to include all 9 numbers ranging from 111 all the way to 999. It turns out that when I started counting the degrees between the 9 closest numbers to one another, I realized that it is exactly 27 degrees. For example, when I counted the lines between 777 and 444, I counted 27 lines including the numbers of 777 and 444. After I had completed my counting between these 9 numbers, which were grouped together in threes, I found that there were only 6 spacings of 27 degrees. This completely matched the number of binaural beats that I had found in the first 18 tones. The 111 intervals in the degree circle hint around about the binaural beats or the six covered wagons mentioned in Numbers 7:3.

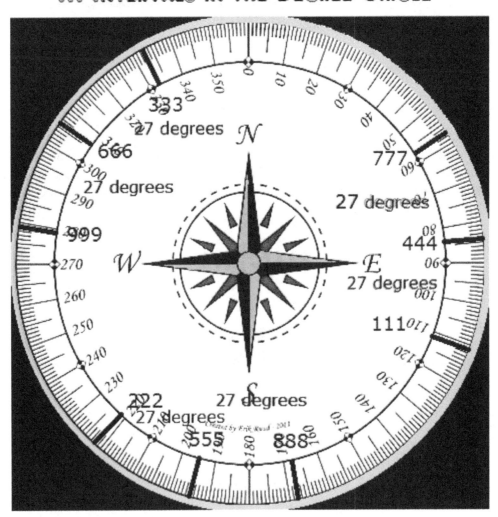

Figure 115

Without the tones' sum being a multiple of 111, we could not find a good foundation to build on with our corner stone, which are the binaural beats of the corner tones for 27 Hz. Hidden within the 111 pattern within the degree circle is the corner stone just waiting to be found. All six of the covered wagons can be uncovered in the 111 foundation number for the tones, so we can see that this number is very special.

In the past I had looked up how many standing stones there are going around the circle at Stonehenge, and I found out that there is thirty. I realized that I need to divide the circle into 30 numbers, so I did the math and found out that it needed to be divided into 12 degree intervals (360/30=12). Once I divided it into 12 degree intervals, I was astonished at what I discovered. There were 2 skip rates encoded into the degrees which are 108 and 324 degrees. I was amazed! I did not realize that Stonehenge could ever be connected to these tones from the Bible, so that has been a surprise to me.

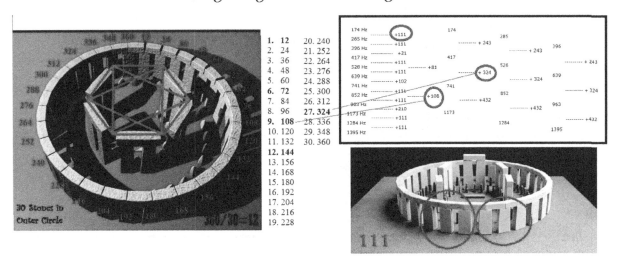

Figure 116

It took me awhile to see a connection between the 111 foundation number of the tones and Stonehenge, but after awhile I understood what my dream was all about. There are 30 standing stones, which meant that the 111 is repeated 10 times around the circle. Also note that the 144 degree stone is directly across from the 324 degree marker, which shows another connection between these tones and New Jerusalem, since the walls measurements are 144 cubits. It is the 10 segments of 111 in the 30 stones that form the foundation underneath the ring stones or circle. Therefore, the foundation number of 111 in the tones is also a foundation for the ring stones, so there is a parallel message between the two.

This information connects with some other research that I had previously done when I researched about the Stonehenge ley line. Ley lines are said to be lines on the earth that carry a tremendous amount of energy or electricity within the Earth. We can think of them as being similar to the nervous system within our body. The more modern name for these ancient ley lines is described in the scientific term of telluric currents. A telluric current is an electric current which moves underground or through the sea.

This Stonehenge ley line goes through the Teotihuacán area of Mexico and through Stone

Mountain, GA, Pilot Mountain, NC, Washington, D.C., Philadelphia, PA, New York, NY and Boston, MA in the United States of America. The line then goes through the center of the circle at Stonehenge at a 108 degree angle, which is, of course, the skip rate in the Solfeggio tones. The line then continues on through Europe and Turkey, and from there it goes into Syria near Damascus and Mount Hermon, which is the Mount Sion (not Mount Zion) mentioned in the Bible as being the mountain that the 144,000 will stand with Jesus.

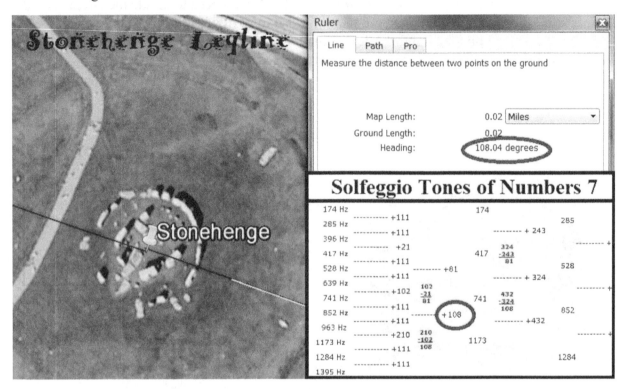

Figure 117

Deuteronomy 4:48

From Aroer, which is by the bank of the river Arnon, even unto mount Sion, which is Hermon,

Revelation 14:1

And I looked, and, lo, a Lamb stood on the mount Sion, and with him an hundred forty and four thousand, having his Father's name written in their foreheads.

Remember that the Mayan ruin of Teotihuacán near Mexico City has a latitude and longitude of 19°41'33"N 98°50'37.68"W, which is very close to this 19.5 degree zone, which shows the marker zone for the base of the tetrahedron energy pattern which is pointing down in the energetic star tetrahedron pattern of the earth.

The fact that this ley line is angled at 108 degrees and goes through the Mount Sion area seems very remarkable to me. The ancient city of Teotihuacan on the ley line has the Pyramid of the Sun and the Pyramid of the Moon, and we can find the diameter to both the sun and moon in the degree circle math which is also associated with Stonehenge's circle. We can find proof in both the degree circle math at Stonehenge and the pyramids at the ancient city of Teotihuacán that shows if we keep rotating around the compass by doubling the 360 degrees of the circle, then we can find the diameter of the moon and the sun.

The Mayan calendar and time system are all based on the degree circle math as well because the measurements for time are the same as the rotations of the compass. The Song of Degrees in Psalms 120-135 has the same degree math as the Mayan Calendar. The Baktun period in the Mayan Calendar consists of 144,000 days, which of course, connects with the 144,000 that will sing the new song in the last days described in the Bible prophecies. You can compare the Mayan Calendar with the degree circle rotations below:

Mayan Calendar

- Kin = 1 Day.
- Uinal = 20 kin = 20 days.
- Tun = 18 uinal = **360 days**.
- Katun = **20 tun** = 360 uinal = **7,200 days**.
- Baktun = 20 katun = **400 tun** = 7,200 uinal = **144,000 days**.

Degree Circle Rotations

- 1. 0-**360**
- 2. 360-720
- 3. 720-1080   *1st 18 Tones*   (moon radius 1080 miles)
- 4. 1080-1440
- 5. 1440-1800
- 6. 1800-2160 (Diameter of the moon 2160 miles- 144,000 marker) *2nd 18 Tones*
- 7. 2160-2520 (Numbers 7:85-86 marker)
- 8. 2520-2880
- 9. 2880-3240 *3rd 18 Tones*
- 10. 3240-3600
- 11. 3600-3960 (72 tones) *4th 18 Tones* 2 rotations?
- 12. 3960-4320
- 13. 4320-4680
- 14. 4680-5040 *5th 18 Tones*
- 15. 5040-5400
- 16. 5400-5760
- 17. 5760-6120 *6th 18 Tones*
- 18. 6120-6480
- 19. 6480-6840
- **20.** 6840-**7200** *7th 18 Tones* 20 Tun?
- **400.** 143,640-**144,000** (144,000/360=400 rotations of the degree circle **400 Tun?**)

These numbers are based on degree circle math. The 360 days of the Tun is equal to the 360 degrees of the circle, and the 7,200 days is equal to the 20 rotations of the degree circle which is called the 20 Tun. The 144,000 days is equal to 400 rotations of the degree circle or compass, and it is called the 400 Tun in the Mayan Calendar. We can see that the Tun of 7,200 days and 144,000 days are the same number as their rotations of the compass. It's also interesting to note that the Tun and Katun of the Mayan Calendar is pronounced as "tune" and "ka-tune." The Song of Degrees is meant to tune our bodies for the a-tone-ment, so either we have an intriguing coincidence, or the Mayan Calendar really is based on the degree circle and the Song of Degrees. Also it's quite fascinating that "ka" in the Egyptian language means soul, and that "ka" in the word merkaba (mer-ka-ba) means spirit body. Perhaps the katun of the 7,200 days is for tuning the soul, and the baktun (ba- means body) is for the 144,000 people who will sing the new song to tune the world. I can see a relationship between Stonehenge, the Mayan Calendar and the Song of Degrees, so therefore, there must be a connection somehow.

I read the book *The United States and Britain in Prophecy* by Herbert W. Armstrong, and he believed that the tribe of Judah throne was once in Ireland and Scotland, and then it later moved to England, which is where the throne remains until Jesus Christ returns to reclaim the throne in Israel. If this is true, then the Israelites could have built Stonehenge in England to mark the ley line and to encode the knowledge of the Song of Degrees.

Throughout the math within the tones, I have found numerous multiples of the number 111, which consists of the numbers 222, 333, 444, 555, 666, 888 and 1110. This is additional proof that 111 is the foundation number for the tones as well as the number 37.

Multiples of 111

```
 444          555          666          888        1110       111 111 21 111 111 102 111 111
                                                               /3  /3  /3  /3  /3  /3  /3  /3
 174          285          396          147         258        37  37   7  37  37  34  37  37
 417          528          639          174         285
+741         +852         +963          417         528              37 X 6 = 222
1332         1665         1998          471         582
                                        714         825
1332/3=444   1665/3=555   1998/3=666   +741        +852
                                       2664        3330

                                       2664/3=888  3330/3=1110

111X4=444   111X5=555   111X6=666   111X8=888   111X10=1110        111X2=222
```

Figure 118

Within the squares of the cube, I also found a 333, 444 and 555 diagonal pattern, and all 18 tones can be found with just the first 3 squares. I realized that not only are the tones being represented horizontally in the first 3 squares, but they are also being represented vertically as well. The last 3 squares only show 3 tones per square, and the same 3 tones are repeated vertically. In the first 3 squares the numbers 333, 444 and 555 go from the left to the right, from the top to the bottom, and in the second 3 squares the numbers can be read from right to left, from the top to the bottom. Basically, the first 3 squares show a clockwise pattern, and the second 3 squares show a counterclockwise pattern. The divisors of all three numbers have some numbers in common, and as you can see from the graphic below the numbers are 1, 3, 37 and 111. I am astounded at all of the interesting patterns that can be found within these tones, and the number 111 or its multiples seems to be everywhere from the skip rates to the tones themselves.

Eighteen Tones and 333, 444 & 555

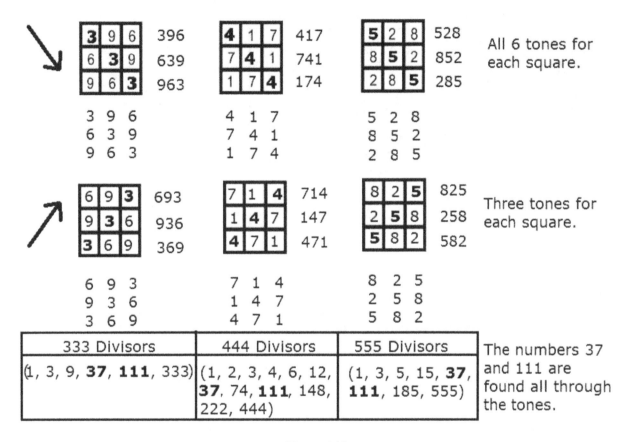

Figure 119

I had a friend that suggested that there might be a pattern within the tones that has something to do with the Schumann resonance. At first I didn't see what the connection could be, but then I realized that there is a significant pattern within these earth sounds. It seemed as if the pattern within the Schumann resonance is based on the number six, and in fact, this number pattern of adding sixes gives us the pattern of repeating sixes. I don't know why no one has ever mentioned that the Schumann resonance has a repeating pattern of 666, but it does. I continued the pattern upwards to see if any of the tones would show up in this pattern, and I very quickly found that 2 of the skip rates of 81 and 111 came up in this mathematical pattern. I continued the pattern of adding 6 to every number, and I was able to find 12 of the Solfeggio tones that fit within that pattern. I am still not sure if this means anything or not, but I can only say that it does match this numerical pattern. If for any reason the Schumann resonance increases, it would increase its frequency rate by sixes due to this being the pattern. The earth was created in six days according to Genesis 1, as the 7th day was just a rest day, so therefore, the Schumann resonance also records this pattern of six, as well as the tones have six counterparts for all of the triad numbers. It's also interesting to note that 33 is a frequency in the Schumann resonance.

This shows an interesting connection to the 33 years that Jesus was here on the planet earth. Within this pattern, I was also able to come up with another skip rate pattern just by subtracting the lower numbers from the higher numbers in the order that they come in each column, and I found some interesting numbers and an interesting pattern. I still do not know if this information means anything at this point, but I thought that I would share it anyway.

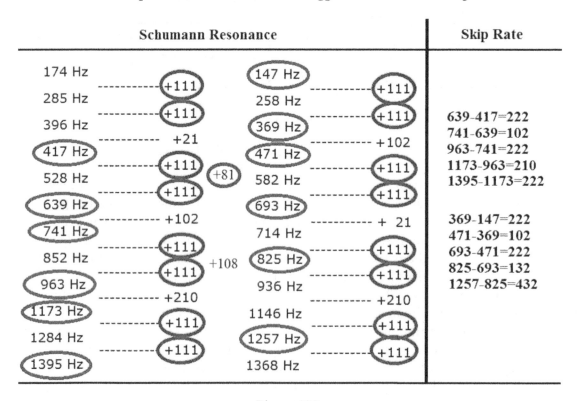

Figure 120

Notice that from this skip rate pattern, the number 222 keeps popping up, so this is showing another trianry number to go with the 21, 102 and 210 skip rates. As I pointed out before, when I added all of the trinary skip rates together with the number 222, then I got the number 888. The trinary code numbers take binary code to the next level, as binary code only allows two choices, but trinary code allows three choices. Trinary code is also encoding the trinity as well as the positive, negative and neutral charges within the tones. The number 432 is the skip rate in the tones, but it is also the musical scale of the ancient people. There have been many ancient instruments that were found by archeologists that were tuned to the 432 Hz frequency scale. I will talk more about this musical scale in another chapter.

There are patterns within the tones that keep it connected to the first 18 triad tones, as I explained before, the second 18 tones has a pattern of *one plus*. The one plus pattern keeps the tones connected to the triad tones because 1 added to the next three numbers gives us the sum of a triad number. The second 18 tones also have a consecutive number pattern associated with its pattern.

The Second Eighteen Tones		Consecutive Numbers Pattern		One Plus Pattern		The First Eighteen Tones	
1173	1146	1 1 7 3	1 1 4 6	1+173=174	1+146=147	174	147
-------111	-----111	1 2 8 4	1 2 5 7	1+284=285	1+257=258	-------111	------111
1284	1257	1 3 9 5	1 3 6 8	1+395=396	1+368=369	285	258
-------111	-----111	1 4 1 6	1 4 7 0	1+416=417	1+470=471	-------111	------111
1395	1368	1 5 2 7	1 5 8 1	1+527=528	1+581=582	396	369
-------21	-----102	1 6 3 8	1 6 9 2	1+638=639	1+692=693	-------21	------102
1416	1470	1 7 4 0	1 7 1 3	1+740=741	1+713=714	417	471
-------111	-----111	1 8 5 1	1 8 2 4	1+851=852	1+824=825	-------111	------111
1527	1581	1 9 6 2	1 9 3 5	1+962=963	1+935=936	528	582
-------111	-----111	1	1			-------111	------111
1638	1692	2	2			639	693
-------102	-----21	3	3			-------102	------21
1740	1713	4	4			741	714
-------111	-----111	5	5			-------111	------111
1851	1824	6	6			852	825
-------111	-----111	7	7			-------111	------111
1962	1935	8	8			963	936
-------210	-----210	9	9			-------210	------210

Figure 121

The tones are also encoded with the number three in many different ways. All of the Solfeggio tones and skip rates are visible by three, and this is also a connection to the trinity. As I showed the 40 degree interval circle encode triangles that are associated with the triad tones, and a triangle has three sides. As you can see from the following diagram, the skip rate number of 432 is a multiple of 144 which is mentioned in Revelation 21:17. The ancient instruments that have been found are tuned to the 432 Hz scale, and one of those notes is actually 144 Hz. I will talk more about this in another chapter.

The number three is also encoded into the net of John 21, so we can see the connections between the trinity number three and the fishing net of the harvest. The number 153 is divisible by 3 and also the number 3 multiplied by consecutive numbers using the Pythagorean skein through number 26 has a sum of 153. The number three is very important in the tones, and therefore, is the most repetitive number encoded within the Song of Degrees. It clearly represents the Father, Holy Spirit and the Son, as well as the positive, negative and neutral charges within atoms. The skips rate numbers of the Trinary code also seem to encode the triple numbers, which is very similar to binary code but has three digits.

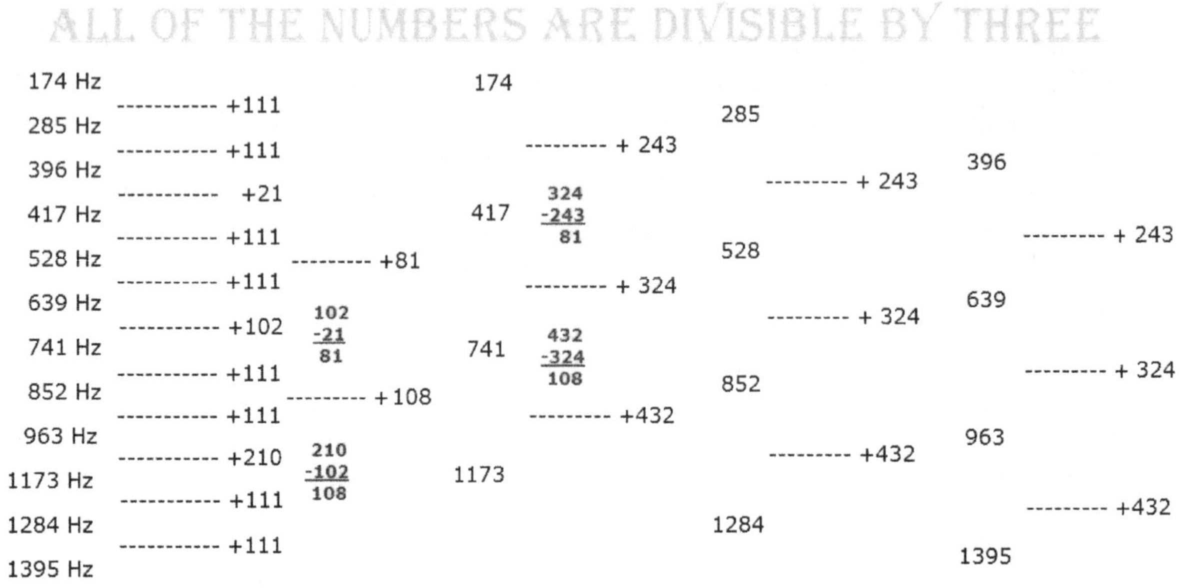

ALL OF THE NUMBERS ARE DIVISIBLE BY THREE

```
174 Hz                              174
        ---------- +111                                285
285 Hz                                      --------- + 243
        ---------- +111                                              396
396 Hz                                                      --------- + 243
        ----------  +21               324
417 Hz                          417  -243                                   --------- + 243
        ---------- +111 --------+81   81
528 Hz                                      --------- + 324          528
        ---------- +111                                              639
639 Hz                           102        --------- + 324
        ---------- +102           -21                                       --------- + 324
741 Hz                            81  741   432
        ---------- +111                    -324                      852
852 Hz                 -------- +108         108
        ---------- +111                      --------- +432          963
963 Hz                                       --------- +432
        ---------- +210           210                                       --------- +432
1173 Hz                          -102  1173
        ---------- +111           108                                 1284
1284 Hz                                                              1395
        ---------- +111
1395 Hz
```

Solfeggio Tones: 174/3=58, 285/3=95, 396/3=132, 417/3=139, 528/3=176, 639/3=213, 741/3=247, 852/3=284, 963/3=321, 1173/3=391, 1284/3=428, 1395/3=465

Skip Rates: 111/3=37, 21/3=7, 102/3=34, 210/3=70, 81/3=27, 108/3=36, 243/3=81, 324/3=108, 432/3=144

Figure 122

One of the more bizarre connections to the Solfeggio tones that I have discovered had to do with a mysterious man that built a castle all by himself out of coral stone in Florida. His name was Ed Leedskalnin, and he built the famous Coral Castle in Homestead, Florida. No one knows how he built this immense complex of stone that weighs tons all by himself, and so it has become an unsolvable mystery to this day. He made a magnetic flywheel that is believed to have produced electricity, and many people have been trying to figure out how this device works, and no one has been able to so far. There is a young man from Australia called Jeremy Stride who was able to decipher the numbers that Ed left on the wall at Coral Castle. He put out a video called *Code 144*, in which he explains that the numbers are the fifteen degree intervals of a circle, and the sums of prime numbers put together. I took a look at his diagram and saw two Solfeggio tone numbers in the sums of prime numbers. The 20th sum of primes and the 24th sum of primes are included within the circle pattern for the flywheel. Another interesting connection to the tones is that Ed's magnetic flywheel has 24 magnets going around the circle at a 15 degree interval which is how six of the tones can be found. Did Ed Leedskalnin know the secret about the tones from the Bible? One rumor was that some boys saw Ed levitating the stones by singing to them.

I added the prime numbers up to 101, and only two of the sums of primes for the triad tones can be found, but they are the same tones that can be found in the 15 degree interval circle. Perhaps Ed managed to figure out that these tones are very powerful and how to use them to levitate the stones, or maybe these tones generated the electricity in the magnetic flywheel. We may never know exactly what Ed did with his flywheel, or if the Solfeggio tones were involved, but it is interesting that two of them can be found in the numerical pattern that he left behind on his wall. Perhaps there can be more tones found by adding the prime numbers past 101, but I am not even going to attempt that project to find out.

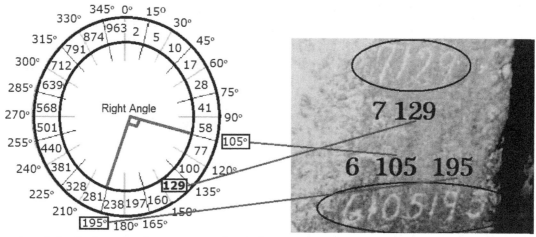

The outer circle displays the degrees around a circle at 15 degree intervals. The inner circle displays the sum of prime numbers.

Ed's Numbers on the Wall

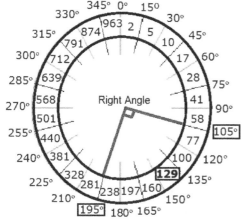

The outer circle displays the degrees around a circle at 15 degree intervals. The inner circle displays the sum of prime numbers.

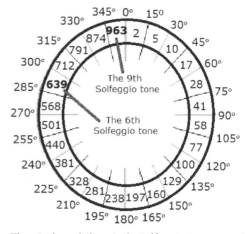

The sixth and the ninth Solfeggio tones can be found in the sums of prime numbers.

Figure 123

I eventually started to work out the pattern beyond the 36 tones and did computations all the way up to 180 tones, so that I could see what the 144th and 153rd tones were going to be. I have not gone beyond the 180 tones at this point. Each subsequent 18 tones group following the first two also have a connection with the first 18 tones or triad tones, as they continue to follow the pattern for the one plus numbers. In the third 18 tones, the sequence would be two plus, and the fourth 18 tones it would be the three plus numbers, and this pattern continues all the way to the180th tone.

On the following page are the sequences of tones from the third 18 tones through the ninth 18 tones. The 144th tone is at the end of the 8th 18 tones, and the 153rd tone is in the 9th 18 tones. The 180 tones would appear to represent a triangle because the angle of all triangles is equal to 180 degrees. Remember that the symbolism of the net number of 153 is represented by the triangle, since it is a triangular number. I believe we are supposed to stop at the triangle number of 180 tones, however, I could be wrong. When I went beyond the 180th tone, I found that it no longer matches the triad tone pattern; so therefore, I wanted to stop the pattern at 180 tones. The 180 tones consist of 28 rotations of the compass or degree circle and also represent the 180 degrees of a triangle. In the Star of David both of the equilateral triangles are 180 degrees which adds up to the 360 degrees of a circle.

The Third Eighteen Tones

Left Speaker	Right Speaker
2172	2145
------111	------111
2283	2256
------111	------111
2394	2367
------21	------102
2415	2469
------111	------111
2526	2580
------111	------111
2637	2691
------102	------21
2739	2712
------111	------111
2850	2823
------111	------111
2961	2934
------210	------210

The Fourth Eighteen Tones

Left Speaker	Right Speaker
3171	3144
------111	-----111
3282	3255
------111	-----111
3393	3366
------21	----102
3414	3468
------111	----111
3525	3579
------111	----111
3636	3690
------102	-----21
3738	3711
------111	-----111
3849	3822
------111	-----111
3960	3933
------210	-----210

The Fifth Eighteen Tones

Left Speaker	Right Speaker
4170	4143
------111	------111
4281	4254
------111	------111
4392	4365
------21	------102
4413	4467
------111	------111
4524	4578
------111	------111
4635	4689
------102	------21
4737	4710
------111	------111
4848	4821
------111	------111
4959	4932
------210	------210

The Sixth Eighteen Tones

Left Speaker	Right Speaker
5169	5142
-----111	-----111
5280	5253
-----111	-----111
5391	5364
-----21	-----102
5412	5466
-----111	-----111
5523	5577
-----111	-----111
5634	5688
-----102	-----21
5736	5709
----111	----111
5847	5820
-----111	-----111
5958	5931
-----210	-----210

The Seventh Eighteen Tones

Left Speaker	Right Speaker
6168	6141
-----111	-----111
6279	6252
-----111	-----111
6390	6363
-----21	-----102
6411	6465
-----111	-----111
6522	6576
-----111	-----111
6633	6687
-----102	-----21
6735	6708
-----111	-----111
6846	6819
-----111	-----111
6957	6930
-----210	-----210

The Eighth Eighteen Tones

Left Speaker	Right Speaker
7167	7140
------111	-----111
7278	7251
------111	-----111
7389	7362
------21	-----102
7410	7464
------111	-----111
7521	7575
------111	-----111
7632	7686
------102	-----21
7734	7707
------111	-----111
7845	7818
------111	-----111
7956	7929
------210	-----210

The Ninth Eighteen Tones

Left Speaker	Right Speaker
8166	8139
------111	------111
8277	8250
------111	------111
8388	8361
------21	------102
8409	8463
------111	------111
8520	8574
------111	------111
8631	8685
------102	------21
8733	8706
------111	------111
8844	8817
------111	------111
8955	8928
------210	------210

The Tenth Eighteen Tones

Left Speaker	Right Speaker
9165	9138
------111	------111
9276	9249
------111	------111
9387	9360
------21	------102
9408	9462
------111	------111
9519	9573
------111	------111
9630	9684
------102	------21
9732	9705
------111	------111
9843	9816
------111	------111
9954	9927
------210	------210

Figure 124

There needs to be perfect balance or the middle way with the tones, as we saw with the binaural beats of the tones. It is important that the tones be displayed in the right and left paradigm, so that we can represent both sides. In a patriarchal society as we have had for centuries, we see unbalance everywhere we look, but the solution is not to bring back a matriarchal society either. What the world needs is balance, and that can only happen in a world where neither dominate, but both sides work together. The Star of David represents unity, as the up triangle represents the masculine side of God, and the lower triangle represents the feminine side of God. The tones are representing the lost feminine side of God which is the Holy Spirit; therefore, the 180 tones represent the triangle pointing down to the 180 degrees within the degree circle.

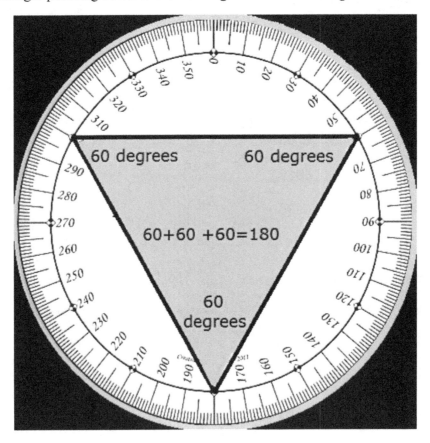

Figure 125

This world has consistently leaned towards a masculine point of view of thinking analytical over intuitively or thinking logically over creatively. We should seek to use both of these perspectives together, until we can bring about the perfect blend of creativity and analytical thinking into one perspective.

In the movie *Contact* there is a scene where Ellie is looking at a galaxy from the spaceship, and she says she has "no words" and states that "They should have sent a poet." Ellie is a scientist, and she thinks mostly analytical, but at the time that she sees something completely beautiful in the universe, she says that she has no words to describe because she couldn't put what she was experiencing into meaningful words. It was at that moment that she thought that perhaps they should have sent a poet because a poet would have the creative ability to describe what they were seeing not just in words but in feelings.

If we view a sunset in a completely scientific way, then we can certainly appreciate the movement of the earth as it revolves on its axis to create day and night, but we would be missing out on the other information within the sunset. However, if we just view the sunset from how we feel, we may start to appreciate how the colorful mirage of light changes as the sky gets darker to display an awesome fireworks explosion of colors painted across the sky. We may feel all kinds of emotions that simply can't be expressed in words, if we are mostly analytical, but if we have the soul of a poet, singer, photographer or artist, then we may be bursting with creative energy. The most intense way to experience the sunset though would definitely be to experience it with both perspectives at the same time. See the majesty of the interplay between the earth and the sun playing peek-a-boo in the darkness of space, while also seeing and describing or displaying the awesome display of colors mingling together in a hazy pattern while the sun sets in the sky.

Just before writing the two paragraphs above, I went to *You Tube* to view the scene from Contact where Ellie is talking about a poet, and to my surprise I couldn't hear any sound whatsoever. All I could see was that Ellie was excited and passionate about what she was seeing, but I couldn't hear her words. Just through her body language alone, I could tell a great many things, but I couldn't really watch it without the words. Likewise, if we just look at the analytical viewpoint to the universe, we can enjoy one aspect that delights the mind, but if we view it from a more intuitive side, then we can enjoy another aspect that delights our soul. The masculine perspective has us exploring how everything works in God's creation, and the feminine perspective explores how it makes us feel. One side brings out the scientist in us, and the other side brings out the artist in us.

When I started to research about the tones, I had to put the patterns on the paper and work them out. Just simply knowing the tones was not enough for me, as I became sidetracked by the visual effect of the tones themselves. It wasn't just simply about listening to them and how it made me feel, but it also became about finding out how they work. In my attempt to figure out how they work, I kept making graphics of the patterns, and some of them really became colorful with numerous geometrical shapes. It was how they made me feel that brought out this creative aspect of the research of these tones, and this is why I don't just describe the tones in words, but why I have made numerous graphics to explain the tones. The patterns that are made by the tones are so beautiful to me, and some of them could perhaps be classified as a type of art featuring numbers and geometry. If I had just viewed these tones from the analytical and mathematical components themselves, then I would have missed out on how they make me feel when I listen to them, or when I make graphics displaying the interesting blueprints and patterns. Making the graphics on the Microsoft Paint program has given me a creative outlet for understanding the tones from a visual perspective, rather than an audio perspective or an analytical perspective of the mathematics within the tones. This is the feminine side of my brain.

There is only one place in the Bible where it talks about the number 180, and it is in a book about a woman named Esther. This verse is symbolic of the feminine triangle in the Star of David.

Esther 1:4 New English Translation (NET Bible)

⁴ He displayed the riches of his royal glory and the splendor of his majestic greatness for a lengthy period of time—a hundred and eighty days, to be exact!

Esther 2

[12] Now when every maid's turn was come to go in to king Ahasuerus, after that she had been twelve months, according to the manner of the women, (for so were the days of their purifications accomplished, to wit, six months with oil of myrrh, and six months with sweet odours, and with other things for the purifying of the women;)

The feminine triangle in the Star of David points down at the 180 degrees spot in the degree circle, so this triangle also represents the bride or church of Christ the King and also about the Holy Spirit being feminine. Jesus baptized with the fire or Holy Spirit, and this purified his bride for the marriage to come.

Matthew 3:11

I indeed baptize you with water unto repentance. but he that cometh after me is mightier than I, whose shoes I am not worthy to bear: he shall baptize you with the Holy Ghost, and with fire:

There are only really nine numbers in our mathematics. Zero is not a number, and any number above nine is only a multiple of the nine numbers. There is a hidden pattern within those nine numbers which shows the Solfeggio tone of 396 Hz.

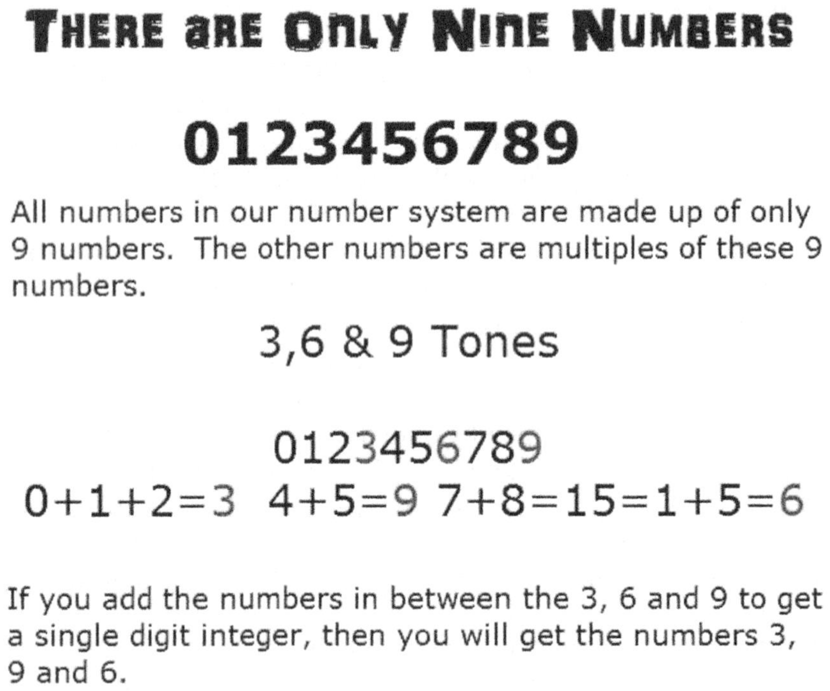

THERE aRE OnLY NInE NUMBERS

0123456789

All numbers in our number system are made up of only 9 numbers. The other numbers are multiples of these 9 numbers.

3,6 & 9 Tones

0123456789
0+1+2=3 4+5=9 7+8=15=1+5=6

If you add the numbers in between the 3, 6 and 9 to get a single digit integer, then you will get the numbers 3, 9 and 6.

Figure 126

Using this pattern, I was able to find more patterns with the triad tones, but only the numbers of 3, 6 and 9 produce another 3, 6 and 9 tone of 396 Hz. The 1, 4 and 7 numbers produce the 528 Hz tone in between and only a 174 Hz tone is made from the sum of the numbers in between the

2, 5 and 8. This suggests that there is more going on in our nine number pattern system, than what we were taught in school.

Two Numbers Apart

                              1 2 3 4 5 6 7 8 9

1 2 3 4 5 6 7 8 9   2+3=5 5+6=11=2 8+9=17=8

1 2 3 4 5 6 7 8 9   1 2 3 4 5 6 7 8 9

1 2 3 4 5 6 7 8 9   1+9=10=1 3+4=7 6+7=13=4

                              1 2 3 4 5 6 7 8 9

                         1+2=3 4+5=9 7+8=15=6

Figure 127

In the next chapter, I will show that the original calendar of the Hebrew people had 360 days of a year, which is also the same 360 days of the degree circle on which we have found the Song of Degrees.

The 360 Day Calendar

There is evidence in the Bible that the ancient Hebrew calendar consisted of 30 day months, which would add up to a 360 day year. This calendar would perfectly go along with the 360 degrees of a circle. In Genesis 7:11, we are told that the flood began on the seventeenth day of the second month, and in Genesis 8:3-4, we are told that the flood waters abated after 150 days, and the ark rested upon the mountains of Ararat on the seventeenth day in the seventh month. Basically, we are being told that from the seventeenth of the second month to the seventeenth of the seventh month was a hundred and fifty days. This means that those 5 months would have been 30 days each to make it add up to 150 days (30X5=150). It is also interesting that we have the net number of 153 encoded in these two verses as well. We know that the number 17 is a multiple of 153 and is associated with this number in many diverse ways. Of course, the flood story is all about water, and these tones work with water.

Genesis 7:11 (KJV)

[11] In the six hundredth year of Noah's life, in the second month, the seventeenth day of the month, the same day were all the fountains of the great deep broken up, and the windows of heaven were opened.

Genesis 8:3-4 (KJV)

[3] And the waters returned from off the earth continually: and after the end of the hundred and fifty days the waters were abated.

[4] And the ark rested in the seventh month, on the seventeenth day of the month, upon the mountains of Ararat.

There were many ancient civilizations that used a 360 day calendar, and even though this calendar does not fit perfectly with the solar year of 365 days or the lunar cycle, I believe this calendar fits perfectly with the precession of the equinox Great year. A Great year would be 25,920 years, which would record the time it takes for the earth's wobble circle to make one rotation. It's interesting to note that the sixth rotation of the compass ends in the number 2160 degrees, which is the number of years in an age of the Great year (25,920/2160=12).

David Wilcock did calculations to find out what would be the time period of one complete rotation of the Milky Way Galaxy, and he believes that it would be approximately 228 million years for one rotation. He calls this a Galactic Cycle. According to his calculations, a Galactic Cycle would be approximately 9,000 Great years of 25,920 year periods. It is obvious to me that the 360 day calendar is following the Great year, which would actually be a more perfect calendar for following the passage of time of our Milky Way Galaxy. In other words, this calendar would be a perfect calendar, not just for our Earth, but for all of the planets in our galaxy. It would be a galactic calendar and not a solar or lunar calendar.

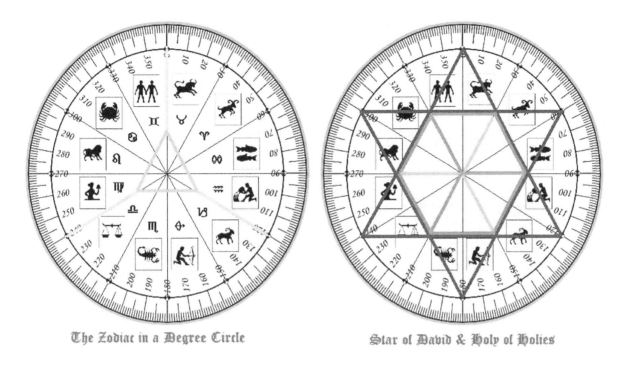

Figure 128

We could think of the degree circle as representing the precession of the equinox in that the earth traces out a complete 360 degree circle for every Great year. During a period of 25,920 years, the earth will point towards twelve constellations in the sky which we call the Zodiac constellations. As you can see, I represented this wobble within the degree circle to show the twelve constellations. Each age is represented by 30 degrees within the degree circle. We have just entered into the Age of Aquarius. Adam and Eve were placed on the Earth during the Age of Taurus. The exodus took place during the Age of Aries. Jesus was born during the Age of Pisces, and we are now in the Age of Aquarius. The tabernacle pattern also records these ages in its star map that I found.

The degree circle represents the Song of Degrees, the calendar for precession of the equinox, the diameter of the moon and the sun, and it represents the geometry of our universe. God's creation was made of circles and spirals, and spirals are only circles in motion. The very science and math of our universe is encoded within the numbers of the 360 degrees of a circle. The ancient Sumerians are credited for giving us the 360 degrees of a circle, but no one knows where they got their information, or if they actually developed this themselves. It is apparent to me that the ancient people knew much more about the passage of time and frequencies than what we know today. These people knew the complexities of God's creation, and how it was all based on this circle and particular numbers associated with the rotations of the compass or degree circle. We know that the Song of Degrees was based on this knowledge, and that somehow hidden within the math of the degree circle is a song so beautiful in its rhythm that it has the power to lift us up in the harvest that is mentioned to occur in the last days. The 144,000 must sing this precious song of higher frequencies to lift the vibration of the earth before the harvest of souls takes place to take us up onto a higher dimensional earth. We know that this song is the net for the fisherman of men, and that it is woven together by these tones for the final atonement of us all.

The Tabernacle Star Map

Orion | Taurus | Aries | Pisces | Aquarius
Age of Taurus | Age of Aries | Age of Pisces | Age of Aquarius

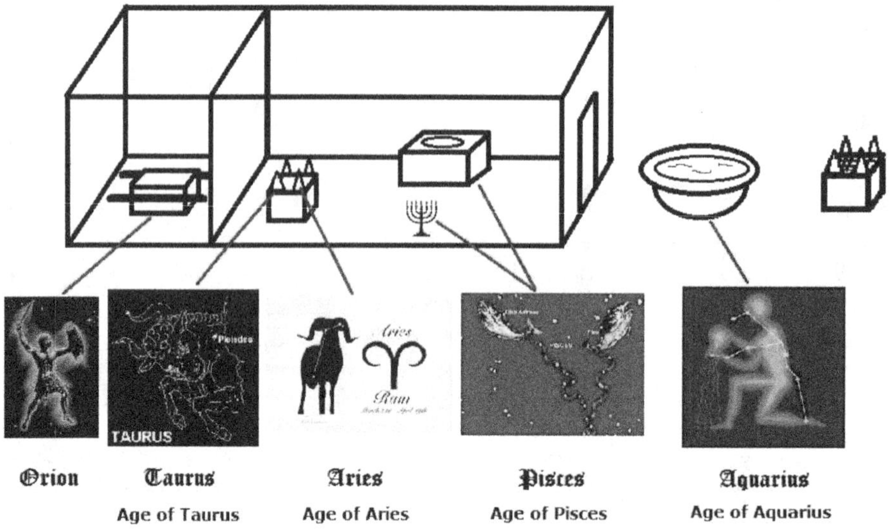

Figure 129

The Age of Aquarius is represented by the water bearer, and the Bronze water laver represents the constellation of Aquarius. This is the last age that is represented in the tabernacle star map, as the Bronze Altar is the same as the Incense Altar. Both of them have the same four horns to represent the constellations of Taurus and Aries. When I was trying to figure out this star map, I realized that the four horns of the Bronze Altar did not match the next constellations. There are two horns of Capricorn but not in Sagittarius, so therefore, I concluded that the same pattern of the Incense Altar was being repeated. After I realized that the two patterns were the same, I automatically wanted to join them together as one. This seems to be another pattern recognition test. Here is the interesting thing: it reminded me of the children's game of matching the symbols that are alike. I realized that if I moved the Bronze Altar on the two dimensional diagram of the tabernacle and put it over the Incense Altar, that it would be like rolling a scroll into a circle to join the two together. It would seem as if this is also pointing out the degree circle. The Bronze Water Laver as well is showing us a circular pattern within the bowl of water. The Bible keeps showing us this same pattern over and over again, and it really is encoded in so many diverse ways. In the tabernacle star map, we are being told that the calendar is circular.

The Mayan Calendar and Aztec Calendar is round which encodes the 360 degree circle into their timekeeping. For some reason I have always been fascinated by the Aztec Calendar every time I saw it somewhere, so when I finally went to Mexico in 2013, I bought a replica of the Aztec Calendar. It was upon bringing it back home and doing more research into the Mayan and Aztec calendars that I realized at some point that it encoded the 360 degrees of a circle. As I pointed out before, the Mayan calendar has the same numbers that the rotations of the degree circle or compass has, so therefore, I realized that their calendar was based on the math of the 360 degree circle. In my chart in a previous chapter, I pointed out that the tun measurement of time was the same as the rotations of the degree circle. The Mayan Long Count calendar measures a year in 360 days, which is really the calendar embedded within the 360 degrees of the circle.

Figure 130

If you look closely in the center of the Aztec calendar, you will see what looks like a modern puzzle piece, and it seems to beckon us to solve the puzzle that is laid out before us in the circle. I counted the sections in the inner ring, and it had 20 pieces, which I automatically knew could refer to the 20 tun. If we rotate around the compass 20 times, then we end up with the number of 7200 degrees, which mimics the 7,200 days in the Mayan calendar. A katun is equal to 20 tun and 360 unial, which is 7,200 days. I got a major surprise when I counted the ring with the eight compass points of the cardinal directions. There were 3 points between each compass arrow, so when I added everything up, I got 36 points. I decided to see how many days are made from 36 rotations of the compass, and I got the number 12,960. For some reason that number looked familiar to me, and I instantly thought that it might have something to do with the precession of the equinox. I divided it into 25,920 of the Great year, and it fitted perfectly. It turned out that 12,960 is half of a Great year. (25,920/12,960=2) Following this hint from the calendar, I was able to calculate the amount of rotations of the compass that would make up a Great Year, and I found out that it would be 72 rotations within the degree circle (360X72=25,920). The Mayan Long Count Calendar and the Aztec Calendar are recording the passage of time in a Great Year.

There is a quote that I found online by Sir Isaac Newton about the ancient 360 day calendar. Newton said, "All nations, before the just length of the solar year was known, reckoned months by the course of the moon, and years by the return of winter and summer, spring and autumn; and in making calendars for their festivals, they reckoned thirty days to a lunar month, and twelve lunar months to a years, taking the nearest round numbers, whence came the division of the ecliptic into 360 degrees."

Genesis 1:14 (KJV)

14 And God said, Let there be lights in the firmament of the heaven to divide the day from the night; and let them be for signs, and for seasons, and for days, and years:

There was a website that I found that showed that the solar year and the lunar year average out to be 360. Although we use a solar calendar today, many ancient people used a lunar calendar, but it's interesting that the 360 day calendar could be an average between the two. The solar year is 365.24 days, and the lunar year (12 lunar months) is 354.37 days. If we add those together, then the sum would be 719.61, which divided by two would be rounded off to 360 days.

$$365.24 \text{ (solar)} + 354.37 \text{ (lunar)} = 719.61 / 2 = 359.8 \text{ days}$$

Many people who study the Bible prophecies are using a 360 day prophetic calendar because the Bible seems to hint around about this in the prophecies. The phrase *time, times and half a time* or *times, times, and an half* refer to one year for a time and two years for times with half a times representing half a year, so put altogether is three years and a half. These phrases are both used in prophetic books of the Bible to show a period of time that would be three and a half years.

Daniel 12:7

*And I heard the man clothed in linen, which was upon the waters of the river, when he held up his right hand and his left hand unto heaven, and sware by him that liveth for ever that it shall be for a **time, times, and an half**; and when he shall have accomplished to scatter the power of the holy people, all these things shall be finished.*

Revelation 12:14

And to the woman were given two wings of a great eagle, that she might fly into the wilderness, *into her place, where she is nourished for a **time, and times, and half** a **time**, from the face of the serpent.*

Other prophetic verses also seem to reiterate the same time period of three and a half years. Here are two verses from the New English Translation (NET) below, which point to a 1,260 day period of time.

Revelation 11:3

*And I will grant my two witnesses authority to prophesy for **1,260** days, dressed in sackcloth."*

Revelation 12:6

*and she fled into the wilderness where a place had been prepared for her by God, so she could be taken care of for **1,260** days.*

If we plot 1,260 days within three and a half rotations of a 360 degree circle, then we find out that 1,260 days would be three and a half years in a 360 day calendar. The third rotation of the compass leaves us at 1,080 degrees, and then when we add 180 degrees to that number to get the half a time in the fourth rotation, we arrive at the 2,160 days. (2160-1080=180)

1. 0-360

2. 360-720

3. 720-1080

4. 1080-1440

1080 degrees+180 degrees=1260 degrees

Time, Times an Half a Time

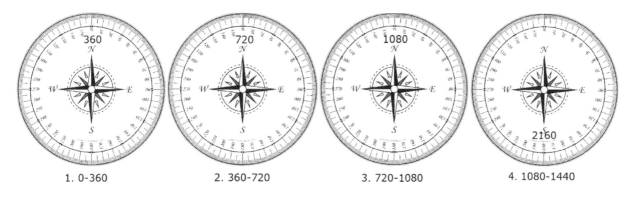

1. 0-360   2. 360-720   3. 720-1080   4. 1080-1440

Figure 131

As you can see the 2,160 days would be exactly 3 ½ years perfectly within the 360 day calendar. Keep in mind that the 2,160 days will be in the last days just before Jesus returns, and this is when the new song of the 144,000 will be sung. This song will contain the tones in the Song of Degrees which, of course, is also found in the 360 degree circle and in the 360 day calendar. It all fits together perfectly!

$$2160/360=3.5$$

I decided to make a graphic of what the ancient Hebrew calendar would have looked like, if it had been put into a 360 degree circle. The twelve months divide up into 30 degree intervals, and within half of those degree points the Star of David and Holy of Holies can be found.

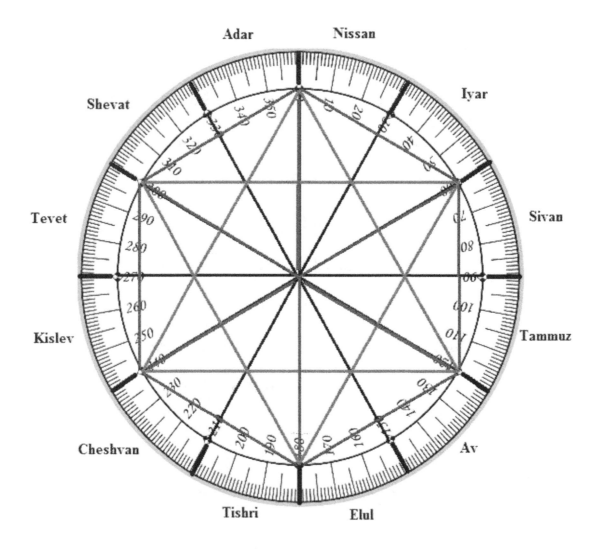

Figure 132

God's 360 day calendar, God's Song of Degrees, God's prophetic timeline and God's tabernacle star map all fit so perfectly within the compass or degree circle. On the day that the 144,000 will sing the new song, they will do so with the rotations of a compass, as they stand on the Bronze Altar to sacrifice their will for God's will. The new song will reflect the compass that was located on the net of the Bronze Altar. This Altar on which they stand will undoubtedly be the wedding altar for the marriage of the Lamb. As they will alter themselves and change in the twinkling of an eye, just as Jesus did in the transfiguration.

Exodus 27:5

*And thou shalt put it under the **compass of the altar** beneath, that the net may be even to the midst of the altar.*

Psalm 26:6

*I will wash mine hands in innocency: so will I **compass thine altar**, O Lord:*

While most Americans work a 40 hour week to support themselves and their families, the 144,000 will work just as hard to learn the secrets of the new song. Our modern day clock is also shown within a circle, as time appears to be cycling over and over during the course of a day. We can think of the 12 hours represented in the degree circle as also representing the ancient calendar with 30 degree intervals, however, in our modern clocks we rotate the compass twice to convey the 24 hours of a day. Over and over again, we see how the cycle of time was conveyed by the ancients and still is being conveyed as a circle. It is perhaps an interesting coincidence then, that 40 hours of a clock is actually 144,000 seconds. There are 60 seconds in a minute, and 60 minutes in an hour with a total of 1,440 minutes in a 24 hour day, which is 86,400 seconds.

60 minutes X 24 hours=1440 minutes (4th rotation of the compass)

60 minutes X 40 hours= 2400 minutes

2400 minutes X 60 seconds= 144,000 (400th rotation of the compass)

We can start to see a relationship between the 360 degree circle, and how we measure time, whether it is on a modern day clock or an ancient calendar. Perhaps the 144,000 will work at learning this new song as hard as working a 40 hour work week which is 144,000 seconds. Nevertheless, they had better hurry because this is the end times, and unfortunately time is almost up. Out of the 7 billion people on our planet, only a precious 144,000 people will learn this new song. Let's hope that they go around in circles to find these mysterious tones.

Music Clues

There are many musical clues that I have found over the years, but because I am not a musician, I do not really completely understand all of these clues. I previously mentioned in another chapter that the Numbers 21 story has the Israelites pitching 4 times before they sang a song to a well. This clue was given in the same book that the tones were encoded which is the book of Numbers, however, all throughout the Bible; we are given the same clues about pitches.

In one pattern recognition tests we are told about three different arks, which all seem to be quite different from one another, however, they all seem to have similarities as well. There is Noah's ark, the ark of bulrushes and the Ark of the Covenant. These first two arks seem to be the most similar in that they both floated on water, and both were made with pitch.

There is a hidden clue that is associated with all three of the arks, and this one has to do with sound. In Joshua 6:4 it says, "**And seven priests shall bear before the ark seven trumpets of rams' horns: and the seventh day ye shall compass the city seven times, and the priests shall blow with the trumpets.**" The obvious clue is that the sound of the trumpets and the Ark of the Covenant is what brought down the walls of Jericho. This is also where I found the clue to rotate the compass six and seven times to find the 36 tones. The hidden clue with the other two arks is just a matter of realizing the specific wording that describes them both, as both of the arks were made with pitch. In Genesis 6:14 it says, "*Make thee an ark of gopher wood; rooms shalt thou make in the ark, and shalt **pitch** it within and without with **pitch***". If we read this verse from a strictly literal point of view, then pitch is a resin that was used to make the ark water tight, which means pitch is a sealant. In the description for the ark of bulrushes we can see that it was made from pitch also. In Exodus 2:3 this verse says, "*And when she could no longer hide him, she took for him an ark of bulrushes, and daubed it with slime and with **pitch**, and put the child therein; and she laid it in the flags by the river's brink.*" Okay, so we can see that both arks were made with a resinous pitch, but remember homonyms are abundant in the King James Version of the Bible, so we have to check all definitions for the word to get another clue that connects us to sound. In Webster's dictionary one of the definitions of pitch says "*the property of a sound and especially a musical tone that is determined by the frequency of the waves producing it: highness or lowness of sound.*" and another definition says "*a standard frequency for tuning instruments.*"

The same hint is recorded within the Sumerian story of the flood, which is found in the eleventh tablet of the Epic of Gilgamesh. In this story of the ark it says, "*Just as dawn began to glow the land assembled around me- the carpenter carried his hatchet, the reed worker carried his (flattening) stone ... the men ... The child carried the **pitch**, the weak brought whatever else was needed.*" In another part of the story, it says that they put "*three times 3,600 (units of) pitch ...into it,*" so we know that pitch was used in the building of this ark as well. The flood and ark story in the Epic of Gilgamesh is an older account of the story than the Bible. One of the differences in this flood story is that Utnapishtim's ark was cube shaped and does not form a normal boat shape as we would suspect. I wrote about this in my online book called *Cube It* which you can find online if you look up the name of my book and my name on Google. Tim Lovett showed on his website where he compared Noah's ark with Utnapishtim's ark to show the difference in the geometrical shape of both the arks. He found that the Utnapishtim's ark was in the shape of a cube which was in contrast to Noah's ark that was in the shape of a rectangular ship. We commonly think of a ship as being in a long rectangular shape with a triangular shape in the front of the ship, so it is quite surprising to think about a cube shaped ship. Could this cube shaped ship refer to something else? The Holy of Holies was also in a cube shape and so is the futuristic city of New Jerusalem, so we have another parallel to connect Utnapishtim's ark to the Holy of Holies in the tabernacle and the Temple as well as a possible prophecy for New Jerusalem.

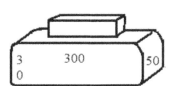

Utnapishtim's Ark

(Epic of Gilgamesh- Tablet 11)

120 L x 120 W x 120 H cubits

"its walls were each 10 times 12 cubits in height, the sides of its top were of equal length, 10 times. It cubits each."

Noah's Ark

(Bible- Genesis 6:15)

300 L x 50 W x 30 H cubits

"The length of the ark shall be three hundred cubits, the breadth of it fifty cubits, and the height of it thirty cubits."

Figure 133

We can clearly see that the oldest story of the flood and ark shows a different blueprint for this ship. The older story is describing a cube made with pitch, which would clearly fit into the blueprint for the Solfeggio tones, as both are made with a pitch and both forms a cube. The other interesting detail of the Sumerian story of the ark is that it says that they put *"three times 3,600 (units of) pitch ...into it."* This number is directly associated with the rotation of the compass, as it is found in the tenth rotation of the degree circle. This clue tells us that the ark was made with three times 3,600 units of pitch, which would be the 30th rotation of the degree circle.

$$3,600 \times 3 = 10800$$

$$10800/360 = 30$$

Utnapishtim's cube ark seems to be describing a ship of a different kind because we do not have sea ships that are cube shaped. Sea ships are always rectangular, and I'm not even sure if a cube shaped ship would even work. It is my feeling that Utnapishtim's cube shaped ark would fit more in line with the Merkaba or light chariot of God, as the star tetrahedron shape of the Merkaba fits completely into a cube. If this is the case and the older ark story is showing the blueprint for the Merkaba, then this ship could perhaps be created with these tones. As we have seen in the geometrical blueprints that are encoded within the tones, we are being shown a cube and Star of David pattern over and over again in many diverse ways, and these are all the shapes that are associated with the mythical Merkaba legends of the Jews. The Book of Ezekiel describes the light chariot of God as containing wheels within wheels, which is also associated with the Solfeggio tones and the Song of Degrees. We know that rotating the compass and degree circle is very similar to rotating a wheel in that we keep going around in circles to rotate the numbers of the degree circle. The ark that is described in the eleventh tablet of the Epic of Gilgamesh could very well be a blueprint for the Solfeggio tones, since these tones encode the cube. The counter rotation patterns within the Solfeggio cube also seems to fit the mythical wheels within wheels of Ezekiel's ship or chariot as well as the counter rotation fields of light that is associated with the Merkaba. We can think of the pitch that was used to make this ark as describing the musical scale ascending into higher and higher frequencies with these tones.

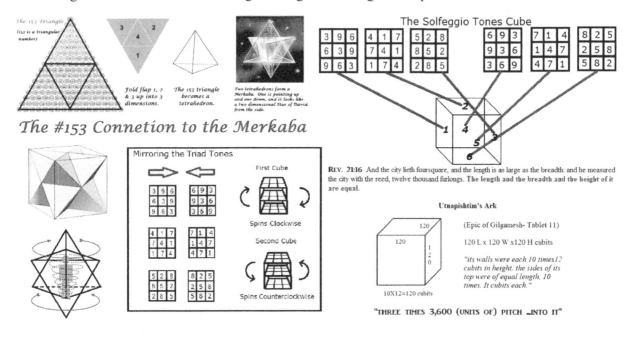

Figure 134

It is obvious that after the 144,000 sing the new song in Revelation 14:3 that the harvest is able to commence in verse 15. I believe that it is the new song that forms the transportation for the church or bride to ascend into heaven. In Revelation 14:15 it says, "And another angel came out of the temple, crying with a loud voice to him that sat on the cloud, Thrust in thy sickle, and reap: for the time is come for thee to reap; for the harvest of the earth is ripe." I would suggest that it is the new song of the 144,000 that precedes the harvest which helps to lift the people up in their vibration rate, so that they may ascend into heaven. Therefore, the cube symbolism that is encoded into these tones is showing us that the new song makes the light chariot of God or

Merkaba for transportation of the church or bride to ascend into heaven. It is then the bride being transported in the cube shaped New Jerusalem from heaven back down to the new earth that is described in Revelation 21. In Revelation 21:2 it says, "**And I John saw the holy city, new Jerusalem, coming down from God out of heaven, prepared as a bride adorned for her husband.**" New Jerusalem is a cube shaped ship that is coming down from heaven and landing onto the new earth, so this describes the light chariot of God or the Merkaba.

REV. 21:2 AND I JOHN SAW THE HOLY CITY, NEW JERUSALEM, COMING DOWN FROM GOD OUT OF HEAVEN, PREPARED AS A BRIDE ADORNED FOR HER HUSBAND.

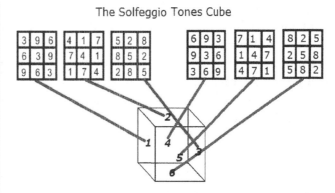

REV. 21:16 AND THE CITY LIETH FOURSQUARE, AND THE LENGTH IS AS LARGE AS THE BREADTH: AND HE MEASURED THE CITY WITH THE REED, TWELVE THOUSAND FURLONGS. THE LENGTH AND THE BREADTH AND THE HEIGHT OF IT ARE EQUAL. (CUBE)

Figure 135

All four arks are associated with sound, but only if we look at these four stories from a symbolic and scientific perspective, then we can find a commonality in the four arks. The math of the tones has been the easiest part of understanding the tones, but I must confess that because I do not know much about music, I have found it harder to understand these musical clues in the Bible. Just recently I was watching a documentary called *The Code* by mathematician Marcus du Sautoy and was astonished to discover a pattern within music that I had never heard before. Mr. Sautoy showed two notes on an oscilloscope with one note at a higher pitch than the other note. He showed that there were twice as many peaks on the sine wave of the higher pitch than the lower pitch, and so therefore, stated that going from one octave to a higher octave shows a pattern of a 1:2 ratio. Using this scale, we can demonstrate the same clue that was shown to us in Numbers 7:7-8 which was found just before the encoded tones verses. If we play each note or tone on a scale where each subsequent note is an octave above the next one, then we will see the same pattern of doubling which is also a main component in counting with binary code. I do not know if these clues of octaves apply to the Solfeggio tones or not, but it is something to keep in mind when studying the tones.

In the book *Healing Codes for the Biological Apocalypse*, it is revealed that these tones may have been associated with the ancient Solfeggio scale or solfège which consisted of six musical notes. This is why these tones are now called the Solfeggio tones. Mr. Puleo mentions a book that he read about the ancient Gregorian chants which was written by Professor Emeritius Willi Apel. In this book, the professor argued that the chants being used today are totally incorrect and undermined the true spirit of the Catholic faith, and also that there were one hundred and fifty two chants that had been lost by the Catholic Church.

Professor Apel wrote, "The origin of the ancient Solfeggio scale can be traced back to a medieval hymn to John the Baptist. The hymn has this peculiarity that the first six lines of the music commenced respectively on the first six successive notes of the scale, and thus the first syllable of each line was sung to a note *one degree higher* than the first syllable of the line that preceded it."

In music, a *scale degree* is the name given to a particular note of a scale, which will specify its position relative to the tonic or main note of the scale. A tonic is the first degree from the scale from which each octave is supposed to begin. Therefore, here we have a different meaning for the Song of Degrees, that does not have to do with the 360 degrees of a circle, which is where we can find the 3, 6 & 9 tones. There is another definition that seems more appropriate when dealing with the musical scale degrees of these tones. The *expression scale step* is sometimes used as a synonym for the scale degree and it may also refer to the distance or interval between two successive scale degrees. In this scale the number of the scale degrees and the distance between them together define a scale. In music theory, a *step* or conjunct motion is defined as the difference in pitch between two consecutive notes of a musical scale, which is the interval between two consecutive scale degrees. The larger intervals are actually called a *skip* or leap. Amazingly, this is what I have done with these tones, when I found the skip rate or the difference between the tones; so therefore, this definition of the scale degree seems to match the definition of the skip rate within the tones.

The original Solfeggio scale was invented by a Benedictine monk named Guido d'Arezzo. The original scale was six ascending notes that were assigned to Ut-Re-Mi-Fa-Sol-La, however, today the Solfeggio scale has seven ascending notes known as Do-Re-Mi-Fa-So-La-Ti. The original six note scales were taken from a hymn to St. John the Baptist, which is called *Ut Queant Laxis* and was written by Paulus Diaconus.

Here is an excerpt from the book *Gregorian Chant* by Willi Apel:

"By degrees these syllables became associated and identified with their respective notes and as each syllable ended in a vowel, they were found to be peculiarly adapted for vocal use. Hence "Ut" was artificially replaced by "Do." Guido of Arezzo was the first to adopt them in the 11th century, and Le Marie, a French musician of the 17th century added "Si" for the seventh note of the scale, in order to complete the series."

"Thus nature and grace illustrate each other, and reveal the great fact that there is a secret ear, more delicate than any "organs of Corti," that can detect sounds invisible as well as inaudible to the senses, and which enables those who possess it to say:

"Sweeter sounds than music knows,

Charm me in Emanuel's name;

All her hopes my spirit owes,

To his birth, and cross, and shame,"

It's obvious to me that the secret ear is referring to the six binaural beats that are found within the twelve tones of the first eighteen tones. Somehow the ancients knew about these secret sounds that are invisible and inaudible, until the brain creates them when listening to the tones in the left and right ears from the tones that are paired or yoked together.

Scale Degree or Expression Scale Step

Triad Tones in Left and Right Channels
Six Tone Groups

Six Binaural Beats

The First Eighteen Tones	
Left Speaker	Right Speaker
174	147
------111	------111
285	258
------111	------111
396	369
------21	------102
417	471
------111	------111
528	582
------111	------111
639	693
------102	------21
741	714
------111	------111
852	825
------111	------111
963	936
------210	------210

174	147
----243	----324
417	471
----324	----243
741	714

285	258
----243	----324
528	582
----324	----243
852	825

396	369
----243	----324
639	693
----324	----243
963	936

174-147= 27	27 Hz
285-258= 27	27 Hz
396-369= 27	27 Hz
471-417= 54	
582-528= 54	
693-639= 54	
741-714= 27	27 Hz
852-825= 27	27 Hz
963-936= 27	27 Hz

Figure 136

In the book *Healing Codes for the Biological Apocalypse,* there is an exercise to do involving Psalms 120-134, which has fifteen chapters in the Song of Degrees. In certain versions of the Bible such as the Authorized King James Version and the Wycliffe Bible, there is a noticeable pattern within the Song of Degrees' chapters. Some chapters say the Song of Degrees, others say the Song of Degrees of David, and one says the Song of Degrees of Solomon.

In this next exercise, underline the title of each chapter in the Song of Degrees to find the pattern. I am going to use the Wycliffe version of the Bible for this exercise, since Wycliffe was my 20th Great Grandfather. Pay close attention to the positions of the name changes to better understand the underlying pattern that is being presented.

Psalm 120-134 Wycliffe Bible (WYC)

120 *The song of degrees.* When I was set in tribulation, I cried to the Lord; and he heard me. (When I was beset with troubles, I cried to the Lord; and he answered me.)

² Lord, deliver thou my soul from wicked lips; and from a guileful tongue. (Lord, save thou me from wicked lips; and from a deceitful tongue.)

³ What shall be given to thee, either what shall be laid to thee; to a guileful tongue? (What shall be given to thee; that is, how shall he punish thee, O deceitful tongue?)

⁴ Sharp arrows of the mighty; with coals that make desolate. (With sharp arrows from the mighty; and with coals that shall make thee desolate.)

⁵ Alas to me! for my dwelling in an alien land is made long, I dwelled with men dwelling in Kedar; (Alas for me! for my stay here in Mesech is prolonged, and I must live among the people,

or in the tents, of Kedar!)

⁶ my soul was much (time) a comeling. I was peaceable with them that hated peace; (I am here too long as a newcomer, *or a stranger*; yea, too long living with those who hate peace.)

⁷ when I spake to them, they impugned, *either against-said*, me without cause. (I am for peace; but whenever I speak of it to them, they be for war.)

121 *The song of degrees.* I raised mine eyes to the hills; from whence help shall come to me. (I raised up my eyes to the hills, *or the mountains*; O where shall I find help?/from where help shall come to me.)

² Mine help *is* of the Lord; that made heaven and earth. (My help *is* from the Lord; who made heaven and earth.)

³ *The Lord* give not thy foot into moving; neither he nap, that keepeth thee. (*The Lord* shall not let thy foot slip, *or stumble*; nor shall he nap, who keepeth thee safe.)

⁴ Lo! he shall not nap, neither sleep; that keepeth Israel. (Lo! he, who keepeth Israel safe; shall not nap, or sleep.)

⁵ The Lord keepeth thee; the Lord is thy protection above thy right hand. (The Lord keepeth thee safe; the Lord is thy protection at thy right hand.)

⁶ The sun shall not burn thee by day; neither the moon by night.

⁷ The Lord keep thee from all evil; the Lord keep thy soul. (The Lord shall keep thee safe from all evil; yea, the Lord shall keep thee safe.)

⁸ The Lord keep thy going in and thy going out; from this time now and into the world. (The Lord shall guard thy coming in, and thy going out; from this time now, and forever.)

122 *The song of degrees of David.* I am glad in these things, that be said to me; We shall go into the house of the Lord. (*The song of degrees for David.* I was glad, when they said to me, We shall go to the House of the Lord.)

² Our feet were standing; in thy halls/in thy foreyards, thou Jerusalem. (And now our feet stand within thy gates, O Jerusalem.)

³ Jerusalem, which is builded as a city; whose partaking thereof is into the same thing. (Jerusalem

is built to be a city, where people be together, *yea, with one heart and mind*.)

⁴ For the lineages, the lineages of the Lord, ascended thither, the witnessing of Israel; to acknowledge to the name of the Lord. (For the tribes, the Lord's tribes, come there to give thanks to the Lord; that is Israel's duty.)

⁵ For they sat there on seats in doom; seats on the house of David. (For the thrones of judgement, *or of justice*, be put there; yea, the thrones of the house of David.)

⁶ Pray ye those things, that be to the peace of Jerusalem; and abundance be to them that love thee. (Pray ye for the peace of Jerusalem; *and say*, May those who love thee prosper, *or have great abundance*.)

⁷ Peace be made in thy strength; and abundance in thy towers. (May there be peace within thy strongholds, *or thy fortresses*; and prosperity within thy palaces.)

⁸ For my brethren and my neighbours; I spake peace of thee. (For the sake of my brothers, *or my kinsmen*, and my neighbours; I say, Peace be with thee.)

⁹ For the house of our Lord God; I sought goods to thee. (For the sake of the House of the Lord our God; I shall seek thy good, *or thy prosperity*/I shall pray for good things for thee.)

123 *The song of degrees.* To thee I have raised mine eyes; that dwellest in heavens. (I raise up my eyes to thee; who livest in heaven.)

² Lo! as the eyes of servants *be* in the hands of their lords. As the eyes of the handmaid *be* in the hands of her lady; so our eyes *be* to our Lord God, till he have mercy on us. (Lo! like the eyes of the servant *look* to the hand of his lord; and like the eyes of the servantess *look* to the hand of her lady; so let our eyes *look* to the Lord our God, until he have mercy upon us.)

³ Lord, have thou mercy on us, have thou mercy on us; for we be much filled with despising (for we be greatly despised).

⁴ For our soul is much filled; *we be* shame to them that be abundant *with riches*, and despising to proud men. (For our soul is filled full, with the scorn of those who have abundant *riches*; and

with disdain from the proud.)

124 *The song of degrees of David.* Israel say now, No but for the Lord was in us; (*The song of degrees for David*. Let Israel say now, If the Lord was not with us/If the Lord had not been for us,)

² no but for the Lord was in us. When men rose up against us; (yea, if the Lord was not with us/if the Lord had not been for us; then when men rose up against us,)

³ in hap they had swallowed us quick. When the strong vengeance of them was wroth against us;

(they would have swallowed us up alive. Yea, when their fury raged against us;)

⁴ in hap water had swallowed us up. Our soul passed through a strand; (the water would have swallowed us up. When the stream had gone up over our heads;)

⁵ in hap our soul had passed through a water unsufferable. (when the insufferable waters had

gone up over our heads.)

⁶ Blessed be the Lord; that gave not us into taking, [(*or*) the catching,] of the teeth of them. (Blessed be the Lord; who did not allow us to be caught by their teeth.)

⁷ Our soul, as a sparrow, is delivered; from the snare of hunters. The snare is all-broken; and we be delivered. (We have escaped, like a sparrow, from the hunter's snare. The snare is all-broken; and we be set free.)

⁸ Our help *is* in the name of the Lord; that made heaven and earth (who made heaven and earth).

125 *The song of degrees.* They that trust in the Lord *be* as the hill of Zion; he shall not be moved [into] without end, that dwelleth in Jerusalem. (They who trust in the Lord *be* like Mount Zion; it cannot be shaken, but it remaineth firm, *or steadfast*, forever.)

² Hills *be* in the compass of it, and the Lord *is* in the compass of his people; from this time now, and into the world. (Like the mountains, *or the hills*, *be* all around Jerusalem, so the Lord *is* all around his people; from this time now, and forever.)

³ For the Lord shall not leave the rod of sinners on the part of just men; that just men hold not forth their hands to wickedness. (For the rod of the sinners shall not remain over the land of the righteous; lest the righteous put forth their hands to wickedness.)

⁴ Lord, do thou well to good men; and to rightful in heart. (Lord, do thou good to good people; yea, to those with an upright heart.)

⁵ But the Lord shall lead them that bow into obligations, with them that work wickedness; peace *be* upon Israel. (But may the Lord lead forth those, who turn aside into depraved ways, with those who do evil. May peace *be* upon Israel.)

126 *The song of degrees.* When the Lord turned the captivity of Zion; we were made as comforted. (When the Lord returned the captives to Zion/When the Lord returned prosperity to Zion; we were made like in a dream.)

² Then our mouth was filled with joy; and our tongue with full out joying. Then they shall say among heathen men; The Lord magnified to do with them. (Then our mouths were filled with joy; and ours tongues with rejoicing. And the heathen said to each other, The Lord hath done great things for them.)

³ The Lord magnified to do with us; we be made glad. (Yea, the Lord did great things for us; and we were glad.)

⁴ Lord, turn thou (again) our captivity; as a strand in the south. (Lord, return thou the captives/return thou our prosperity; like the streams return to the south.)

⁵ They that sow in tears; shall reap in full out joying. (Then they who sowed in tears; shall reap with rejoicing.)

⁶ They going, went, and wept; sending their seeds. But they coming, shall come with full out joying; bearing their handfuls (They going, went, and wept; sending out their seeds. But when they shall return, they shall come back rejoicing; carrying their harvest.)

127 *The song of degrees of Solomon.* No but the Lord build the house; they that built it have travailed in vain. No but the Lord keepeth the city; he waketh in vain that keepeth it./But if the Lord build the house; they that built it have travailed in vain. But (if) the Lord keepeth the city; he waketh in vain that keepeth it. (*The song of degrees for Solomon.* Unless the Lord build the house; those who have built it, have laboured in vain. Unless the Lord guardeth the city; he who standeth watch, guardeth in vain.)

² It is vain to you to rise before the light; rise ye after ye have set, that eat the bread of sorrow. When he shall give sleep to his loved; (It is useless for you to rise before the light; and then to stay up late, only so that ye can eat the bread of sorrows. For he giveth to his beloved; even while they sleep.)

³ lo! the heritage of the Lord *is* sons, the meed *is* the fruit of womb. (Lo! sons and daughters *be* thy inheritance/*be* thy gift from the Lord; yea, the fruit of thy womb *is* his reward to you.)

⁴ As arrows *be* in the hand of the mighty; so the sons of them that be shaken out. (Like arrows *be* in the hand of the mighty; so be the sons and daughters that a man hath when he is young.)

⁵ Blessed *is* the man, that hath [full-]filled his desire of those; he shall not be shamed, when he shall speak to his enemies in the gate. (Happy *is* the man who hath filled his quiver full of them; he shall not be put to shame, *or defeated*, when he shall speak to his enemies in court.)

128 *The song of degrees.* Blessed *be* all men, that dread the Lord; that go in his ways. (Happy *be* all those, who fear the Lord/who revere the Lord; and who go in his ways.)

² For thou shalt eat the travails of thine hands; thou art blessed, and it shall be well to thee. (For thou shalt eat the fruit of thy labour; thou shalt be happy, and it shall be well with thee.)

³ Thy wife *shall be* as a plenteous vine; in the sides of thine house. Thy sons as the new springs of olive trees; in the compass of thy board. (Thy wife *shall be* like a fruitful vine; by the side of thy house. And thy sons and thy daughters shall *be* like the new branches of olive trees; all around thy table.)

⁴ Lo! so a man shall be blessed; that dreadeth the Lord. (Lo! so shall the man be blessed; who feareth the Lord/who hath reverence for the Lord.)

⁵ The Lord bless thee from Zion; and see thou the goods of Jerusalem in all the days of thy life. (May the Lord bless thee from Zion; and may thou see the prosperity of Jerusalem/and may thou share in the prosperity of Jerusalem, all the days of thy life.)

⁶ And see thou the sons of thy sons; *see thou* peace on Israel. (And may thou see the sons of thy sons/the children of thy children. May peace *be* upon Israel.)

129 *The song of degrees.* Israel say now; Oft they have fought against me from my youth. (Let Israel say now; they have often fought against me from my youth.)

² Oft they [have] fought against me from my youth; and soothly they might not to me (Yea, they have often fought against me from my youth; but truly they could never overcome me.)

³ Sinners forged on my back; they made long their wickedness. (The sinners scourged my back; they made their furrows deep and long in me.)

⁴ The Lord is just, (he) shall beat (together) the nolls of sinners; (But the Lord is just, and he shall free me from the bonds of the wicked;)

⁵ all that hate Zion be they shamed, and turned aback. (let all who hate Zion be put to shame, and be turned, *or driven*, back.)

⁶ Be they made as the hay of housetops; that dried up, before that it be drawn up. (Be they made like the grass on the rooftops; it dried up, before that it could be pulled up.)

⁷ Of which hay he that shall reap, shall not fill his hand; and he that shall gather handfuls, *shall not fill* his bosom. (Of which grass he who shall reap, shall not get a handful; and he who shall gather handfuls, *shall not get* an armful.)

⁸ And they that passed forth said not, The blessing of the Lord *be* on you; we blessed you in the name of the Lord. (And so they who pass by, shall never say, The blessing of the Lord *be* upon you; we bless you in the name of the Lord.)

130 *The song of degrees.* Lord, I cried to thee from the depths;

² Lord, hear thou my voice. Thine ears be made attentive into the voice of my beseeching (Let thy ears be made attentive to the words of my plea).

³ Lord, if thou keepest wickednesses; Lord, who shall sustain, *or abide*? (Lord, if thou keepest a record of our wickednesses; then Lord, who shall survive?/then Lord, who will not be condemned?)

⁴ For mercy is at thee; (But there is mercy with thee, and I stand in awe of thee;)

⁵ and, Lord, for thy law I abode thee. My soul sustained in his word; (yea, Lord, I wait for thee. My soul is sustained, and I hope, and I trust, in his word.)

⁶ my soul hoped in the Lord. From the morrowtide keeping till to the night; (My soul waiteth for the Lord, more eagerly than those who wait for the morning light; yea, *more eagerly* than those who stand guard, *or be on watch*, until the morning light.)

⁷ Israel hope in the Lord. For why mercy *is* at the Lord; and plenteous redemption *is* at him. (Israel, trust in the Lord. For there *is* always love with the Lord; and there *is* plentiful redemption with him.)

⁸ And he shall again-buy Israel; from all the wickednesses thereof. (And he shall redeem the people of Israel; from all their wickednesses.)

131 *The song of degrees to David.* Lord, mine heart is not enhanced; neither mine eyes be raised. Neither I went in great things; neither in marvels above me. (*The song of degrees for David.* Lord, my heart is not exalted, *or puffed up*; nor be my eyes raised up. And I do not concern myself with great things; nor with marvellous things that be so high above me.)

² If I feeled not meekly; but [I] enhanced my soul. As a child weaned on his mother; so yielding *be* in my soul. (I went forth humbly; and I did not exalt my soul. Like a weaned child upon his mother; so *is* the yielding in my soul.)

³ Israel, hope in the Lord; from this time now and into the world. (Israel, trust in the Lord; from this time now and forever.)

132 *The song of degrees.* Lord, have thou mind on David; and of all his mildness. (Lord, remember David; and all his troubles and tribulations.)

² As he swore to the Lord; he made a vow to [the] God of Jacob.

³ I shall not enter into the tabernacle of mine house; I shall not ascend into the bed of my resting.

⁴ I shall not give sleep to mine eyes; and napping to mine eyelids. (I shall not give sleep to my eyes; or napping to my eyelids.)

⁵ And rest to my temples, till I find a place to the Lord; a tabernacle to [the] God of Jacob. (Until I find a place for the Lord; yea, a dwelling place for the Mighty God of Jacob.)

⁶ Lo! we heard that (the) *ark of (the) testament* (is) in Ephratah [Lo! we have heard (of) it in Ephratah]; we found it in the fields of the wood. (Lo! we have heard that the Covenant Box is in Ephratah; we found it in the fields of Jaar, *or of Jearim*.)

⁷ We shall enter into the tabernacle of him (We shall go into his Tabernacle, *or his dwelling place*); we shall worship in the place, where his feet stood.

⁸ Lord, rise thou into thy rest; thou, and the ark of thine hallowing. (Arise, O Lord, and come back to thy resting place; thou, and the Ark of thy power.)

⁹ Thy priests be clothed with rightfulness; and thy saints make full out joy. (Let thy priests be clothed in righteousness; and thy saints rejoice.)

¹⁰ For David, thy servant; turn thou not away the face of thy christ. (For the sake of thy servant David; turn thou not away thy face from thy anointed *king*.)

¹¹ The Lord swore (in) truth to David, and he shall not make him [in] vain; Of the fruit of thy womb I shall set on thy seat. (The Lord swore truthfully to David, and he did not say in vain, I shall put the fruit of thy womb upon thy throne.)

¹² If thy sons shall keep my testament; and my witnessings, these which I shall teach them. And the sons of them till into the world; they shall set on thy seat. (And if thy sons shall keep my covenant, and obey my teachings, which I shall teach them; then their sons shall sit on thy throne forever.)

¹³ For the Lord chose Zion; he chose it into (a) dwelling to himself (he chose it for his dwelling place).

¹⁴ This is my rest into the world of world (This shall be my resting place forever and ever); I shall dwell here, for I chose it.

¹⁵ I blessing shall bless the widow of it; I shall [ful]fill with loaves the poor men of it. (I blessing shall bless *Zion's* widows; and I shall fulfill her poor with bread.)

¹⁶ I shall clothe with health the priests thereof; and the holy men thereof shall make full out joy in full out joying/in full out rejoicing. (I shall clothe her priests with salvation, *or with deliverance*; and her holy men shall make great joy rejoicing.)

¹⁷ Thither I shall bring forth the horn of David; I [have] made ready a lantern to my christ (I have prepared a lantern for my anointed *king*).

¹⁸ I shall clothe his enemies with shame; but mine hallowing shall flower out on him (but a shining crown shall be upon his head).

133 *The song of degrees.* Lo! how good and how merry *it is*; that brethren dwell together. (Lo! how good and how pleasant *it is*; for brothers, *or God's people*, to live together *in unity, or in harmony*.)

² As ointment in the head; that goeth down into the beard, into the beard of Aaron. That goeth down into the collar of his cloth; (Like ointment on the head, that goeth down onto the beard, onto Aaron's beard; yea, that goeth down onto the collar of his cloak.)

³ as the dew of Hermon, that goeth down into the hill of Zion. For there the Lord sent blessing; and life till into the world, *that is, without end.* (Like the dew of Mount Hermon, that goeth down onto the hills of Zion. For there the Lord sent blessing; and life forevermore.)

134 *The song of degrees.* Lo! now bless ye the Lord; all the servants of the Lord. Ye that stand in the house of the Lord; in the halls/in the foreyards of the house of our God (Ye who stand in the House of the Lord; night after night).

² In nights raise your hands into holy things; and bless ye the Lord. (Raise up your hands in the holy place; and bless ye the Lord.)

³ The Lord bless thee from Zion; the which *Lord* made heaven and earth. (May the Lord bless thee from Zion; the *Lord* who made heaven and earth.)

The Song of Degrees in Psalms 120-134 makes a specific pattern that seems to highlight the triad pattern within the first eighteen tones, as well as the six note scale of the Solfeggio tones. In the book *Healing Codes for the Biological Apocalypse*, Horowitz calls the Song of Degrees of Solomon a stanza break in the poem, but it could also represent a rest period or pause in the song.

Here is the list.

120 *The song of degrees.*

121 *The song of degrees.*

122 *The song of degrees of David.*

123 *The song of degrees.*

124 *The song of degrees of David.*

125 *The song of degrees.*

126 *The song of degrees.*

127 *The song of degrees of Solomon.*

128 *The song of degrees.*

129 *The song of degrees.*

130 *The song of degrees.*

131 *The song of degrees to David.*

132 *The song of degrees.*

133 *The song of degrees.*

134 *The song of degrees.*

There is a difference between the King James Version and the Wycliffe version of the Bible. In the KJV there are two Song of Degrees of David before and after the stanza break with the song of degrees of Solomon. Horowitz says that if we subtract one of the repetitious Song of Degrees of David from both the top and the bottom, then we have six degrees above and six degrees below the stanza. This matches the six musical notes of the Solfeggio scale.

The Wycliffe version is different in that it only has three Song of degrees of David, and two are above and one is below; however, it also demonstrates the exact same thing as the KJV but in a different way. You can see the pattern from my graphic below:

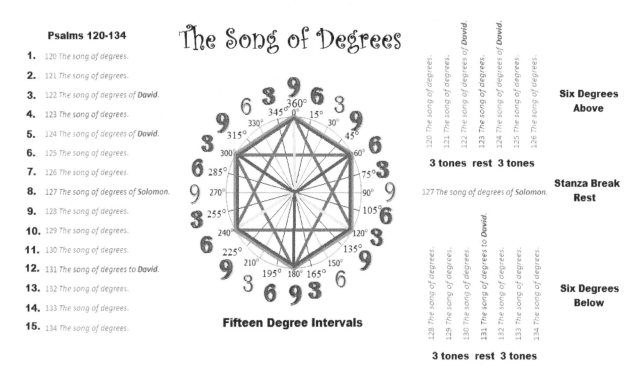

Figure 137

The degrees of the tones appear to be separated at three tone intervals as well as separated at six degrees above and below the stanza. This appears to be encoding the triad tones and the three sides of the triangle associated with the triad tones. In chapters 120 through 126, the two songs of degrees of David are outlining the middle stanza in chapter 123 and in chapters 128 through 134 the song of Degrees to David is the middle stanza break in chapter 131. Chapters 123, 127 and 131 appear to be rests or pauses in between the tones, so therefore, it seems to be a musical pattern similar to "123, 123, 123 and123" type of a beat within the tones. Chapter 123 is the first stanza break in the pattern of the song, and it also seems to be hinting around at the rhythm or beat to the song. This divides it into four sections, which could be demonstrating the beats or beasts around the throne of God, if we consider that beast could be an anagram for beats. The four sections of three within the Wycliffe pattern are mimicking the four beasts with six wings around the throne of God, which are the four Star of David patterns found within the Song of

Degrees. These beats of the three tones and the pauses in between them shows the possible rhythm or tempo of the song.

In terms of music, the beat is the basic unit that measures off the time or the regular pulse of the music. Music is organized into measures recognized by an accented downbeat such as 123, 123… or 1234, 1234…, so the Wycliffe clue could be showing us that the song has three beats per measure which is ¾ time. This is known as a triple meter and is often counted as 123. It is interesting that Chapter 123 is the first rest or stanza break in the Song of Degrees because the number of the chapter also seems to be hinting around about the beat of the song being counted as 123. The three beats per measure would fit the pattern within the tones of threes, but it also could be symbolic of the trinity as well.

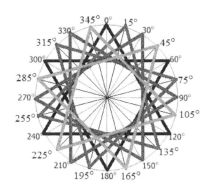

THE 24 POINTS ON A DEGREE CIRCLE

Rev. 4:8 And the four beasts had each of them six wings about him; and they were full of eyes within: and they rest not day and night, saying, Holy, holy, holy, Lord God Almighty, which was, and is, and is to come.

There are 4 Star of David's or beast used in this graphic, and each of the vertices is one of the 24 points or elders in the degree circle. Each Star of David contains 6 vertices or wings. The word Holy comes out to 60 in English gematria, and the Star of David is made up of 60 degree angles.

Could beast be an angram for beats?

In music and music theory, the **beat** is the basic unit of time, the pulse of the *mensural level*[1] (or *beat level*).[2] In popular use, the beat can refer to a variety of related concepts including: tempo, meter, rhythm and groove.

http://en.wikipedia.org/wiki/Beat_(music)

Could wings be an anagram for swing?

In music terms, the word "swing" refers to a bouncing groove that can be created in the rhythm of music.

http://blog.dubspot.com/swing-creative-use-of-groove-quantization/

Figure 138

The trinity beat within the tones are actually three beats as one, and the positive, negative and neutral theme that I found throughout the 3, 6 and 9 pattern of the tones is denoting the electrical qualities of the Seraphim Angels or fiery serpents that are singing Holy, Holy, Holy around the throne of God. This is an electrical beat for the elect of God. The 1, 4 and 7 tones represent the Son of God, and all of those tones are neutral, whereas the 2, 5 and 8 tones represent the Father, and the 3, 6 and 9 tones represent the feminine Holy Spirit or Mother. The tones representing the Father in the trinity are positive and the tones representing the Holy Spirit are negative. Each beat of 123 in the scale is literally representing the trinity, but the neutral beats representing the Son of God that is Jesus Christ is also representing the Bride of Christ as well, so therefore, the Son represents masculine and feminine qualities together as one. The a-tone-ment of Christ is all about the at-one-ment. In the music of the tones, the three beats represent one beat as a segment, so in other words, three are one.

There is a clue to an ancient music scale within the skip rate for the triad tones of the Solfeggio tones. Archeologists have found instruments at ancient archeological sites that were tuned to the 432 Hz scale in Egypt and Greece. The 432 skip rate is found within the triad tones with the 243 and the 324 pattern, which makes the 12 tone pattern to continue the tones beyond the first 18 triad tones. I have read that 432 Hz is in the range of the color purple, which is also the color associated with royalty.

In this next exercise, divide 432 with the number 3 to find a very important number from the Bible.

$$432/3=\underline{\quad\quad}$$

The next graphic shows the 432 skip rate within the triad tones which is made from the wraparound pattern of the number 324 in the sequence. Notice that the triad skip rate pattern of the numbers 243, 324 and 432 also shows the same pattern within the tones skip rates of 81 and 108.

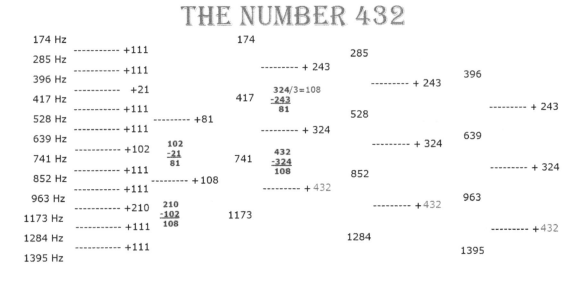

Figure 139

The number 432 is associated with the number 144 which is found in Revelation 21:17 in the Bible. The walls of New Jerusalem are measured in 144 cubits, and there are 12 walls altogether, so each 3 walls would total to the number 432. In other words 432 is a multiple of the number 144, and it also fits into the trinity pattern that we have seen associated with the triad tones. These patterns of threes are very significant to the tones, as all tones and skip rates are divisible by three. This pattern with the number 432 Hz shows us another connection to New Jerusalem and these tones from the Bible.

In Pythagorean tuning the frequency of 432 is the note A which would be the letter Alpha in Greek. Jesus says that he is the Alpha and the Omega or the beginning and the end, so this could also be a symbolic reference to Jesus as the Alpha. The pattern in Pythagorean tuning brings out many patterns within the tones and the Bible's clues, including some of the skip rates, the binary numbers of Numbers 7:7-8 and the numbers for the rotations of the compass or degree circle. Also, included in the tones is the number 144, which is the measurement of New Jerusalem's walls.

In the next graphic, the key of A has a pattern of 27, 54, 108, 216, 432, 864, 1728 and 3456, which has several of the skip rates. The first two in the scale are 27 and 54 which are the skip rates in the binaural beats of the tones. The number 108 is a skip rate in the tones, and 432 is a skip rate in the triad tones. The numbers 108 and 864 are multiples of the moon and sun's diameter, so we can see a connection between the measurements of the diameter of the moon and sun and the musical scale associated with Pythagorean tuning and the skip rates of the Solfeggio tones.

The key of C shows the same pattern of Numbers 7:7-8 with the binary numbers of doubling the numbers of oxen and wagons. This fits in within the binary number of 111 which is found in the skip rates of the tones. We can clearly see that the C notes are the same numbers that we use for our memory storage systems in computers.

Pythagorean Tuning

G	A	B	C	D	E	F#
24	27	30	32	36	40	45
48	54	60	64	72	80	90
96	108	120	128	144	160	180
192	216	240	256	288	320	360
384	432	480	512	576	640	720
768	864	960	1024	1152	1280	1440
1536	1728	1920	2048	2304	2560	2880
3072	3456	3840	4096	4608	5120	5760

Figure 140

The key of D shows the measurements for the walls of New Jerusalem and the key of A shows the actual measurements of the twelve walls or faces of the hypercube altogether. (144X12=1728) The key of F shows the rotations of the compass or degree circle, which is 360 degrees of one circle, 720 for two rotations, and 1440 for four rotations, 2880 for 8 rotations and 5760 for 16 rotations. Again, we can see the same binary pattern for Numbers7:7-8 in the rotation pattern of 1, 2, 4 and 8 rotations of the compass.

In the Pythagorean tuning chart, there is a definite pattern in the fractions with the numerator representing the Solfeggio tones skip rates and the denominator representing the binary counting numbers. These are both patterns presented to us in Numbers 7; so therefore, this scale shows an encoded musical scale that comes out of the math within these tones or numbers. Pythagorean tuning represents Numbers 7 beautifully; however, we must realize that this represents an ancient musical scale and not a new one. This encoded information probably does not represent the new song of the 144,000, but it does have information that is important to know with these numbers that are found in Numbers 7 of the Bible.

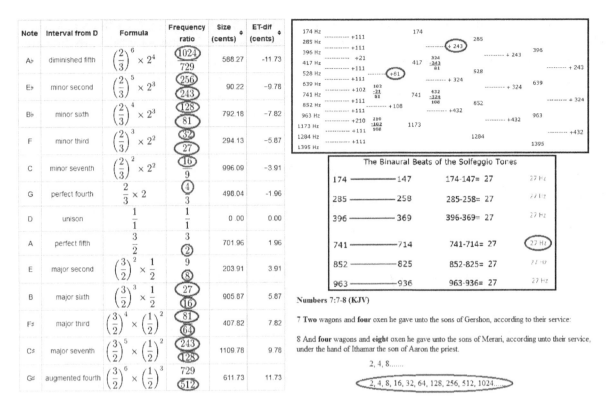

Figure 141

Another interesting connection with the number 432 is that it is a multiple of the sun and the moon. Keep in mind that the sun is an analogy of the Son and the moon is an analogy for the Church of Christ and the 144,000, as the moon reflects the light of the sun and Christ's followers are reflecting the light of the Son.

Try this exercise below to see the significance of the number 432.

Approximate Diameter of the Sun 864,000 miles

$$864,000/432=\_\_\_\_$$

Approximate Diameter of the Moon 2,160 miles

$$2160/432=\_\_$$

Again we can see that the sun and the moon are encoded into this celestial music of the Bible, and that there is special significance attached to the math within God's Creation. Everything in God's Creation has a specific blueprint, and the math of the degree circle encodes this Divine design. The number 432 multiplied by 2,000 is the mean diameter of the sun and the number 432 multiplied by 5 is the diameter of the moon. Jesus Christ tones for the atonement are literally the light of the universe because their skip rates are showing us a comparison to the sun and moon which give us light on the earth. The Son gives all of the Light to the entire Creation.

In this chapter, I have shown some musical clues that I have found in the Bible and beyond, and these clues may help the 144,000 to find the musical scale for the new song. The keys to the new song are encoded all throughout the Bible for people that have eyes to see and ears to hear. All that it takes to decode all of the clues to the song is given in simple math, and like I have written before, math does not lie. You can change the parables of the Bible and delete or add information, but the true core of the math encoded in the Bible will give the reader all that they need to know to find the truth. The math of the tones shows us beautiful blueprints that at the core are very simple to understand, but when we start to put the pieces of this puzzle together, we start to see the complexity of it all. The mathematical and geometrical patterns within the tones are amazing to me, and I am in awe of the Creator's design of our universe.

The Science of Sound

On July 8, 1680 Robert Hooke, who was a philosopher, architect and a polymath, observed the nodal patterns associated with vibration on glass plates. He ran a bow along the edge of a glass plate that was covered with flour, and he saw specific patterns that emerged from the sound or vibrations. A German physicist and musician named Ernst Chladni, who is often called the *father of acoustics*, repeated the experiments of Hooke. Chladni's technique consisted of drawing a bow over a piece of metal that was covered in sand, and his technique was first published in 1787 in his book *Discoveries in the Theory of Sound*. The patterns that were formed by these geometrical patterns in the sand are now called *Chladni figures*.

These earlier experiments with sound have modernly led to the science of cymatics, which studies the vibration patterns that emerge from playing certain frequencies. Cymatics is a Greek term which means "wave" to describe the acoustic effects of sound waves. The term was coined by Hans Jenny, who was a physician and natural scientist that studied the geometrical patterns that were made by sound waves in different mediums, such as fluids, powders and liquid paste. He concluded from his studies that "This is not an unregulated chaos; it is a dynamic but ordered pattern." In 1967, Jenny published his first volume of *Cymatics: The Study of Wave Phenomena*, and in 1972 he published his second volume which contained photographic documentation of the effects of sound vibrations. Jenny also made a tonoscope to show the patterns that are made from specific sounds or vibrations. The low tones on the tonoscope showed simple and clear shapes, and the higher tones formed more complex geometrical structures. There is a video on YouTube called *Cymatics - Bringing Matter to Life with Sound* that shows the geometrical shapes that are made from certain frequencies or tones that are played on a tonoscope. This video that was made by Hans Jenny in the 60's also shows shapes and patterns that are moving and changing as the frequencies increase to higher or lower pitches. I was astonished by the beautiful geometrical shapes that are formed from sound waves the first time I saw this video on YouTube. Jenny's work in recording the geometrical shapes that are made by sound into photos and videos shows how sound forms matter into very simple shapes or quite complex shapes as the frequencies increase to higher and higher pitches. This was the first time that scientific proof could be shown to support the Bible's verses that show that the creation of our universe could have most definitely been formed through sound or the Word of God.

Genesis 1 (KJV)

1 In the beginning God created the heaven and the earth.

² And the earth was without form, and void; and darkness was upon the face of the deep. And the Spirit of God moved upon the face of the waters.

³ And God said, Let there be light: and there was light.

The Bible tells us that there was a void before the creation and that the earth had no form until God spoke and said "Let there be light." In videos about cymatics, we can actually see form or shapes that suddenly appear out of nothing when certain frequencies start to play. In the science of cymatics, we can actually visually see how the creation of our universe started to take shape by the sounds of God's Words.

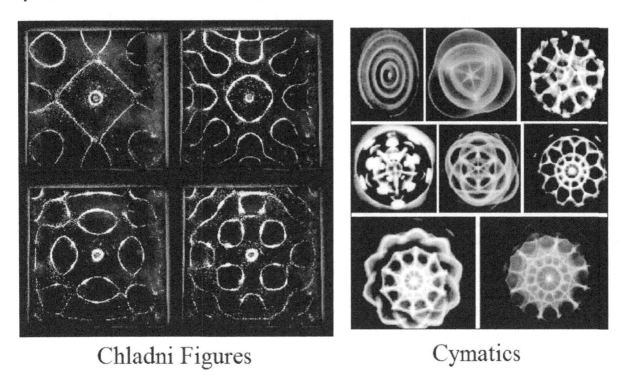

Chladni Figures   Cymatics

Figure 142

Jenny also found out that when the vowels of the ancient languages of Hebrew and Sanskrit were pronounced that the sand actually took the shape of those letters in Hebrew and Sanskrit. Somehow the ancient Hebrews and Indians must have known that the sound for these letters would form those shapes in different mediums. This shows that perhaps some ancient languages might have been used to show the connection between sounds and written languages. Are the languages of Hebrew and Sanskrit sacred languages based on the cymatics of sounds?

The ancient book called the *Sefer Yetzirah,* which means the *Book of Formation*, also attributes the Hebrew language as being a Holy language that was used in the formation or creation of our universe by God. The book was written most likely in the 2nd century AD according to Christopher P. Benton, who said that the grammatical form places its origin closer to the period of the Mishna, although according to tradition, this book was originally ascribed to the patriarch Abraham. What I find interesting about this book is that it puts a great emphasis on the sounds of the Hebrew letters themselves, and how these sounds formed the universe, so therefore, it is almost as if the writer or writers of this document were aware of the importance of sound in the formation of our universe. This ancient book actually supports the work of Hans Jenny in his discovery that the vowels of the Hebrew letters formed in the sand from the pronunciation of each letter. The modern science of Cymatics prove the Bible's verses that say the Word of God formed all of the Creation, and also that the Sefer Yetzirah's attempt to explain the importance of the sounds that are created from the pronunciation of the Hebrew letters.

Sefer Yetzirah CHAPTER II

1. The foundations are the twenty-two letters, three mothers, seven double, and twelve single letters. Three mothers, namely A, M, SH, these are Air, Water, and Fire: Mute as Water, Hissing as Fire, and Air of a spiritual type, is as the tongue of a balance standing erect between them pointing out the equilibrium which exists.

2. He hath formed, weighed, transmuted, composed, and created with these twenty-two letters every living being and every soul yet uncreated.

3. Twenty-two letters are formed by the voice, impressed on the air, and audibly uttered in five situations, in the throat, guttural sounds; in the palate, palatals; by the tongue, linguals; through the teeth, dentals; and by the lips, labial sounds.

There is a CD called *The Divine Name: Sounds of the God Code*, which was made by Jonathan Goldman and Gregg Braden. This CD intones God's name or Tetragrammaton with vowels rather than the consonants of God's name. God's name in Hebrew is Yud Hey Vav Hey (יהוה) and is considered to be unspeakable. Mr. Goldman discovered that the ancient Tetragrammaton of God's name was not pronounced by the consonants but by the vowels. In the CD booklet, he says, "What if the sounding of the Divine name transcended the limitations produced by consonants, language, and speech, and was in fact, a tonal name- one that was simply unpronounceable because it was a harmonically related tone that could not be spoken." He asked the question, "What if the Name had to be sung?" The CD booklet explains that the name of God is encoded in the singing of just four vowels with the repetious singing of EEE-AH-OOO-AYE. He says, "Thus, by simply sounding EEE-AH-OOO-AYE, the entire spectrum of vowels and their corresponding harmonics can be created." The first sounds of EEE and AH sounds like "Yah" and the second two sounds od OOO and AYE sounds like "Way", which forms God's Hebrew name that is pronounced as Yah Way. Mr. Goldman's work also seems to support the discovery that Mr. Jenny made in cymatics with finding that the Hebrew vowels actually create the letters themselves in matter. It seems to be the vowels that are the most powerful letters in language.

There is a Gnostic Christian book called *The Discourse on the Eighth and Ninth* that is included with the Nag Hammadi Library of books that were found buried in clay jars in Egypt. It also seems to confirm that God's name is sung with the vowel sounds. At first, when I started reading the Gnostic Christian books, I was perplexed by some of the books including the vowel sounds. At the time, I did not understand and just dismissed it all together as being rather silly; however, after I bought *The Divine Name* CD, I began to realize that this was the silent name of God that was unspeakable according to the legends of the Tetragrammaton. God's name is formed from the signing of the vowel sounds. In this book, it also shows that God's unspeakable name was sung in a hymn. It is also interesting to note that the number nine is brought up in the title of the book, as if it is a clue to the Divine nine pattern within the Solfeggio tones.

"Grace! After these things, I give thanks by singing a hymn to you. For I have received life from you, when you made me wise. I praise you. I call your name that is hidden within me:

A O EE O EEE

ooo iii oooo

ooooo

ooooo uuuuuu oo

oooooooo

oooooooo

oo.

You are the one who exists with the spirit. I sing a hymn to you reverently."

The belief in the Jewish, Christian and Muslim religions that God created the universe with words isn't the only religions that believe that sound played a pivotal role in the creation of our universe. The Hindu belief of the Indians also says that sound is what created our universe, and their belief is that the Om or Aum sound was the first sound of the creation. I was watching a video about the Sri Yantra on YouTube which is called *Mystery of Sri Yantra Unlocked- proof* by Cymatics Production, and all of the numbers that were popping out of the math within the Sri Yantra are the same ones that are encoded in the math of the Solfeggio tones. It's fascinating! I highly recommend for the reader to watch this video to understand more about how these numbers are encoded in the Sri Yantra. Here are some graphics to help demonstrate the math in the Sri Yantra:

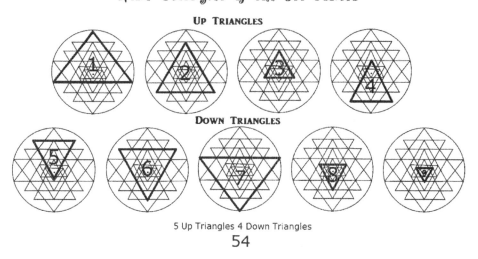

Figure 143

There are nine triangles in the Sri Yantra mandala, and there are columns of nine tones in each eighteen grouping of segments within the tones. Each triangle has 3 vertices, so therefore, there are 27 vertices in the Sri Yantra. (9X3=27) The number 27 is the skip rate for the binaural beats in the Solfeggio tones and one of the notes of A major in the Pythagorean tuning scale. There are 5 down triangles and 4 up triangles, which could represent the number 54 in the scale and as a skip rate in the binaural beats of the tones. The four doors of the Sri Yantra multiplied with the 27 vertices will give the number 108 which is also a skip rate in the Solfeggio tones. We can see a clear pattern within the numbers in the Sri Yantra which is beckoning us to discover the ancient musical scale for the note of A major in the Pythagorean musical scale.

27, 54, 108…….

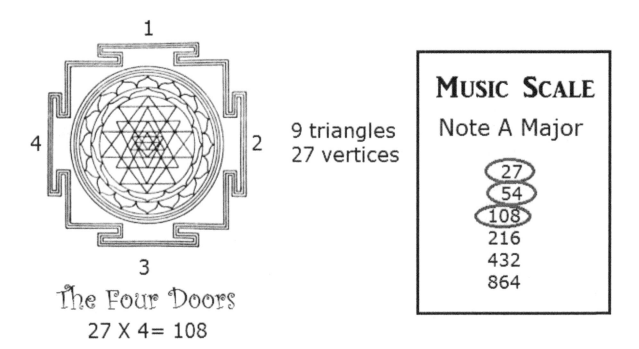

Figure 144

The Hindu belief that our universe was created with sound, and also the fact that the vowels in the Sanskrit language form the letters in various mediums show us that the ancient Hindu people were also well aware of the cymatics of sounds. The mandala of the Sri Yantra shows further proof that they were also aware of the same ancient musical scale that was encoded within the Bible.

The physicists have come up with a way to explain our universe based solely on sound or vibrations, and this theory has been given the title *String Theory*. In string theory the particles are replaced by one-dimensional objects called strings, and the mass and charge of the particle is determined by the underlying vibrational state of the string. Another addition to string theory is called *M-Theory*, and this theory states that these strings vibrate in multiple dimensions. The vibration of the string actually determines whether it appears as matter or as energy, so in other words, a higher frequency vibrating string would be seen as a wave, while a lower frequency vibrating string would be seen as a particle. This would perhaps explain particle wave duality even better, as the vibrational string can appear as either a particle or a wave based solely on its vibrational rate. In this theory that is based on mathematical elegance, it is surmised that the universe is actually made up of 11 dimensions altogether.

I watched a video online in which physicist Michio Kaku describes String Theory and M-Theory and was amused at his eloquent description of those theories. I have put some of the transcript from that video below. The video is from the Big Think website, and it is called *The Universe Is a Symphony of Vibrating Strings*. I highly recommend watching this video.

Michio Kaku: *I work in something called String Theory, that's what I do for a living. In fact, that's my day job. I'm the co-founder of String Field Theory, one of the main branches of String Theory. The latest version of String Theory is called M-Theory, "M" for membrane. So we now realize that strings can coexist with membranes. So the subatomic particles we see in nature, the quarks, the electrons are nothing but musical notes on a tiny vibrating string.*

What is physics? Physics is nothing but the laws of harmony that you can write on vibrating strings. What is chemistry? Chemistry is nothing but the melodies you can play on interacting vibrating strings. What is the universe? The universe is a symphony of vibrating strings. And then what is the mind of God that Albert Einstein eloquently wrote about for the last 30 years of his life? We now, for the first time in history have a candidate for the mind of God. It is, cosmic music resonating through 11 dimensional hyperspace.

So first of all, we are nothing but melodies. We are nothing but cosmic music played out on vibrating strings and membranes. Obeying the laws of physics, which is nothing but the laws of harmony of vibrating strings.

It's interesting to me that M-theory seems to corroborate what Jesus said about our universe in John 14. This theory comes from mathematical calculations and formulas that suggest that there are higher dimensions beyond the three dimensional universe that we now live.

John 14

² In my Father's house are many mansions: if it were not so, I would have told you. I go to prepare a place for you.

³ And if I go and prepare a place for you, I will come again, and receive you unto myself; that where I am, there ye may be also.

If we replace the word house with the word universe or creation and replace the word mansions with the word dimensions, then this verse would say the exact same thing that the physicists are now saying. In this more modern interpretation or translation, we can see that Jesus is going to take us to perhaps a higher dimension. Going from a house to a mansion seems to describe going from a smaller place to a much bigger place. This more modern translation would best describe Heaven as being in another dimension, rather than in this universe. With the Hubble telescope we have peered into the outer limits of the universe only to find an infinite amount of galaxies spreading further and further into the depths of space. Heaven is neither in the sky as some paintings suggest, nor does it seem to be out there in the vastness of space, so perhaps the theory that Heaven is hidden or folded up within a higher dimension of our universe seems to fit better with our modern day theories of physics.

"In my Father's Creation are many dimensions"

We must keep in mind when we are studying our Bible that we are not in God's original creation due to the fall of mankind. We could think of string theory in this way. We were once higher vibrational strings as a wave or in the spirit, but after the fall of mankind, our vibrating strings slowed down or fell in their vibrational rate, and we became particles of matter in a physical form. We no longer could see in that higher dimension that we call Heaven because we fell down into a lower dimension. Perhaps the fall in our vibration would best describe the fall of mankind and also about the fallen angels. The ascension of mankind could then be described in the new song of the 144,000, as being a higher frequency song, which could possibly tune our bodies into higher and higher vibrational states of being that would ascend us up the musical scale of pitches into the higher dimension.

I had a friend that suggested that I research about the Schumann Resonance, and so I did just that and was amazed at the information that I found. The Schumann resonances are actually electromagnetic resonances that are generated and excited by lightning discharges that occur within the area between the earth's surface and the ionosphere. I had always heard that the Schumann resonance was around 7.8 Hz, which rounds off to 8 Hz, but after studying more I found out that the Schumann resonance is more of a range that can vary slightly from many varied factors. The frequencies can range anywhere from 3 Hz to 60 Hz; however, these extremely low frequencies appear to peak at certain intervals that have a very distinctive pattern. The pattern of peaks within the Schumann resonance range appears to go up the scale by frequencies of sixes. It actually forms the repeating pattern of 666, which we know to be a Bible number that is the sign of the beast in the book of Revelation. This intrigued me when I realized this pattern; after all, we are living on a lower dimensional earth ever since the fall of mankind occurred.

I began to wonder what would happen if I continued this six interval pattern, and so I continued the pattern beyond the frequency range of the Schumann resonance on the Earth to see where it would lead. I was astonished to find that twelve of the Solfeggio tones fit into the Schumann resonance pattern, and two skip rates came up as well. I do not know if this information is pertinent to the new song or not, but nevertheless, I will include a graphic showing which tones correspond to the scale of the Schumann resonance.

In stands to reason that if the fall of mankind was caused by the lowering of Adam and Eve's vibration rate, then perhaps we need to increase our vibration rate and the frequency of the earth. There is a theory that has been talked about all over the internet that says that we must find a way to increase our vibration rate to ascend. If this is true, then it would possibly have to be done in resonance with the natural tones of the earth. The twelve tones that belong within the Schumann resonance pattern may help to increase the frequencies of the earth and perhaps help bring the earth into a higher dimension to create the new earth. If this is so, then perhaps singing the new song will help to give birth to the new earth.

First 12 Solfeggio Tones	Second 12 Solfeggio Tones	Schumann Resonance
174 Hz	147 Hz	8 (7.8)
----------- +111	----------- +111	---------6
285 Hz	258 Hz	14
----------- +111	----------- +111	---------6
396 Hz	369 Hz	20
----------- +21	----------- +102	---------6
417 Hz	471 Hz	26
----------- +111 (+81)	----------- +111	---------6
528 Hz	582 Hz	33
----------- +111	----------- +111	---------6
639 Hz	693 Hz	39
----------- +102	----------- + 21	---------6
741 Hz	714 Hz	45
----------- +111	----------- +111	**Continue Pattern**
852 Hz +108	825 Hz	
----------- +111	----------- +111	
963 Hz	936 Hz	
----------- +210	----------- +210	
1173 Hz	1146 Hz	
----------- +111	----------- +111	
1284 Hz	1257 Hz	
----------- +111	----------- +111	
1395 Hz	1368 Hz	

Schumann resonance pattern of +6 has 12 of the Solfeggio tones and 2 of the skip rate numbers.

Figure 145

Today sound is being used for healing and diagnostic medical sonography in the medical community. Sound waves are used to break up kidney stones inside the kidney, bladder, or ureter in a process called Lithotripsy. In Ultrasound, high frequency sound waves are also being used for imaging inside of the body to determine the size, shape and consistency of soft tissues and organs. Ultrasound is most often used in pregnancy to see how the fetus is growing and positioned inside of the womb, as well as to determine the sex of the baby.

Although sound can be used for positive medical purposes, it is also being used in a negative way as a deterrent against loitering of young people and crowd control with activists during protests. A device called the Mosquito uses sound that is only audible to teens and young adults to drive away loiterers. Another device called the LRAD sound cannon is being used for crowd control and has been used against activists in the United States. Both the Mosquito and the sound cannon devices are considered controversial, and the sound cannon may have potentially long term effects for permanent hearing loss. Although, the LRAD sound cannon has been used in a positive way to deter birds from hanging around airports to prevent bird strikes that can potentially cause devastating airplane crashes.

We are living in a modern society that is bombarded by sounds all around us in the air with technology that is beaming sound waves around us every day. We are surrounded by cell phone towers and tall towers emitting broadcast signals for television and radio. In addition to these sound waves, our ionosphere has been bombarded by technological stations around the world that are emitting high frequency signals and bouncing them off the ionosphere. These high power radio frequency transmitters are being used to analyze the ionosphere and investigate the potential to develop technology for the purpose of radio communication and surveillance. Research facilities like HAARP in Alaska or EISCAT in Norway have been using this kind of technology for years now; however, HAARP recently closed its facility.

Conspiracy theorists have claimed that this kind of technology is capable of modifying weather, causing earthquakes and being used for mind control. Conspiracy theorists further prove their claims by citing evidence about a top secret government experiment called the Montauk Project. According to a whistle blower named Preston Nichols, who claims to have worked on the project years ago, these secret experiments conducted by the United States government involved emitting sound waves from an antenna and aiming it at a nearby town to observe the behavioral effects in the people from playing certain frequencies. Preston B. Nichols chronicles his experiences in a book called *The Montauk Project: Experiments in Time*.

Oddly enough, in the book of Daniel in the Bible, we have a bizarre story about a king trying to control people when he plays music. The king **Nebuchadnezzar** makes a decree that people should bow down and worship a golden image every time they hear the sound of the cornet, flute, harp, sackbut, psaltery, dulcimer and all kinds of music. Many biblical scholars agree that the book of Daniel seems to be a prophetic book, and is quite similar to the book of Revelation, which is also a prophetic book in the New Testament. Could this story be prophetic for the last days? Could the governments of the world actually be using sounds and music to control the population of the world? We can only speculate.

Daniel 3

[10] *Thou, O king, hast made a decree, that every man that shall hear the sound of the cornet, flute, harp (HAARP?), sackbut, psaltery, and dulcimer, and all kinds of music, shall fall down and worship the golden image:*

[11] *And whoso falleth not down and worshippeth, that he should be cast into the midst of a burning fiery furnace.*

In this chapter, I have attempted to explain the science of sound, and how we can see in the study of cymatics that sound waves really do have the power to shape the world around us into form and geometry. Sound and mathematics are intricately woven throughout our universe and therefore, sound is the universe in which we are living. Everything in our universe is in motion through the pages of time that we are now flowing on our linear course towards the end times. Motion and vibration are basically just sound, and therefore, all of our awesome and vast universe is singing. The problem is that we are singing off key and at lower frequencies due to the fall of mankind. We perhaps need to learn to sing the new song to increase our vibration rate, so that we may ascend. One thing that I have learned from the science of sound is that we are all singing, and indeed the entire universe is singing. We just need to learn to sing in harmony with God to ascend back up into the higher dimension from which we fell. There is one thing that we need to remember. We don't just sing the new song…..we should become the new song. The 144,000 will set the new song in motion, but we will eventually sing the new song as well. They will be the conductors of the new song, which we all must eventually sing.

Afterword

It's astonishing to me that I am writing a book about the mathematical clues that are encoded within the Bible, and it amazes me that I actually comprehend all of this information. It is a testament to God Himself that this book has actually been written due to the fact that I have never been a math person until the last few years of my life. When I was in second grade, I went to math lab because I had a lot of trouble with understanding mathematics. The truth is that I very much hated math back then, and I thought it was quite boring and maybe even a form of educational torture. I absolutely never wanted to do any mathematical assignments or homework and had it not been for the fact that schools make us learn this stuff, I would have never pursued it on my own. If someone had told me that I would be writing a math book someday, I would have laughed for hours at the very idea. I had a learning disability when I was younger and at one point in second grade the school suggested that I be put in special education, so that I could get the help that I needed, but thankfully my parents refused their offer to put me in special ed, and my mom started helping me with my homework and studying. It took years to completely overcome my learning disability, but by middle school I was making the B honor roll and doing quite well in school. I sometimes wonder what would have happened to me if I had been put in special education. I wonder if I would have even graduated from high school, or would I have ever overcome my difficulties. In most part I owe my thanks to my mother who was very diligent in helping me with my learning difficulties. I eventually did overcome my difficulties with math, and by high school I was making A's in geometry and algebra, but I still hated math. The problem with the way that math is taught in school is that it is totally boring with all of the repetition and never really applying it towards anything exciting. I was a total space case when I was in school, and had they actually applied a math lesson to something in astronomy, then it might have piqued my interest; however, when it came to math assignments, it was always about doing a page or two of nothing but boring math problems. I used to look at those math assignments and think, "How am I going to get all of these problems done?" All I ever saw was a bunch of numbers filling the paper, and there was nothing ever creative or fun about it at all.

When I started looking at the mathematical patterns that were made within the tones, it actually became exciting to me. It was more than just the numbers themselves, I think it was the creative and entertaining patterns that was getting the most of my attention. It became more than math….it became a work of art. I started to realize through pattern recognition that these were much, much more than just tones, but that these numbers themselves hid more than what appeared at the surface. This led me to dig deeper and deeper until I was able to find layers of information encoded within these tones. It actually started to take more of the shape of a vast treasure hunt in which I was able to start finding many precious gems hidden within the m̲ of the tones themselves. It has felt like I am putting together a giant puzzle by adding that I can find in the hopes that maybe someday I will complete this puzzle and be̲ⁿ see the whole picture. I still feel that I don't have the whole picture yet, but I̲ ҄y Grail of the resolved to continuing the hunt for all of the pieces of the puzzle, until the ҄he new song. someday understand how it all comes together as a whole. This would ̲ᴏf tones themselves if someone ever does find all of the pieces to this r̲

Perhaps I will never be able to find all of the pieces to this mystery, but I can promise the world and God that I will never stop trying. According to the Bible, only 144,000 will be able to learn this new song, and that is only a precious few in a world of over 7 billion people. If this song was so easy, then the Bible wouldn't have told us that so few people would be able to learn it.

Revelation 14:3 (KJV)

³ And they sung as it were a new song before the throne, and before the four beasts, and the elders: and no man could learn that song but the hundred and forty and four thousand, which were redeemed from the earth.

Over the years I have studied the research that has been done to discover the science of sound, and I can tell you that sound is much, much more than what we were taught about in school. In John 1:1 it says, "In the beginning was the Word, and the Word was with God, and the Word was God." It was the sound of God's Word that created the universe that we are now living, and it is sound that creates the different geometrical patterns that are found in matter and all throughout the universe.

During the time of writing this book, I was able to buy a triplex for $28,900. I am going to live in one apartment, and my son is going to live in the middle apartment, and the basement apartment is going to be used for storage, games and exercise equipment. What is interesting about this triplex is that it is 4,320 square foot, and that happens to be the degree number at the end of the twelfth rotation of the degree circle or the beginning of the thirteenth degree circle. I see this as highlighting the twelve apostles going around Jesus Christ, which is visible in the thirteen circles of the Metatron's cube graphic. We found pictures of Jesus in the basement apartment, and both my son and I hung up a picture of Jesus beside the entry door to our apartments. My son's picture is of Jesus knocking on a door, and it was painted on a tree slice. The picture that I hung in my apartment is of Jesus as a shepherd, and I feel that I am an assistant shepherd as are so many of his followers. It's interesting that we bought this at the time that I am writing a book about Jesus tones or keys that he gave to humankind. In December of 2014 I was awakened early in the morning and told that I wouldn't be here much longer. I was so happy. At the time, I thought maybe the Lord was telling me that I was going to die soon, or that the rapture would be happening soon, but now I understand that it was His plan for my son and me to move to this triplex. It's interesting, because all throughout these tones, I kept finding the pattern of threes and the trinity, and now I have bought a triplex. Each apartment is 1,440 square feet, which is a multiple of the number 144 that is the cubit measurement of the walls of New Jerusalem. This house has come to symbolize the years of work that I have done with the tones and the writing of this book. It seems so much more than a synchronicity that I bought this triplex at this time. It almost seems like it is the physical personification of the Song of Degrees that is written in stones, whereas the Song of Degrees is written in tones. The power of these tones, as each set of three tones has a positive, a negative and a neutral tone which is just the way electricity is in the electricity or energy that runs through the body when listening to them. I recently got an estimate by an electrician to convert all three electric meters into just one meter that I won't be getting three electric bills and three water bills. It seemed interesting to me that this is also what I believe the tones are designed to do. The tones seem to be used for Jesus a-tone-ment, which is also meant to develop the at-one-ment of Christ. These tones or keys were designed by Jesus to bring us at one with God. Talking with the electrician about converting the three meters into one is much like the trinity tones becoming as one beat around the throne of God. All are one, and one is all.

Many people can't see the forest for the trees, but I see that it takes every tree to make a forest, and I am just one of those trees, while Christ is the forest. He will bring all of God's Creation back into at-one-ment with God. I know that with the new song, Jesus will soon be back to take us to the place he has prepared for his bride, and we will be as ONE. As I begin to move into this triplex, I know that this is a temporary shelter that the Lord has prepared for my son and me to live. But someday soon, we will join Jesus Christ in the sky and will be freed from this terrible prison because we have the keys to the Kingdom of God.

My son found a triangular pin when we were cleaning out a storage area. This storage area had boxes that were filled with objects that had been damaged or tarnished by smoke and soot from a fire that had occurred in the home around 20 years ago. This stuff had probably been sitting out there for 20 years since that fire. The boxes practically crumbled when we started cleaning out that area. I recognized the symbol. It was a triangle pin that was given to members of the Knights of Pythias. My mom had found out in her ancestry research that her grandfather, my great grandfather, was a member of the Knights of Pythias in West Virginia. Some of my ancestors were buried in a Knights of Pythias Cemetery at Junior, West Virginia. The symbol of the triangle is divided into four parts, and in fact, it resembles the diagram that I did of the 153 triangle divided into four parts to represent the two dimensional diagram of a three dimensional tetrahedron. The outer triangles contain the letters of F, C and B and the middle triangle has a knight. These letters are supposed to represent friendship, charity and benevolence, but I see these letters in a different way. To me the F, C and B would represent the Father, Christ and his

Bride and the middle triangle would represent the Holy Spirit. I can see the three triangles folding upwards to make the three dimensional tetrahedron that is a part of the ancient Merkaba or the light chariot of God and the bride ascending upward to join Christ and God for the at-one-ment. I find it interesting that we found a triangle pin in a triplex we bought because these tones contain all of these symbols of three within this new song. This triangular pin is yet another synchronicity that has happened from buying this new home.

The last three and a half years of my life have been very difficult for me due to dealing with the worst experience of my life. God has given me life experiences that have been both challenging and difficult; however, I have been able to overcome all of the obstacles and plough through them with His help. A lot of people would have given up a long time ago, but so far I haven't. I am the parent and caretaker of a son who has many different issues in his life. My son has Type One: Diabetes, a seizure disorder, Autism, Intermittent Explosive Disorder and Obsessive Compulsive Disorder. Any one of these problems alone is hard to deal with, but put them all together in one person, and it seems almost impossible at times. Fortunately though, I have grown stronger through all of these problems, and I have learned to deal with all of these issues just one day at a time. God has been my strength though this life, Jesus has been my rock, the Holy Spirit has been my instructor and the Angels have been my messengers, protectors and guides.

I've had to deal with low blood sugar, high blood sugar, seizures due to severe insulin reactions, giving shots for about 14 years, excessive school problems, terrible violent tantrums, excessive hand washing and shower routines, which has led to horrible mold problems and issues beyond these.

As if this wasn't enough to deal with for years as a single parent, I have encountered some problems in the last three and a half years of my life that makes these entire problems look simple. It's been so horrible that I don't talk about much of it at all, but my son talks about it every day. It's been so painful of an experience for my son, me and my parents that I find it difficult to cope altogether. I have virtually had to separate myself from it all and ignore most of what my son says day after day due to his obsession with this topic. I've had to deal with depression for most of my adult life, but in 2014 I had to deal with the worst depression episode that I have ever known. I was literally crying every day for months, and I didn't know what to do. I started seeing a counselor to help me, and after awhile I decided to take white powder gold to help me overcome it. It worked, and I was able to begin working on my research about the tones again.

Due to the environment that I have been living within for most of my adult life, I have become accustomed to dealing with unusual and difficult situations. My life has been anything but normal. I see my research with the tones as being a way to help God and Jesus defeat Satan and the demons. I see freedom in these tones and the new song, as it is the new song that is sung before the harvest or rapture. I see these musical keys that Jesus has given us as the keys to unlock the prison that we have been living in our entire lives, since the fall of mankind. This is not God's kingdom that we have been living through, and I can't imagine anything worse than living away from God. This life has been one of good and evil, but I wish to know neither. I wish to have the neutral life that we had in the beginning in the Garden of Eden. Here, I can't know good without evil or evil without good, but I care not for the extremes that I face in this place. I just want to know a life where I exist in harmony with God.

A year and a half ago my son was in jail for 10 months, and this was when I was thrust into the worst depression of my life. I only wished at that time that I could free him from his misery. His only crime was that he had fought the new world order for three years and was writing very revealing articles about corruption in our government. He was set up for something that he did not do. It has always been my job to help my son in any way possible that I can, but in 2014 I felt powerless to help him at all. My hands were tied, and I was forced to watch my son go through the worst experience of his life. There is nothing more defeating than watching your son being arrested and put in jail when he is innocent. I now know just a little of what the Virgin Mary must have gone through when she experienced her son being arrested, imprisoned, tortured and then killed. I witnessed through phone calls my son complaining about the jail not giving him his insulin sometimes and only giving him half of what he needed. I witnessed talking to him on the phone when he was having an insulin reaction and not being able to do anything to help him. The jail did not take very good care of him at all. It was hell knowing that my son was being tortured in that place, and I am surprised that he didn't die in there with all of the medical malpractice that took place. There is nothing worse than watching your son suffer in jail and not being able to help him. I do not know how Mary got through watching her son go through that experience, and I don't know how our Father got through that as well.

Luke 21:12 (KJV)

^{12} But before all these, they shall lay their hands on you, and persecute you, delivering you up to the synagogues, and into prisons, being brought before kings and rulers for my name's sake.

There have been many good people that have had to endure time in prison, and their only crime was that they fought against the corrupt system of the governments or religions. Jesus turned over the tables of the moneychangers at the Temple because he saw how the Pharisees were allowing the Temple to be used as a store to make money. He said, "It is written, My house shall be called the house of prayer; but ye have made it a den of thieves." The Pharisees plotted against him to get him arrested not very long after that incident, and they succeeded. Later many of the Apostles also ended up in prison because they were preaching the Word of God, just like Jesus did. In the last century, we have seen other people who fought for peace and civil rights have to endure prison time as well. Mahatma Gandhi, Martin Luther King Jr. and Nelson Mandela all spent time in prison or jail when they were innocent of any wrong doing, and all fought for the rights of the people. I'm proud to say that my son also had the courage to speak out about the corruption and any wrong doing towards the people of this earth, and he has suffered greatly for doing so. He is one of the few people that have chosen to speak out against the evil that is being done in this world.

"The world will not be destroyed by those who do evil, but by those who watch them without doing anything"

— Albert Einstein

One day I went to the jail to visit my son and was told that I could not see him due to them not having his paperwork. I left the jail disappointed, but then I saw a shiny Star of David lying on the steps just outside of the jail. It was during the time period of Hanukkah, but how did a decorative and shiny Star of David end up on the steps outside of the jail? I took it as a good sign from God and picked up that Star of David to keep. I went home and looked up more about the Star of David and found out that this was on a shield that was given to King David to protect him in war. My son's middle name is David, so I took it as a promise that God was protecting my son while he was in jail. That Star of David was something that I looked at a lot when my son was in jail. It made me feel better on the bad days, and I knew that I needed to just trust God to get us through this horrible experience. God did get my son through everything, and today he is free.

This same Star of David is what I found within the Song of Degrees, and I know that it is there for our protection in these most horrible times. I find that all of us are in a prison down here and are trapped within this lower dimension away from God, and that has been hell for me. I seek to help with this new song by assisting the 144,000 in any way that I can. God told me years ago that I would be doing this work, and I am. It is my hope that this new song will help to free us from this world, so that we may go back home to the Garden and back to God. I see these keys as freeing us all from Satan's jail. I see these keys as unlocking this physical prison that we now live. I see these keys as representing our FREEDOM.

I have often read the words to the speech that Martin Luther King, Jr. spoke in 1963 as an inspiration to overcome the current predicament of all mankind. I leave you with his most eloquent words in which he spoke of the day when we will all be able to sing with new meaning. It's interesting that the year that he spoke those words was in 1**963**, which oddly enough has a Solfeggio tone in the date following a one.

Let freedom ring….please sing! May we all sing as one?

And this will be the day -- this will be the day when all of God's children will be able to sing with new meaning:

My country 'tis of thee, sweet land of liberty, of thee I sing.

Land where my fathers died, land of the Pilgrim's pride,

From every mountainside, let freedom ring!

And if America is to be a great nation, this must become true.

And so let freedom ring from the prodigious hilltops of New Hampshire.

Let freedom ring from the mighty mountains of New York.

Let freedom ring from the heightening Alleghenies of Pennsylvania.

Let freedom ring from the snow-capped Rockies of Colorado.

Let freedom ring from the curvaceous slopes of California.

But not only that:

Let freedom ring from Stone Mountain of Georgia.

Let freedom ring from Lookout Mountain of Tennessee.

Let freedom ring from every hill and molehill of Mississippi.

From every mountainside, let freedom ring.

And when this happens, and when we allow freedom ring, when we let it ring from every village and every hamlet, from every state and every city, we will be able to speed up that day when all of God's children, black men and white men, Jews and Gentiles, Protestants and Catholics, will be able to join hands and sing in the words of the old Negro spiritual:

>   *Free at last! Free at last!*
>
>   *Thank God Almighty, we are free at last!*[3]

  -Martin Luther King, Jr.- I Have A Dream Speech - 1963

Made in the USA
Las Vegas, NV
12 October 2023